Don't Go

Abraham Aamidor

STEPHEN F. AUSTIN STATE UNIVERSITY PRESS

All characters, living or dead, and events described in this book, other than well-known historical references, are fictional, with the exception of references to Prof. William Hardenberg, formerly of Southern Illinois University.

PUBLISHED BY STEPHEN F. AUSTIN STATE UNIVERSITY PRESS
P.O. Box 13007 SFA Station
Nacogdoches, Texas 75962
sfapress@sfasu.edu

Managing Editor: Kimberly Verhines

Distributed by Texas A&M Consortium
www.tamupress.com

ISBN: 978-1-62288-929-7

ACKNOWLEDGMENTS

"John Gardner's Last Ride": *The Gettysburg Review,*

"Diary of a Triage Patient": *The Antioch Review*

"Alleys": *Vermont Literary Review*

"My Stupid Life Dot Com": *Chicago Quarterly Review*

'Siddhartha": *The Gettysburg Review*

"Sacrificing Isaac": *Amoskeag: the Journal of Southern New Hampshire University*

"The Sound Transit 594": *The Broad River Review*

'Best Jewtown Hot Dogs": *Prick of the Spindle*

"Nietzsche's Dog": *The Main Street Rag*

CONTENTS

To Shirley, Joe and David,
and to all good people because I believe there are many.

JOHN GARDNER'S LAST RIDE

JOHN GARDNER STOOD ALONGSIDE his Harley-Davidson motorcycle, the classic, 700-pound Road King model snatched from a 1950s Broderick Crawford TV police drama, the kind of fat-tired, loud-mouthed killer cycle with fenders like those on a Model A Ford and decorative chrome rails surrounding hard fiberglass saddlebags in back, and he knew he had forgotten something, but didn't know what it was.

How can I know I've forgotten something, but not know what it is, he thought. Gardner rubbed the stubble on his chin and reflected on this. He hadn't bothered to shave for class, but he usually didn't and his students always seemed to understand. In fact, they'd be disappointed if he showed up shaven. They had signed up for classes with John Gardner the icon, no ordinary creative writing teacher. Gardner smiled to himself. *They're buying my act,* he thought. Then he squinted. He hadn't wanted his life to become an act. *What did I want my life to mean?* he wondered. *I've forgotten.* He thought about how dry and lumpy he looked at 49, like a child's Pla-Doh left out in kindergarten too long.

Gardner went back into the kitchen of his little farm house, meaning a house that once belonged to a man who had worked the land but had long ago given up and gone to town. Now writers liked to rent houses like that, which sometimes made Gardner feel uncomfortable, except that he really liked the house and, besides, it was no affectation because he had grown up on a farm, not in a stray, safe university town. A proper farm wife would have kept the house better than this, though. Chipped porcelain plates and tin pots with baked porcelain finishes, the kind cowboys always ate from out on the range, were piled high in the sink, and a red gingham plastic tablecloth draped a square wooden table with loose legs in the middle of the room. Gardner noticed his quarter-bent briar pipe resting on its side inside a small Cinzano ashtray on the table's top. Ash had fallen from the bowl, distributing itself nicely according to all the probability professors' predictions. He inhaled through his nostrils and combed his fingers through his foppish, prematurely white head of hair and he furled his brow. *How can I know I've forgotten something if I've forgotten what it is?* he continued to muse.

A countertop clock radio, with its almond-colored plastic body and dial hands on a round face in front, blared in the background. "It is now 2 pm. Leading the news this afternoon is word that Bashir Gemayel, president-elect of Lebanon, was killed in an explosion in Beirut today," a news reader intoned dryly. Gardner noticed the announcer's cadence and his baritone voice, not completely eviscerated by the cheap, 3 ½ inch speaker inside the plastic body of the $14.95 Sears Roebuck radio.

Bashir Gemayel, Gardner silently echoed. Pictures of Ronald Reagan and Ariel Sharon fluttered in his mind; he tried to banish these images while he scanned the room further. There, then and there, at the feet of an old painted cupboard and just out of sight behind the table where he took his meals, was the old rucksack he had bought from a camp store in the Shawnee National Forest during his Carbondale days teaching at Southern Illinois University. It was what he was looking for. *Where are memories stored?* Gardner hoisted the rucksack and slung it over one shoulder, then trudged back out the screen door toward his Harley.

The ride to Binghamton was about 28 miles. Gardner, wearing his tight-fitting Marlon Brando motorcycle jacket, slipped his arms through the straps of the rucksack harness while he rolled his shoulders so it would rest more easily on his spine. It was a waxed cotton import from Germany, desert tan and streaked with sweat and oily stains and encrusted with bits of bug.

The chrome on the long, dual mufflers sparkled in the sun. Leaning on its long kickstand, its front forks and wheels turned in just a few degrees, the Harley-Davidson looked like a horse watering at the trough, caught in the decisive moment in a perfect photograph, standing still in time, not like some inanimate object but a living, breathing beast standing still in time. Gardner squatted on his knees so he could inspect the tires, first the

---

front and then in back, and he looked between the treads, even rubbing the tips of his fingers against the rubber for any stones or shards of glass. Then he straightened up and unscrewed the gas cap. He peered into the filler tube to see how much fuel he had left; he watched as the indifferent fumes distorted the air like a desert mirage. He had half a tank, more than enough to get him to Binghamton. Up Route 92, over to Route 171, and US 11 into the Empire State. Gardner liked the adventure of following a route he could draw on a piece of folded paper like a treasure map, and in his mind he ticked off all the mile markers and landmarks along the way. It was more of a journey that way, a real adventure, he knew. *Melville would ride a motorcycle like this if he were alive today,* Gardner told himself. *This is how Melville would have gone to sea, because you can't go to sea anymore. You can only ride a motorcycle from here all the way to the horizon and still not catch it.* Gardner looked both lovingly and longingly at his Harley, the way actor Warren Oates, a runaway middle-age man on the road to nowhere, looked at his Pontiac GTO in "Two Lane Blacktop." Then he admonished himself – he had no idea what Melville would be like in modern times. He only knew he wanted to be back there with Melville, back in the 1830s, and this was the best he could do.

The Harley spit and hiccupped and chuffed to life, clearing its throat with every twist of the grip at Gardner's right hand. *A right hand – you use that to wield a scythe across the wheat, you use your right hand to write a love letter,* Gardner thought. He was pleased that he was right-handed because that's the hand one used to twist a throttle with.

As the Harley settled into an uneven idle Gardner sat upright in the wide cruiser seat and cast his eyes skyward. A few thin clouds swirled in the milky Wedgwoodian firmament. He felt the soft breeze against his skin and he could hear a thin whistling, too. Gardner turned his head to the rows of silver maple and tulip poplar in the windbreak at the west end of his property; he turned his head slowly like a lover who knew his lover was looking at him. It was the leaves. The temperature was in the 70s, perfect because it did nothing to draw attention to itself. *But it draws my attention.* He would talk to his students about Tolstoy, he concluded.

Gardner shifted the motorcycle into first gear, tapping the rubber-tipped lever with the sole of his boot, and he and the Harley began rolling forward. He turned the bike in a wide arch, still weaving a bit while he tried to steer at slow speed with the high handlebars he had mounted on the bike after he bought it, and he pulled onto the gravel path leading away from his house and toward the county road in front. Then he stopped, rested his right leg on the ground while he shifted into neutral with his left, tapping the gear lever up with the hard leather cap toe of his boot this time, up into neutral, and he pushed out the kick stand with his boot and dismounted. *Fuck. I'm always forgetting something.*

"The Death of Ivan Illyich," its dust jacket creased and stained with grease, leaned against the inside of a simple, open bookcase in Gardner's living room. He gazed at the stillness, their eternity, and he stepped over the debris on the carpet in the middle of the living room and plucked the book from the second shelf. He slid off his rucksack and stuffed it inside, then again put on the backpack and turned to leave. He remembered as a child getting ready for school like this, when he was young and innocent and earnest. Before leaving he stopped in the kitchen at the refrigerator, pulled a can of beer from the inside door panel, and took it to the counter top near the sink. He opened a drawer at his side, grabbed a can opener, and punched holes on either side of the top of the can. Gardner took a long swig, stopped to breathe, then poured more beer down his throat before leaving the half-emptied can on the counter.

There was a slight gap between the edge of the gravel path leading from Gardner's house and the paved county road; when the front tire of the Harley rolled over the gap the front forks compressed slightly and Gardner instinctively blipped the throttle while he gripped the handlebar more tightly. The rear tire kicked up a few pieces of gravel and the engine sounded like a bull snorting, but he soon regained control.

Gardner pointed the motorcycle north, then opened up the throttle with zest. The Harley picked up speed easily, traveling true and straight now, and Gardner was happy. He'd arrive in Binghamton in less than 30 minutes and he would ruminate all the way there, unless he saw two horses playing and kicking behind a white fence, then he might slow down and gaze. The constant, deep-throated bleat of the Harley would follow him all the way up Route 92 like a second shadow. The motorcycle drove steadily on, its heft making him staunch against the wind. Feet flat on the floorboards, hands on the handlebar grips and his bum locked in place on the deep saddle – motorcycle and rider were one, not spiritually but physically, which is spiritually in the instance, and Gardner was quietly exultant in the embrace.

Tolstoy found God late in life. That and working the land. Gardner was thinking about his lecture later that afternoon. *God can't teach us anything, but what can a man's faith in God teach us?* It would be a good discussion topic.

Gardner tried not to think about reviews of his latest novel. Nobody liked "Mickelsson's Ghosts." *They loved me before.* He smiled; he was thinking of "Grendel." He had written "Grendel" only to please the critics, to show that he could give them what they wanted, sort of like a young Picasso painting in a classical style, which he could do very well, thank you very much and all that, but it wasn't Picasso. Gardner never believed in Grendel. It was just an academic exercise. The fact is he had sucked their collective dick, and sucked it hard, and the Academy thought they owned him, now and forever. *I'm no longer the darling ingénue of the literati. I don't validate them anymore.* Yet Picasso had got them to suck his dick. *Maybe I'm just not Picasso.* Gardner was not immune to self-doubt.

Gardner would arrive in Binghamton in 22 minutes. *I live among a generation of writers that thinks everything is bullshit,* he ruminated, thinking of other writers then current, those role models and benchmarks his students aspired to surpass. *They have everything and still they say, 'You know what? It's all bullshit.'* Tolstoy had searched for meaning in life and the good that might be in people, even people who weren't very good, or brave, or intelligent enough to see three moves ahead in a game of chess. Tolstoy had achieved success and said it didn't matter after all, and they had achieved success and said it didn't matter after all, but Tolstoy and these other people weren't saying the same thing. *Tolstoy said there were more important things in life. They're saying nothing is important.*

How glad Gardner was that he had been born on a farm. Life was not bullshit. *In the end your life does have meaning,* he reminded himself, affirming it like a kind of Doubting Thomas who, once having discovered a truth, does not want to let this thing go. Even Whitehead knew better. Your life did matter because you actually lived it. *People who talk about bullshit, they're the bullshitters. What kind of courage does it take to write that values are bullshit, life is bullshit, "I'm Chevy Chase and you're not" bullshit? It takes no courage today to say everything is bullshit. It takes courage to say everything is not bullshit. Tolstoy understood this. The highest purpose of art is to make people good by choice. The salt of the earth understand this. I understand this, and that's why they hate me now. Fuck Gore Vidal.*

He drove on toward Oakland at 65 miles per hour, fast enough for a two-lane country road and a heavy motorcycle that really didn't like fast sweeping curves. Only a few cars passed him in the other direction. Not much was happening. He noticed that, he noticed the nothingness, which presented a paradox. *How do you notice nothing? It must be the absence of things. But, which things?* Gardner thought of all the people all over the world who, right then – right then, it amazed him – were working and struggling and fighting and dying, billions of people, a billion people here and a billion people there, just like Sen. Dirksen said, and pretty soon you're talking about a lot of people, which is not really what Dirksen said, but was a kind of pun Gardner liked, if it was a pun. He smiled. He had learned about Everett Dirksen while out on a little paddle boat on Campus Lake in Carbondale one hot August afternoon with humidity higher than in New Orleans, or at least St. Louis. *I don't make enough jokes in my novels*, he reflected.

The two-lane blacktop Gardner traveled down had a slight shoulder on either side, then drainage ditches backed up by farmers' fields. On his left a green John Deere harvester brought in the corn. *Pretty early*, Gardner thought, though he understood. It had been a hot and dry, a long, hot, dry summer and the corn wasn't going to get any better than this. Gardner looked at the solitary figure behind the glass-lined cab in the harvester. The man wore a wide-brim straw hat and didn't seem to move. *Your life matters*, Gardner thought. The leaves and husks on the corn stalks hadn't been green since July. They were the color of straw themselves now and just as dry. On his right Gardner saw another farmer driving a small tractor, dark blue so it must have been an old Ford, and he watched it pull a cultipacker that rolled the seed for winter wheat into the firm earth. He couldn't make out the driver too well through the billowing dust, though. This was a Thomas Hart Benton mural, but not as crowded, not as stiff, because Benton's paintings always were stiff in spite of the lank, rubbery figures that populated his landscape. At least Benton knew decent people when he met them. *Regional art is fascism? What bullshit the Academy had put art through in the 1930s. Now they're after me. I have values. That's almost as bad as fascism, isn't it? Benton's real failures were artistic, not political. He thought he was making soup, not art. He just threw in the ingredients. I could have taught Thomas Hart Benton a thing or two.*

Gardner loved the rapid pulse of his motorcycle. He could feel the engine beating through the floorboards, through the handlebar grips, even in the seat of his pants. He liked the movement. *When the bird mated with the ox a motorcycle was created.* Yet he was late heeding a turn in the road just outside Susquehanna. There is a point, when trying to negotiate a turn on a motorcycle, when you know you cannot negotiate the turn. Gardner always looked through a turn, at the exit point, just as all motorcyclists are taught, and not at the apex and certainly never at the front wheel as it enters the turn. Look through the turn and the rest will take care of itself. *Look through the turn.* But Gardner did not look through the turn until it was late. He saw the lip of the road and the painted white stripe at the edge and he saw the narrow, grassy shoulder just beyond already upon him. *How odd*, he thought. Space was enveloping him; it was like watching a movie, but in very slow motion. Everything just came closer, swallowing him up, the volcano and the giant whale all in one. *It's so smooth everything coming down around me*, he thought.

Gardner thought of Alice and the looking glass, he thought of the lion, the witch and the wardrobe. Enter, the whisperer whispered to him, though he no longer had a choice in the matter. He sat up straight on the motorcycle and went over the lip of the paved road. He went smoothly over the shoulder, too. Gardner reflected how supple the motorcycle felt crossing the shoulder, how peaceful the afternoon was, too, how the afternoon would absorb this interesting development of traveling on a motorcycle as it left the paved road and leaped from a narrow shoulder, this development that was happening to him right now, just as things were happening in the lives of billions of people all over the world at that very moment. Then the front wheel of the big Harley-Davidson Broderick Crawford police special motorcycle hit the far side of the drainage ditch about half way up. The front forks buckled, and Gardner flew over the handlebars as if he was catapulted, only the catapult was to follow closely behind him. Motorcycle and operator, the snake and the woman, the means and the end, they all bounced and tumbled on the farmer's field like junk tossed from a passing car.

The Sears Roebuck radio on the kitchen counter back in the old farm house showed 10 minutes past 2 just then and Willie Nelson's "Always on My Mind" pined from its cheap, 3 ½ inch speaker. Silver maple leaves turned in the wind, and dust billowed from farmers' fields everywhere.

DIARY OF A TRIAGE PATIENT

I CAST MY EYES TOWARD the endless blue sky, deep and present, I hear the squawk of seagulls circling above, I who lie limply in the sand as brittle sea water gurgles and foams, just me, my boots and all the dead cuttlefish.

"Hang in there, buddy," says a man in olive drab as he bends low over me. He's blocking the sun, still I can make out his pale, shaded face, stubbled beard like charred wood, and a pleated surgical mask that's slipped below his chin, now it's like a cowboy's kerchief around his neck, and there's a pretty woman standing over his shoulder, can't be a nurse because she's also dressed in drab, not white.

But she is a nurse, of course.

I want to speak to the doctor – he's fortysomething, 45 or 50, my father's age, though he looks nothing like him – but I can't speak, my tongue must be hanging out like a dog's, my throat is scratchy like a rusty pipe, my jaw is hard like an anvil.

What did the nurse say? The doctor steps away from me and they are conferring, conspiratorially, and I can see their silhouettes out of the corner of one eye, the sun behind them now, it glinting on the tips of waves lapping onto the shore, licking my skin, ebb and flow.

They're talking about me, very hushed, but their mumbling is like gravel in my ears.

I try to remember how I got here even before I know where I am. And what is it that's dripping from a hot slice of pie on my left cheek, warm and syrupy but also salty and bloody like squeezed meat, like blood itself.

Which it is, of course.

I tilt my head toward the triage team – yes, fuck, that's what they are, and I can hear the projectiles whistle and whine overhead and these two don't flinch at all – and I turn up my ears like antennae to hear them but it's all garbled, gruff hushed whispers without emotion or sympathy. I roll my head left and right, bodies are scattered like driftwood, faces not quite human except for the very young ones. They can't all be dead, I tell myself. Maybe the doctor can save me. I want to suck the salt water from my uniform.

Before, it was before when my stomach turned as I waited for the signal to go in and my head wanted to explode, and I fought to keep from letting slip my rifle from my hand. Some of the other men were seasick and not all could reach over the gunwales; I worried about stepping in their yellow green putrid chunky vomit but at least it took my mind off my own misery. Willoughby whimpering is the last thing I remember before we hit the beach, when the front ramp dropped onto the water like a giant slab and I was shunted forward by men charging into the heavy, sloshy water. At first nothing came from the opposite direction, which is always the direction of hell in war. Then something came. A man is on your left and then he's no longer there. Is that him, face down in the water?

Have you ever been a hero? Me neither. "I'm no hero." I'm in my old high school gymnasium, I can hear myself speaking to gaggles of children and rows of fat-bottomed teachers and jowly civic leaders, even the lunch ladies who've come from the kitchen to hear me, bunting hanging from the high running track and all the national, state, military, school ("Go Red Devils"), even UAW flags on staffs in the corner of the portable stage while the Mayor, the superintendent, my Congressman and his wife and an ecumenical preacher who have come to celebrate my sacrifice point to me in a wheelchair and laud my heroism and yet when I'm asked to speak I don't know what it is I'm supposed to have done at all. "I'm no hero," I say and the applause is almost thunderous, almost as loud as the first blasts from the mortar fire and heavy machine guns that made me shit my pants.

This is where it comes back to me, the smell of hot metal, the sting of black smoke in my eyes, the cries and whimpers of stooped and fallen men all around me. Yes, I'd stopped to drag someone out of the line of fire. I did that. Limp, listless, laden - was he already dead? His boots plowed the earth beneath him as I dragged.

That's him over there, on my right. Yeah, that's him. Right over there! I think. It's a man with no arm and only half a head.

"Fella, are you all right?" I'd asked.

"Leave him," someone ahead of me yelled. "He's dead meat."

Carrion. I looked it up in a dictionary once, it was part of a class assignment when I was younger. We were reading a book about World War I.

I look at my hands. Are they still stained, slimed with vitreous humor and blood serum, urine and bits of cartilage like wet clay? He was just some guy. Poor fuck. Who'll tell his parents?

The triage doctor is on one knee again peering into my eyes. He's holding my eyelids back but I see him quite well. He's not so old after all, maybe only thirtysomething, and he has keen blue eyes himself, like mine, like people always told me I have, they're not pale or grayish at all but sparkle like sapphire, and the stubble on his beard and square chin is manly, not dirty. He wears no cap; his thick black hair is quaffed on top. He's a movie star and he lifts my head in what must be broad hands and he puts his nose close to my mouth to smell my breath, then he gently rests my head against the heavy wet sand again. I can see the wind tease his hair as he turns to look at the nurse, it must be the nurse, but she is out of view. I am looking only at the doctor.

"Stavik, get in," the sergeant has yelled. It's hardly a trench, more like the space behind a berm, but I flop down beside him. I'd heard of bullets whizzing by overhead, hearing their hissing noise and Doppler changes, maybe it was just a Hollywood movie, but I only hear little popping noises in the background and I taste the bitter acid air with my tongue.

"There's too many of them," I say to the sergeant.

"Doesn't matter," he replies. "When your number's up it's up."

What? What the fuck is he talking about? The sergeant sticks his head up over the littlest of little ridges in front of us and poof, ping, splat, his number's up.

Get in line to pray to Jesus.

I try to accommodate my pain. It surges like hot waves under the surface of my skin, it vibrates and pulsates in slow motion and it's in all my muscles. It hums. It's sharp, too, razor wire pulled through as easily as a needle and thread, now it's worms poking through my flesh, and my mouth and sinuses are stuffed with cotton wool. I begin to breathe more rapidly, hyperventilate they call it, and the doctor, whose back is to me, turns and casts his eyes down. Say something, Doc. I don't want to die.

We'd hid out in a small barn behind a stone farm house as we listened to the sounds, orders barked in an alien tongue and boot heels stomping in the hard earth getting closer. Where's the straw, I'd wondered. I'll hide under the straw with all the horse shit. Rakes, shovels, rope, even a thick padded leather horse collar, but no straw; light sprayed between the boards in the walls like the salmon run in fall. No, it was just dust particles spinning in the air like galaxies.

"I ain't swmmin' in that," I'd said as a boy.

"You afraid of a few turtles and tadpoles?"

"There's all that junk in the water!"

I don't know where it was, or when. I didn't want to swim in the brackish, muddy water in a little lagoon back in the woods somewhere in the heat of a torrid summer but I forced myself to just so no one would say I wouldn't. I don't think that made me brave, either. I'm no hero. I'm not brave at all. I just want to go home. Doc, am I dying? I promise I'll be brave.

In Sunday school they talked about Paradise and it never was the pearly gates or cumulus clouds against a deep blue sky and Jesus himself sitting on a throne of gold as he leans forward to offer his pure, white hand, now fully cleansed of blood, no signs of iron spikes that pierced his hands at all, he's reaching out to receive his flock – well, sometimes it was that – but mostly it was this, a little trail deep in the woods under a green canopy of renewal and growth gently wending its way to the promised place. It's in the certainty of each step you take, the firmness of commitment one makes when you know you're glory bound. But I never liked swimming in that murky lagoon.

"GO GET THE BALL!" someone on the sidelines yelled; maybe it was the coach.

"That was your ball!" the center fielder admonished me moments later. "You gotta get those, Jason."

I'd made the team, it was only Junior Varsity, sometimes I got to play right field or pinch hit in a lopsided game, but a lot of kids didn't even get that far. That's what Dad told me, he was my rock, my Jesus, and I said, "Yeah, I guess so," and, anyway, I got a hit the day I let a ball go by in the gap. It was my ball, I know.

Dad couldn't always make it to the games but that's not a complaint, no "Poor me" bullshit coming. He'd come to a lot of games, but often he had to work overtime in the factory. I played with a lot of kids from the factory. We all had the same story. Work was steady, Coach was a former Presbyterian minister who now taught high school history, and we held hands and prayed before each game, then shook hands with the other team after, win or lose.

"Do your homework?" Mom always would ask.

"I finished it at school."

"And what kind of home-work is it that you can finish at school? You got your books with you?"

"Yes, Ma'am."

"Well, go to your room and you can come down when you finish."

"Can I have a piece of pie first?"

We had cotton print curtains in the little kitchen window over the sink, a window that looked out into the fenced back yard and dog run. I could stare there, the wind rustling the dry leaves in the Black Gum and Hackberry trees, and on the second floor I had my own room and bed, felt pennants from any team and posters from the Indianapolis 500 on the walls, too. And windows – I could look out at the same Gum and Hackberry trees and even beyond.

I'D HEARD OF PEOPLE getting Conscientious Objector status to the war. Coach talked about it in class once.

"That's shit," Teddy Kovacs blurted out. "My brother's on a submarine right now in the Pacific and some piece of shit is gonna sit out the war while he's dodging depth charges every day?"

"But you've all read the anti-war poetry of Wilfred Owen and Siegfried Sassoon in English class, haven't you?" Coach said. "They fought and they saw that war was evil."

No one said anything further, not at first, and then I raised my hand.

"Yes, Jason," Coach said. He was a kindly man, tall and a bit overweight and his hair was cut short and he always dressed in a light gray suit with heavy black leather shoes for class but he was never overbearing and our old school building had high, coffered ceilings and tall windows that faced full elm trees on the boulevard outside and I'd raised my hand because this is what I felt I had to tell the teacher and the rest of the class: "But they fought anyway. That's the important thing, isn't it?"

I didn't mind my Army physical. No, not at all, not that it was a time to complain. The fun part was when the doctor stuck his finger up my anus. Not because it sort of felt good, which it did, but all the other boys would laugh every time the doctor would do it to any of them.

"I wouldn't want your job, Doc."

"Yeah, they couldn't pay me enough."

We all spent what seemed like hours going from station to station, padding on hard linoleum floors, at ease against subway-tiled walls dressed only in our white cotton skivvies while doctors probed every orifice and scoured every inch of our skin under a square magnifying glass or a round photographer's loupe or took urine samples and swabbed our mouths and even checked for toe fungus.

I'd left my glasses at home but it didn't matter because my eyes weren't that bad. I'd thought about it, though.

Letters to Catherine: I have to write Catherine. She's my girl, see. I didn't have a girlfriend when I went in, and I'd never been further with a girl then sticking my hand under her bra in the darkened balcony of our local Bijou, which was called The Terminal Theater because it was near the end of a railroad spur line, right in town it is, but the USO had forwarded me a letter from Catherine mixed in with the oatmeal cookies and sweet toffee squares that were hand-wrapped in bits of wax paper and I'd wanted to write her back. There had been a last name and a full address but the USO had redacted that. Still, they allowed that it was Catherine from Maine and in my mind I wrote her all the time. "Hey, Cath, wish you were here, ha." I didn't want to know how old she was but her penmanship was pretty good so she wasn't a little girl.

Hey, Cath, remember that time we visited that place, there were all those people, it was great, wasn't it? Do you still have a pageboy haircut?

I think she spelled her name with a "C."

I feel myself starved for air; am I? I'm breathing rapidly again, short, guttural growls, but air is coming through my nostrils and I'm not panicking. Two men arrive, they lift my litter, tell me they're moving me to a staging area, "Hang in there, Buddy," one says, but after a while I realize I've been cast aside, written off. I hear someone yowling down the line and I look to my left, not at the first man but the one after him. I think he's the one moaning, it sounds like a tree bending and creaking in a strong wind, then more yowling and moaning, I've heard it many times, but no one is bent over the boy's body to comfort him. The priest is farther down yet; he's on his knees waving his arms, kissing his trinket, doing his voodoo thing. We're not Catholic, but they're all right, I guess. The doctor will come back for me soon. I'm calm. I think I'll rest now.

I HIKE PAST ROTTING logs, mostly tulip poplar and red oak, but beech trees are more likely to crack in the middle when toppled by the wind and still stick up from the ground like broken spears, and I step over the mushy fallen leaves from all the autumns past, growth of the soil stuff, and the late afternoon light streaks through the nimble branches and leaves on twisting petioles like everyone knows light streaks through the forest when the sun is starting to get low in the sky and I have to cross a creek, there are sycamore trees that announce it, yellowed peeling paper-thin bark, but it is a still staunch beech tree I am after, my very own.

Everybody knows beech trees. They're the ones with gray skin, a gray hide, that you can etch names into, "Bobby loves Martha" inside the scratched outline of a heart, that kind of stuff, and it'll last forever, as long as the tree will last, I guess that means as long as anything ever lasts. I'd carved my name in that tree once. I'd walked alone there, or I was walking along the trickling edge of the creek, it was early autumn then and the water was low and there was more gravel in the riverbed than sand and old half-pint booze bottles and used condoms were exposed on the banks and I'd thought that was horrible but mysterious, too, and I'd stopped to lean my back against a big beech tree that looked to the west, over the water and toward the other side. I looked out at the water, too, channels of water always moving just like Heraclitus said, at least that's what my high school English teacher said he said, which was good enough for me when I was in high school, and the sun shone on the tiny tips of the gently rippling water in this unnamed eternity, bubbles over the eddies popping like child's play, becoming and being at the same time, the beloved always a contradiction. I want to be buried beside my beech tree.

A newspaper reporter is interviewing me: "How do you feel?" he asks. His eyes are intense, wide-eyed, and he has bushy eyebrows; that's all I notice under his brown felt fedora. He's got a stubby pencil in one hand and a little flip notebook in the other.

It's what's he doesn't say that's unsettling. *How do you feel now that you're dying?*

"Well, it's been a good life, sir," I say. "We're going to lose a lot of good men today and I don't want anyone to think I'm anything special. The important thing is that we will prevail in the end."

I look to my right and left; my head swivels now, it's not hard to turn at all, my breathing is relaxed. There are no trees nearby, just a tree line off in the distance, limbs blurring into each other, little more than watercolor strokes. I want to go to my little trail lined with leaves that wave to me like the hand of a queen, like friends who've been expecting me.

I hear footsteps. Not the click-clack, click-clack of hard-soled shoes and high heels on the Terrazzo flooring in some fancy office building lobby, not the sodden sounds of men marching through a muddy field, either. Just the dull thud and drag of boots on wet sand. I look up hopefully.

Mom used to make hot chocolate when I'd come in from skating on the makeshift ice rink next to the fire station every winter; it was an empty lot that the firemen would fill with water when it got cold enough. They'd build up a little dirt berm on all four sides to hold in the water, they knew when a hard freeze was coming, which was always before Christmas, sometimes even by Thanksgiving. "Give it a couple more days, son," a firefighter once told me, then he tousled my hair and smiled very warmly at me.

"Did you fall down?" Mom would tease when I'd come in after skating all afternoon. If it was a Sunday Dad would look at me and smile, too, then he'd hide his face behind the folded pages of his favorite newspaper. It was never warmer inside the house than it was on those days, my cheeks never redder.

"Come 'ere, let me rub your feet," Dad would say after a bit. My ice skates were dumped in a cardboard box dripping melt into the bottom, but the bottom was covered with last week's newspapers so it wouldn't leak out.

"Stop it!" I'd always cry when Dad would tickle my feet.

"Well, at least you don't have frostbite," he'd say.

I didn't want him to stop. We had a small fire in a small fireplace and Mom often served apple pie of a Sunday. I liked it best if it was a bright and sunny cold December day.

I wonder if Catherine would have had sex with me, you know, if she'd known that I'd end up like this. I would have been nice about it. Guys talked about how their girlfriends didn't want to do it, but they'd do it when they saw their men really were shipping out. They knew all along that the men would be going, of course, after Basic, after the last visit home to settle things, but seeing is believing. Some of the guys received letters saying their old ladies now were pregnant – that's what we'd call their girls if they were pregnant, even if they weren't married yet – but some guys got pissed and said the girls had wanted to get pregnant all along, that they'd been tricked by feminine wiles, not carnal desires, not that many of them knew the right words, but that's what they were saying. I think the guys didn't want to admit that they'd just wanted to get laid all along. I never wanted to before, that is, before I'd be married. But now I wanted to.

"Doc, I'm cold," I call out. "Can you get me a blanket? I just want a fucking blanket!" I didn't think I had the wind to shout like that, but I guess I do. It feels good to have that little bit of strength left. I'm not done yet, ha. But I'm cold. The nurse brings me a woolen throw and lays it over me, folding it back neatly at the shoulders. I think she's a nurse. She doesn't look like the other nurse, though.

"Thanks, Babe," I say with my eyes. She smiles, her cheeks blush pink, puff up, and strands of brassy hair fall across her face. She sweeps her hand softly across my forehead and wipes the scum from the edge of my lips with the tips of her fingers; I think she wipes her hand on her skirt afterward. I want to ask if she loves me. I know it's silly but she's so beautiful. The wind is in her hair now and we are sailing away; we've pushed off the shore and we will go where the wind leads us. She's not on her knees, more like crouching, her knees spread and pointed upward and her white stockings are smudged and dirty but I can tell they're white stockings and I can make out her very, very shapely calves. Her shoes are queer, though. Why do you wear such clunky leather shoes, I want to ask, heels as thick as hooves, leather like a trucker's wallet? Are you a nun? She wipes my face with a wet cloth and she rises to walk away. She's wearing a plain drab skirt, no pleats though it is wrinkled, and there are those sooty white stockings. The skirt flaps a little as she walks away and she recedes into the canvas again. You're so beautiful.

But still I am cold. I laugh. I can laugh! That's good, isn't it? It's more of a chuckle but the thing is that this is not really cold. When I delivered papers as a boy I was cold. It was so cold one morning, 37 below, they said, it really was, and I'd gotten up at 4:30 in the morning to deliver my paper route. I waited at the street corner three blocks from home for the delivery truck to drop off my load and I'd have waited until dawn because I had to be responsible, just like Mom and Dad always said I had to be. I split the money with them, too, I didn't mind and, besides, I knew they were just saving the money for me when I'd grow up and need it more. You're still saving it for me, I know! Mom put my fingers in a little bowl of tepid water when I came back home empty-handed that morning; Dad had come to fetch me. I'd been outside only for a few minutes, but that's a long time when it's 37 below. I wanted Mom and Dad to be proud of me. And they were. They are.

I write a letter home; I know there is no Catherine to write to first.

"Well, Pops, I tried to do the right thing, to fit in. Tell Mom I love her. I know you love me."

ALLEYS

A LIGHT DRIZZLE OUTSIDE my window, temperature hovering around 40 degrees Fahrenheit, just a thin, cold soup, uninviting and fretful.

It's the last day of the Matisse exhibit Downtown and I decide to see the "Blue Nude," on loan from the Baltimore Museum of Art.

The drive into the city is easy – traffic is light on a Sunday afternoon, the Colts are on TV and they're having a good year – but the lines inside the exhibit hall are long. I stand behind other art patrons, mostly middle-age couples dressed in down jackets and heavy flannel pants or skirts, some younger hipsters in tight jeans and Chuck Taylors, and a group of us are told that it will be another ninety minutes before we can see the Matisse painting, his paper cut-outs, too. I pay for my ticket, check the time stamp, and I wander other collections.

The Indianapolis Museum of Art is as much about anthropology and multiculturalism as art per se. Small Veracruz and Moche sculptures from the pre-Columbian era, African wood carvings featuring totems with big breasts, and enough Regional pieces from Thomas Hart Benton and Edward Hopper to satisfy anyone who loves America from the early 20th century, which is people like me. But there also are enough flower pots and fruit bowl still lifes to fill every hospital waiting room in the city and I blow by these like a leaf in the wind.

I have time for a coffee but on the way to the cafeteria I stumble across a student art exhibit, unheralded but there. Student art exhibits are the sign of a small-time museum, perhaps, yet every artist has to start somewhere, sort of like everyone has had a first day on the job at least once in their lives. Besides, anyone can like Matisse today, but what was he before he became "Matisse?" I stop and look.

There are the inevitable Brown County forests, almost a basic test for every artist trained in Indiana – the broad hills and rich hardwood stands, the log cabins, too, and horses feeding in a meadow. "Oh, no, not another Brown County scene," I tell myself. "What year is this? Nineteen Ought Six?"

I wince at a painting of a checkered flag being furiously waved, the winning race car blurred and elongated as it crosses the finish line, anxious fans leaning far over the railings in the stands to catch all the action – isn't LeRoy Nieman dead, I ask myself. Well, they're art school students. They're trying. Yet a few will be good, which is all that matters to history.

I continue canvassing the room, moving methodically from one framed picture to the next. I see a nude, perhaps it's of the artist's girlfriend. I appreciate the model's bored expression as she languishes before the easel, the fourth wall in any painting, but also the integrity of her little belly pouch and slightly sagging breasts. The model has been placed on top of an unmade bed, her left knee raised in front and her arms wrapped around her leg as she stares blankly at the artist, at me, too. The corona around her long, unkempt hair is due to the window light coming in from behind her – the effect is subtle, not overdone, but there. The artist has some talent.

And then there is a painting of an alley, three-flats and six-flats on either side of a dry river bed arroyo paved with cracked asphalt blacktop over worn original cobblestones, detached garages with old style swinging wood doors on iron hinges, warped wooden telephone poles up and down like tired, heavy hearted soldiers after a long campaign, the insulated wires strung between them drooping in the invisible, still air, birds perched on them, Blackbirds or sparrows, I don't know, and none is in flight, just perched, looking this way and that way, their indifferent moment, a repudiation of Cartier-Bresson for sure.

I stop and look at this one longer.

The picture is drawn from the perspective of the artist standing on a third floor back porch near one end of the alley looking down and across, a wonderful sweep to such a small, ordinarily unimposing place. It's at heart Cubist, but the geometry is more subtly embedded in the structures themselves than made dominant or independent. The colors are natural and earthy, not artificially optimistic, a bit sooty like life in older American neighborhoods itself, all the stronger for it. I don't want to leave this painting.

I look again at the red brown bricks in the exterior apartment walls, their rough textures and the pitted tuck pointing, the windows, too, only a few are open, some a little, some a little more, but there are no people visible in them, not sticking their heads out a window to check the weather or breathe the fresh morning air, nor is anyone standing on a back porch hanging laundry even though laundry lines are visible, nor backing a car out of a garage below, not even kids kicking a can down the alley. There is just the hint of people's lives in those open windows, the prominent telephone wires, or are they electric wires, the substantial debris and litter in the alley, too, and I think the artist has left out the main thing, the people.

I have known alleys like this before. I have walked down them many times in my life.

"QUARTER SAYS YOU MISS IT." That's what Michael, my 10-year-old best buddy when I was 10-years-old, would say when we played baseball in an alley behind his house on the northwest side of Chicago. Hit a rubber ball straight past the pitcher and that's a double, but a homer if you hit it across Ainslie and into the next alley. Hit it into a neighbor's back yard and you had to get the ball yourself; it was an automatic out, as well.

Still, it was baseball, especially if you had a wood bat by Hillerich & Bradsby, which I did, I'd bought it the winter before with money I made shoveling snow, and a Rawlings leather glove, which I'd received as a nice birthday gift the summer before.

"Quarter says you miss it." Michael and I would add up our debts when the season ended around the first snowfall in November and square up that way but, of course, we always came out even.

My alley was between Drake and Central Park, about a mile away. Girls would walk down that alley in summer dressed in their tan or navy blue gym shorts, the kind with flouncy bottoms and tight elastic hems like cut-off bloomers, everyone on their way to or from the A & P on Lawrence Avenue, or maybe just headed to the neighborhood playground a couple of blocks south.

"Uh, high, Barbara," I said to a girl I knew from school when we crossed paths in that alley one day, her playfully curly hair unkempt by the wind, skin smooth as a sea shell. I stood in awe, stood nervously as I waited for her to acknowledge me, her coterie of other cute girls standing guard behind her and, if I remember correctly, I tried to ignore it at the time, but I think they were giggling, probably at me.

"And where are you headed?" she asked without saying my name. I recall her sipping soda through a straw from a tall, waxy paper cup just then, very coquettish as she looked over the rim of her cup and into my eyes.

"Oh, just to the store to get some milk," I replied. "We're out of milk." It was a gratuitous explanation of my need to go to the store, to be in the alley just then – *See, I'm not stalking you* – and I pointed up to the third floor back porch of my apartment just behind us in the alley. "That's where I live," I added.

Later – not that day, not that week, but not so long after – my brand new Ranger bicycle, which I had dutifully locked to a porch post at the bottom of my apartment's back steps, was stolen, the chain just snipped in two, the bike stealthily stolen and gone forever just like the girl.

You cut through alleys to get places faster; you slink through them to avoid being seen. You hear things from the bottom of alleys you can't easily hear from the street in front – shouting, crying, demanding, people tinkering with their cars and motorcycles, even the clink of china plates and silver flatware at dinner time.

I didn't think of alleys when I went away to college, but I was reminded of them after I moved to Indianapolis for a job. I worked Downtown and the alleys there were a bit different than what I recalled from my youth, darker, grittier, deeper. More imposing. I lived in the suburbs so I had no alley of my own. "If I were to make a movie in Indianapolis, something noirish, I'd film only in the alleys," I told a photographer friend from the local paper.

Behind the big bank buildings; behind Monument Circle in the center of the city, alleys leading to it like spokes in a wheel; behind the block-long Indianapolis Star building, too, where my photographer friend parked his 4-wheel-drive vehicle each day.

Downtown teems only during lunch in Indianapolis, making that the best time to slink through one for the full film noir effect, as counter-intuitive as that might seem, not hidden by the dark so much as by the blindness of others, hidden from view like a refugee in Europe (circa 1938, that is), alone known only to the delivery truck drivers and garbage collectors, rats the size of moles your only friends, an antithesis to the playfulness of the neighborhood alleys from my youth but a necessarily stark contrast to shake me out of my stupor.

A beggar has taken a break, maybe he'd gone back of a tall building to pee and now he's smoking a fag except it's gone out and all he has in his mouth is the butt. He looks hard at me, yet under sleepy eyes. I know he's going to hit me up for pocket change and I don't want to be cowered, I don't want to show that I'm afraid of a homeless bum beggar doing timeout hidden from the rest of humanity behind an insurance company's new tower and I'm intent on ignoring him, which I do.

"Hey, how you doin'," he says to me with a bit of a flip of his head as I pass by, as I walk a line near enough to him so as not to look like I'm trying to avoid him but not getting too close to him, either. "Hey, how you doin'." That's all he says, then he takes another draw on his unlit cigarette butt and looks away. To think, I was steeling myself to say, "I don't have any," cigarettes or change.

I once caught a couple fornicating in an alley in Downtown Indianapolis, fellatio, actually, right behind a Quiznos. The man was well-dressed, leaned against the wall while the girl did him below. He held his cigarette in the air jauntily like Franklin Roosevelt. I wasn't quick enough to say to him, "Hey, how you doin'."

Harry Belafonte once vied for love in alleys like these in "The World, the Flesh and the Devil," a doomsday film far ahead of its time, being racially and gender balanced like the TV news today, a white man, a black man, and a really beautiful, classy chick, take your pick who was who in the title, but all that was left of New York City in this noirish film were its alleys and these three survivors, the only question in the minds of the audience who would get the girl.

And the outlines of the alleys in the aerial shots were like traces of canals on Mars.

I remember the day I found the Dead Sea Scrolls in a dust devil behind the Bank One building, torn newspaper pages spinning in a sorcerer's vortex, actually a story in *The Indianapolis Star* all about alleys. I didn't normally pick up old newspaper pages from among the detritus in alleys, I wasn't someone who slept under loading docks or huddled against the walls of a tall building to deflect the icy winds in winter, but this was a Dead Sea Scroll, or could have been.

"It's hard to imagine America before the 1950s without alleys – they were as essential to cities and neighborhoods as fire hydrants and sidewalks," the story began. It was in the Living section of the paper. "Yet the post-World War II era ushered in a new type of streetscape: suburban subdivisions with attached garages dominating the fronts of new homes. Alleys were increasingly seen as avenues of crime, places where luckless people came to pick through your garbage, or worse."

Well, it was a page from the Satanic Verses I was reading, the original deal, not Salman Rushdie's novel. Alleys are a war zone; they're like the plumbing that carries our shit to sea. They don't even have stop signs, no law and order at all.

The last time I walked behind the Bank One building – I was on my way to Starbucks – there was a shoot-out. At first I heard a loud screeching voice, maybe it was someone calling out a name, followed by the sound of caps, but real ones, the way they talk about capping someone in the inner city, then a real fusillade of fire, followed by quiet and a stillness all around me. It happened so fast, clichés usually being true, it was so other-worldly that I didn't react at first. Yet when one of the gunmen ran up to me, stopping and turning his head left and right, a real 9-mm pistol in his hand, black and semi-gloss shiny, I retreated to an iron dumpster behind me and hid from view, covered my eyes, too. I heard footsteps, the shooter running away, but other shooters running up to the same spot near me and the sound of bullets flying again. Then I heard a woman scream, then weep, and I cautiously came out of my hole and saw her bent over what appeared to be a freshly fallen corpse. I heard more footsteps around the corner, the sound of men in leather-soled shoes, but receding, merging into the normal din and hum of the day before finally disappearing. A delivery truck approached the crime scene from the other end of the alley, stopped in front of the bereaved woman and the very deceased man, and then he slowly drove around the obstruction. I ran up to the lady.

"What happened?" I asked her.

"You don't know?" she replied. The woman, tall, young and thin, dressed in a silky black shift under an unbuttoned fur coat with huge collar, maybe Russian Sable, she looked at me plaintively, her tears smearing her thick eyeliner.

I shook my head.

"I don't know, either," she said with a heavy sigh. "I was just coming out of the club and I saw this man killed and it's so sad."

"Well, I guess we should call the police," I said and I pulled out my cell phone to call the police. They arrived in about five minutes, not very impressive, and in the meantime the lady in the black dress and fur coat and I directed light traffic around the corpse, a couple of people stopping briefly to ask what happened before moving on, and when the police arrived we each dutifully gave our statements. The crime scene investigators soon arrived, all wearing blue latex gloves just like on TV, and they collected all the bullet casings – they found many – and an ambulance arrived next to take the body away.

"We'll be in touch if we need more information," one of the officers said to us. They never called, but The Indianapolis Star reported the next day that the deceased was a travel agency executive believed to be heavily in debt to local loan sharks. The US Attorney would investigate, the article said. It was the 67th murder in the city that year. The date was September 12. The article included a picture of the crime scene, the corpse covered in a white sheet-like thing, the police huddling nearby, and if you looked closely you might have been able to make out me comforting the crying woman as we stood under an awning by a wall. My photographer friend from the newspaper had recorded the image.

I DECIDED TO BUY The painting of the neighborhood alley on display at the student art exhibit the day I went to see Matisse's "Blue Nude." I struggled to make out the name of the artist, but ultimately I made out the name, "A. Levitt." I looked for the nearest docent. I wanted to buy the painting, I told him. "How do I go about doing that?" I asked. He didn't know, so I asked where I could find a curator. The docent directed me the museum office, said someone there might be able to help me. I thanked him and wended my way to the office on the floor below; finding the door ajar I entered unannounced and spied a woman working silently at a desk in the corner. She was a mature woman – I think that's the preferred term today – very slim and well-dressed in a designer wool suit, her short gray hair unharmed by chemicals and precisely snipped at the ends. She wore half-frame reading glasses low on her nose; when she looked up at me she didn't need to remove them. I was afraid she'd be startled to see a stranger in the museum's suite of administration offices on a Sunday afternoon but she remained very composed.

"May I help you?" she said.

I turned and looked over my shoulder, a habit I guess I'd never overcome, and I pointed in the general direction of the student art exhibit gallery on the floor above. "It's that painting, the one of the alley," I said. "Is it for sale?"

"Ah, the Levitt painting," she said, rising smoothly from her chair. "I liked that one myself. So real, so honest."

"Do you know where he drew it?" I asked.

"She," the woman corrected me. "Andrea Levitt. It's near the old art school, up by 19th Street and Talbott. It's the same alley and it's a bit different. That's what distinguishes good art, don't you think?"

"Well, I don't know, really," I said. "I just like alleys."

The woman walked around me to a metal cabinet and pulled out a file. "Let's see what the story is, then," she said. "My name is Susan. And you are?"

"Albert, you know, like the Royal Albert Hall," I said.

It's obvious – I still was the little boy in the alley behind my old apartment on Drake Avenue. The woman smiled softly. "I see," she said.

Susan perused the file she had pulled. "Yes, here it is," she said. "It's called 'The Alley,' price $750, no discounts." She looked at me over her half-frame reading glasses.

I didn't hesitate. "I'll take it," I said.

Susan waved a finger at me. "No, you can't," she said. "It's sold." She closed the manila file and turned to insert it in its place in the metal file cabinet.

"Then who's the buyer?" I asked, speaking somewhat insistently. "I can guarantee him a quick profit. Or her."

Susan shook her head at me. "We can't divulge that kind of information," she said. "Anyway, the buyer is 'Anonymous.'"

"Give me the contact information for the artist, then," I said. "Maybe she has other paintings of alleys. Artists like to make sales."

"You're very eager," the woman – Susan – said, again looking presciently at me over her half-frame reading glasses. She handed me the artist's card; the young lady had recently graduated from art school in Indianapolis and had moved to Chicago.

I thanked Susan and I checked my watch; I had missed the last admission to the Matisse exhibit and his "Blue Nude."

I wanted to drive home via alleys in the city at least until I reached A. Levitt's alley at 19th and Talbott, but the winos standing beside fires they'd lit in 55-gallon oil drums, the furtive looks from youths, their slumped shoulders, hands in pockets, ambling by in their hoodies, and all the overturned stolen grocery carts I had to maneuver around before I arrived at the Levitt place convinced me otherwise. I turned to Meridian Street, the main north-south thoroughfare, and drove straight home instead. The article in The Star was right; it was my memories of alleys that were tainted, both sentimental and maudlin. A. Levitt had been mindful of the past – yes, I appreciated that, it was valid – but she was unfettered by the kinds of positive associations I had made over the years, the promise that America once was and for which I still pined. She had suspended disbelief in the things I thought I knew but she wanted proof that something better remained, which may have been the secret message behind no people in her painting.

A light drizzle outside my window when I get home, temperature hovering around 40 degrees Fahrenheit, just a thin, cold soup, uninviting and fretful. Where will I go now?

MY STUPID LIFE DOT COM

I'M SUFFOCATING UNDER this deluge of publicity for Twitter and Facebook and Blogger and all the rest. I mean, you can't read anything online, whether it's a story about human trafficking in Asia or the latest item about "The Bachelorette" on ABC's web site, that doesn't ask if you "Like" the story or want to be a "Fan" of the web site. You can't watch "Wheel of Fortune" without being prompted to get clues for tomorrow's show on Twitter. You just can't avoid this stuff, right?

So, I'm walking up State Street one day after work and all the young women are wearing long sweaters that cover the tops of their fannies and black leotards about two microns thick and they're all on their smart phones texting someone about something, or they're listening to Lady Gaga on iTunes or searching the internet for the nearest designer jeans store.

I get it, I get it, the whole Facebook and Twitter thing and blogging about your life experience at age 16. The old guy in the cubicle next to me at the call center where I work says his daughter just started a blog herself. It's about celebrities, the people they're dating, what's their next big movie project, things like that. She gets her information from other blogs, then writes everything down in her blog. Papa is so proud.

I thought of offering to help the girl with her blog because I'm pretty good with software, actually, plus I haven't been on a real date in six months. But then I saw her picture tacked to the inside wall of the man's cubicle. Uh, I don't think so, I told myself. I graduated from the University of Illinois in Urbana-Champaign with a degree in finance and a minor in HTML four years ago and, of course, am always looking to hook up with someone. I go to alumni mixers, but either I'm the youngest guy there or I have to look away because I hope the ugly girls don't spot me first.

I work with enough young women at the call center, sure, but what kind of conversation am I going to strike up with them by the candy machine on the third floor? "Hey, do you work here? Oh, yeah? Me, too. What kind of work do you do? Customer service? That's what I do! By the way, you're really fat."

Customer service is all anyone does here all day. It's just such a shitty job that the number one unwritten rule we all have and respect is *never talk about this job.* We all sit inside the same cookie-cutter cubicles with fabric-coated sound-deadening walls that don't absorb any noise and take complaints from people who say their packages didn't arrive on time, or we have to listen to some really loud, old guy who says he never ordered the item that came in the mail, how does he send it back, who would ever want to buy something like *that!*

Heh, heh, you probably think my name is Dilbert. Actually, I put up a picture of Dilbert outside my cubicle one day but they made me take it down. It's like I work on "The Office" on TV, like I work for the really crazy guy. No, not Steve Carell, but Rainn Wilson, who's really sick. One older woman I work with thought it was pretty funny that I put up a Dilbert cartoon, though. One older woman! After I thanked her and turned back to my computerized incoming call program on the monitor in front of me, one of the older CRT monitors because the company hasn't switched to flat screens yet, I noticed she still was standing next to the prefab wall section, leaning on it on one arm and kind of swaying her hips. I think she was coming on to me. I mean, she's at least 40, maybe even 45. I want to date someone named Chloe or Madison, not June Bug. I hope she didn't see me smirking as I tried not to look up at her.

Actually, I'm just working at the call center until I go back to school for my MBA. Still, you probably do think I'm a Dilbert. That I feed my cats when I get home every day after work. Well, no. In fact, I don't even own a cat. I do rent a basement garden apartment on the far-Northwestside from a very nice Yugoslavian couple who came to America 20 years ago and worked their way up as janitors to buy up half the street where I live, though. I keep my apartment clean and I do not buy anything from IKEA because their knock-down furniture isn't any better than what I can get at Target, thank you very much. I prepare my own meals, too – pan-fried fish, broasted chicken, or just scrambled eggs in a big iron skillet – plus vegetarian baked beans, creamed corn from a can, stuff like that. Maybe Chef Ramsey wouldn't approve, but I eat all right.

And, no, I don't call the phone sex lines or watch pornography. I don't even have cable.

Well, I did call a phone sex line once. They switched me over almost immediately to a $2.99 per minute line but I hung up right away and the charge never even appeared on my phone bill. Another time I called a dating service but they wanted my credit card number and I wouldn't give it to them. The girl on the other end then suggested she would give me phone sex if I gave her my card number, but I had to ask, "What is that, anyway? What is phone sex?" She just asked me, very calmly, if I was dressed and suggested that, if I was, I should get undressed and then I could give her my credit card number.

She was unflappable, I'll give her that.

Actually, I don't watch much TV at all. Everybody is your friend on TV. Why is Nate Berkus smiling all the time, and who is Nate Berkus, anyway? "We're having a *par-tee*," Oprah used to say. That's what TV is, a big, virtual party and we're all invited. Except no one watching is really there. I'm not at their stupid parties and neither are you if you're watching TV at home in the middle of the afternoon still dressed in your underwear. When I work the late shift I always get up at the regular time and brush my teeth and get dressed just like it's a regular day, and then I watch daytime TV sometimes.

So, it's a Friday night and the closest I've had to a date in months is the 40-year-old woman who works in a cubicle near me Downtown and, maybe, this other woman who works at a call center for a cheesy dating service. "Are you going out tonight?" Mrs. Kaczynski asked me recently. She's the Slav who owns my apartment with her husband. She's trying to be motherly, I know. But the Kaczynskis have a beautiful daughter, I mean tall and buxom but not ridiculous, with womanly hips but not egregious like Jennifer Lopez, and raven black hair with a cute bob in front like Katy Perry. She drives a late-model 328i, too. Not new, but clean. She comes home from time to time and I can hear them all yelling in Serbian or Slavic or maybe Russian, I don't know, but the truth is I've never been formally introduced to the daughter. She just snaps a kind of curt smile at me when she passes me on the walkway leading up to the apartment building. In fact, I've only ever spoken to her once. That was when I had to ask her to move her car so a store could deliver a piece of furniture to me.

What's the use, right? All the chicks – I know no one uses the word "chicks" anymore but I see on TV that the late '50s and early '60s are hip again, if you can dig that – want someone who has a gear job and cool car and lots of trendy friends. I think that's where Facebook and Twitter come in. Look at me! I'm on Facebook. Look at me! I have a blog. Look at me – I'm tweeting to you live while hosting the Oscars! What category are we presenting now? I don't know – I'm too cool to give a damn.

What is it Lenin said? If you can't beat 'em, join 'em? (Hee, hee. That wasn't Lenin. Don't you think I know that?) I decided I would launch a blog myself. The prospect immediately engaged me. What tags should I use? Hollywood entertainment? Fantasy sports? International relations and the prospects for Middle East peace?

Should I allow comments? Will my site be moderated?

First, I did some research. There are 70 million blogs in America today. But only about 1 and ½ million appear to be active. According to DSM-IV, the Diagnostic and Statistical Manual of mental disorders, about 1 in every 10 Americans is addicted to a blog. The best treatment option is drug therapy together with peer counseling hosted by a trained and licensed facilitator. Hey, maybe that's how I'll meet girls – I'll go to a 12-step group for people addicted to blogs. I remember Katie Couric asking a guest on TV who suffered from sex addiction if that isn't where guys just go to meet women who are sex addicts.

I decided I needed a really catchy title, something different that might actually go viral on the Internet. If you go viral on the Internet then "Live! With Regis and Kelly," or whoever replaces Regis, will feature you in a segment. "Imagine that!" Regis would say with mock surprise and exasperation all at the same time. "How in the world did you name a blog that?" he'd add. He'd slap the top of his desk with the palm of his hand and shake his head incredulously, then finish by saying, "Oh, well," and move on.

Yeah, I'd start my own blog. Maybe I'd name it "Stud in the City." I could write about the best places to meet girls and hook up with them. People would contact me and ask, "Where is the best place in Chicago to hook-up with girls?" and I'd be able to tell 'em.

Well, no. Too juvenile, of course, like something every fat kid in an early Steven Spielberg movie would try.

How about, "The Chicago Literary Society. Established 2011." That might attract a better class of girl.

Hmm. Sounds like something a University of Chicago grad would come up with. Scratch that.

Maybe, "Calories burned per mile walked adjusted for the temperature humidity index: A Chicago guide."

Yeah, that could be a title. I mean, it would be more of a chart than a blog, I know, but it would be useful. People would write me and say, "Hey, Joey, we all know it's cooler in Chicago along Lake Michigan, but isn't the humidity higher there because of all that water? If so, how many calories would I burn in a 10-minute walk to the Starbucks at the corner of Clark and Chestnut?"

I could do the math and publish a credible number, then wait for other people reading my blog to comment. Some might be hostile – I'd have to accept that. "Where the fuck did that number come from, Joey? Don't you know that if you walk to Starbucks and order an Ice Peppermint White Chocolate Mocha it's 400 calories? Subtract your stinking 27 and ½ calories for walking there and you're still gonna die from obesity-related illnesses before you're 55. You suck, Joey."

Full disclosure here: My name is not Joey. I just thought that would be a friendly name for a blogger. Everybody knows a Joey, from the old Sinatra movie "Pal Joey" to cute kangaroo Joeys. But my name is really Sherman. Maybe I'll call myself Master Master Chicago Blaster, like a rapper's name, even if that is kind of a '90s rapper name. OK, that's not very good, either. I'm still working on a *nom de plume*. It can come later.

Basically, the reason I want to do a blog is because my stupid life sucks. But that has to be true for lots of people who are on Facebook or Twitter or Creeper or even Linkedin ("Uh, no, I'm not looking for a job. I couldn't be happier with my present job.") or any other social media web site. Those people can't have a life, either, or else they wouldn't be wasting their time online.

Then it hit me. Wasn't it Vladimir Putin who said the best ideas are always the simplest? Maybe it was Warren Buffett. Anyway, I would do a blog called "My Stupid Life Dot Com." People would relate to that. They'd get it right way. You know what I'm sayin'?

"Oh, yeah, do I know what you're sayin'? I know what you're sayin'! My stupid life sucks, too. Oh, yeah."

You have to read the latter quote in a whining, rising voice, somewhat like the George Costanza character from "Seinfeld." There are a lot of people like George Costanza out there.

Ah, "Seinfeld." Just the greatest TV comedy of all time.

Anyway, I could feel my life starting to turn around as I lay on my Target futon and made notes to myself in a spiral binder. I would buy a domain name, download a free template for my web site, then hire a national company to host it for a small monthly fee. *Cha ching!*

My Stupid Life Dot Com. It just came to me like that, you know? It's not like I'd want my followers to think that I think I'm better than they are. We're all poor *shlubs*, right? I'd invite people to share tales from their stupid lives with me. I'd make the really clever people Contributors and let them post to my blog directly. We'd all become fans of each other on Facebook. And the people who just visit the site? If they register then they can post comments, I decided. It was all coming together. You can imagine how good I felt. As Abu Mazen said, you gotta take a lemon and make lemonade out of it.

I called in sick the next day at work. I don't know what I told my boss, actually. Maybe I said my grandmother died. Maybe I said, "*Your* grandmother died and I'm going to *her* funeral." Yeah, I don't remember what I told him. But he said, "Whoa, Sherman. It's not like you to call in sick. What happened? You almost get laid last night?"

Yeah, that's how they treat me at work. But not much longer. "I really like your blog, Sherman." That's what they'll be saying in the future. "Can I be the Chick of the Month on your blog, Sherman?"

So, I was fishing round on the Internet and I typed in "my stupid life dot com." (Hey, the only reason I keep spelling out "dot," which I know is very annoying, is in case you're reading this online and you have a spam filter that blocks web sites. Are we OK with that?) Yeah, I type "my stupid life dot com" into Google and holy shit, it pops right up. Someone else has got a blog called, "My Stupid Life Dot Com." It pops up right away. The guy is showing pictures of his ugly sister and the rear end of his 1991 Honda Accord that he backed into a telephone pole. What an idiot!

But he owns the domain name.

I'm heartsick. Or broken. Whatever. My one big, fat chance to be somebody and it's gone faster than spit on a hot griddle.

I go into work the next day. My boss says something smart to me and I just smile. "Real cute," I tell him. I go to my cubicle and there's a slice of apple pie on a small ceramic plate wrapped in cellophane right on my desk. A card next to it reads, "Hope you're feeling better," written in nice calligraphy with a fine ink pen. It has to be from my middle-age suitor. I decide to take it back to her but it looks pretty good so I hesitate, then decide that I can eat it after all. But not before break. They don't like us talking to customers with our mouths full.

THE DAYS PASS BY and I still don't have a blog or a date. My highlight at work is the guy who demands to know why the brown belt he ordered was more like an olive green, and he claimed that it wasn't really a 38 inch belt at all, but more like 37 inches. He measured it against a belt he was sure was

38 inches, one he bought at Nordstrom, so that one had to be correct. He said he didn't like to order online or via catalogues because you can't really measure things ("Now, can you?" he asked with real flair, as if he was saying something profound, or at least catchy) but he decided to take a chance.

I have to tell you something about my call center before going forward with this tidbit. We're a contract call center, meaning we take calls for lots of companies. Obviously, we don't make clothing or belts or any consumer items in Chicago. I mean, the old German tailors died off long ago and no one will work in sweat shops anymore in America, even if there is no other work for people on the wrong slope of the bell curve. Besides the large clothing catalogue and web site we take calls for, we represent a Taiwanese bicycle manufacturer, a Venezuelan gasoline company, an Israeli mineral baths producer, and a Chinese computer reseller. We don't know anything about any of these products, but when people call in we ask the nature of their complaint, check a couple of boxes on the computer screen, and wait for responses to appear. Usually, the response is just to mail it back, but in the case of bicycles we tell them to go to an authorized local bicycle shop that may or may not be in their city. In the case of computers we give them a phone number for the technical assistance department, but usually people already have tried that and no one ever answers.

I told the guy with the belt to mail it back. I told him this even before going through the on-screen protocol. I would log everything into the computer later because that's how they measure productivity at work – how many calls you received, how many answers you gave. Once you identify which catalogue or web site they've ordered from you have to tell them for speedier service they can always log back on to their computers and check the frequently answered questions section.

Anyway, the guy with the belt became hysterical. I don't mean hysterical ha-ha. I mean hysterical peculiar. "Why should I have to mail it back to you?" he's demanding. "You people shouldn't advertise faulty products like this in the first place." I can tell he's getting heated, maybe even frothing at the mouth.

"Just send it back for an exchange or complete refund," I repeat. I'm pretty calm. This is not the first nut case I've ever had to deal with.

"Oh, yeah?" he counters. "I paid postage just to receive this merchandise. I'm not going to pay more just to mail it back, plus the cost of an envelope plus I gotta put gasoline in my Plymouth just to get to the Post Office. What do you think of that!?"

He's challenging me. The ball's in my court. What am I going to say to him? But I don't really care what he does. I'm just there to state policy. Why doesn't he understand that? There is no contest, there's nothing personal going on between me and him.

"You full of shit people," he now says. I can hear him breathing deeply. It's more than exasperation. Maybe he's psychotic. We have a right to hang up on loons, but I want to hear this guy. Yeah, lemme have it. I don't care what the guy says.

"Yeah, you're so full of shit at Braverman Belts and Haberdashery," the man continues. "You think I'm ever gonna order from you again? You think I'm gonna *recommend* you to anyone?" He emphasized the word "recommend."

Well, that's the kind of stuff I put up with at work. On the train ride home I recommit to developing a blog that I know will connect with people. I believe I will succeed because I look around me at all the other people on the train and, yes, some are happy and laughing and talking in an animated and bright-eyed way on their cell phones, going, "*Yeah? Yeah? Really?*" like maybe someone had an orgasm, but most are unhappy, unhappy and downcast and beaten, the new wretched of the earth in this vacuous, meaningless world we all inhabit.

I immediately go to my computer when I arrive home. My stupid life my ass, I'm thinking. I don't care who owns that name. I'll come up with something close enough, close enough to attract attention and make everyone forget this other site. I'm getting really excited. In fact, I'm salivating, maybe even frothing at the mouth. "My Stupid Life Sucks Dot Com." Yeah, that's what I'll call it. I mean, this is the Internet. I can use a word like "sucks." I'm not coddling stupid consumers back at the call center. I like the new name a lot.

"Hey, dude, I dig your crazy web site." I can imagine people saying that, or chicks pointing at me as I walk confidently by them feeling 10 feet tall and they say, "Hey, check him out. That's the guy who runs 'My Stupid Life Sucks Dot Com.' You think we should go up and introduce ourselves?"

I go to Network Solutions to register the domain name. I can't wait.

What the fuck! Somebody already has registered "My Stupid Life Sucks Dot Com." The site's not even up yet but some douche bag has registered the name. He thinks he can pay $7.95 a month forever and keep that name all for himself?

The next day at work just sucks. I can't get into any of these phone calls. I mean, usually there's one caller who stands out as so ridiculous, so stupid, that I can forget my troubles and just laugh at him or her all day. Mildred comes to my cubicle at about 11. Mildred is the middle-age woman I've been telling you about. She just had a guy who says his Chinese-made computer stopped working just before he threw it out the window and even though the warranty's expired he wants to send it back to us for a full refund. In pieces. "Like we're going to do that," Mildred tells me, sounding very much like Roseanne Barr, which is not a good thing. Mildred is not actually that fat, or even really an old lady yet. She catches me looking at her full hips and fleshy thighs under her skirt and they're definitely sending a message to me, and then I sense that she's winking at me behind a veil of implied sexuality. It's getting very surreal very quickly and she doesn't appear to be offended at all by my staring. She turns with a confident flair and walks out of the cubicle.

What am I thinking? I commit to developing another version of My Stupid Life Dot Com right then and there.

It's the weekend and I really want to get this right. What about "My Fucking Stupid Life Sucks Dot Com?" I ask myself. I quickly type in the words in Google. Shit. Someone has that, too.

How about "My Stupid Life Sucks and You're a Shithead, Too, Dot Com?" Oh, that name I can have! No one has registered "My Stupid Life Sucks and You're a Shithead, Too, Dot Com." But it's not a serious candidate. I can't insult the people I'm trying to seduce, so to speak.

How about, "Our Stupid Lives Suck Dot Com?" Yes, it's kind of negative, too, but it also shows communion. It's like the difference between the young Woody Allen and the young Chevy Chase. Whereas Woody Allen humor was always premised on the belief that we're all schmucks, Chevy Chase humor was premised on the notion that *you're* a schmuck. I decide to save that one, but I realize there may be a problem in making it too obvious that we're all losers.

Really, all I know is that the title has to include the words "My Stupid Life." That's all I know for sure.

More days roll by in what seems like a long march toward dejection while I search for the boundaries of my dreams.

"Sherman, Sherman. Are you home?" I hear loud rapping on my front door at home one evening. Is this the moment? The Blog Angel has come to deliver the Good News of online success forever. My wait is over. I quickly turn off the TV and jump up from my bed to answer the door.

"Oh, hi, Mrs. Kaczynski," I say. I should have recognized the accent but I guess I heard what I wanted to hear. "Sherman, do you have a flashlight? Our daughter's car won't start and we have to look under the hood."

This is how they came to America and bought up half of Chicago? They don't even have their own flashlight? That's what I'm thinking but not what

I say. "Oh, sure, Mrs. Kaczynski," I say. "I'll come down and help." I'm as earnest as a Boy Scout, as quick as a trigger.

"Oh, no, Janek knows how to fix things," she replies. "The battery died in our flashlight, that's all."

"It's no trouble," I insist. But Mrs. Kaczynski seems impatient now.

"Just get the flashlight, Sherman," she says. "Our daughter is in a hurry. She has a big date in Marina City."

I next decide to call my blog "My Fucking Stupid Life Really Does Suck Dot Com." I think about this title all day when I return to work but conclude I must investigate the legal ramifications of using one of George Carlin's seven dirty words on the Internet, even if the Internet is not radio. I'm afraid to search on a company computer, though. Employers own all tools to do your job in the call center business, not to mention the means of production per se. Yet imagine my dismay when I get home and run to my computer only to learn that "My Fucking Stupid Life Really Does Suck Dot Com" is taken. It's taken. Some guy in Sweden has it. What's a Swede got to be unhappy about? And why doesn't he call it "My Fooking Shtupid Life Really Does Suck Dot Com?" They all speak English with an accent over there, don't they?

I even find a similarly titled blog in Malaysia. It's called, "Fucking Stupid Life Really Sucking Big Dot Com."

I'm really unhappy now. I mope around the city the next several weekends and people just stare at me or walk closer to the edge of the street when I pass by. At work people congregate near my cubicle and talk in whispers while they steal glances in my direction. Even my boss is worried. I can tell because he has stopped making fun of me.

"OK, OK, I'll tell you what the matter is," I finally scream from the top of my desk after I climb up on it. I can see across entire room and into almost all of the other cubicles. I hear rustling sounds all around, then I see heads popping up over the walls of those cubicles as people stand up to see what's going on. A curious lot, people are, but that's not the same as giving a damn, is it?

"Yeah, I'll tell you what's wrong. All I want to do is start one fucking stupid little blog online, just like any other sane human being in his twenties might do today. But, oh no, you have to name your blog. And it has to be a name no one else has. All these other stupid people with their own blogs, even ones that aren't active, they can name their blogs anything they want and then you can't have that name. It's not fair. Fucking unfair is what it is."

I immediately feel better having gotten it off my chest. Cathartic, even.

I just let it all out, just like the magazines all say you have to do sometimes. But Big John O'Hara, a thirtysomething hunk of a guy, a big, tall dude with a bulked up chest and tiny waist who wears suspenders all the time at work, comes up the aisle and stops at the front of my cubicle. "Why don't you just name it 'My Stupid Life Dot Com,' Sherm?" he says to me. Then he walks off nonchalant-like.

I can hear the laughter from the other cubicles and a little wave of chatter as O'Hara moves down the aisle and passes by other workers on his way to his big office in the corner. O'Hara is the chief administrator for the call center branch where I work, my supervisor's supervisor, in other words. It's just so humiliating. They must be saying, "Good one, John," or, "What a dork, John." Everybody always is sucking up to John, you know. They don't care about me. I bury my head on my desk and begin backtracking in my mind to the very first time I thought I might have a blog. What was I thinking, really? The chances of having a successful blog and getting linked to Yahoo! or The Huffington Post are like landing on The New York Times best seller list, or winning the Megabucks Lottery or something. I'd have to hire professional web site developers and marketing experts and invest thousands and on and on just to have a chance.

My mind is drifting off into all kinds of end of life scenarios when I hear a light tapping sound behind me. It's Mildred. She's dressed in a silky blue polka dot blouse and a tight black skirt and she's done something with her hair, too. Her hair is shorter and especially richer, like she's started rubbing goop on it or something, like she's using all those infusion products they advertise on TV all the time. And she's wearing horn-rimmed glasses, but with very narrow lenses, the very trendy kind that all the roller girls like these days. She's pouting, too, giving me a kind of sympathetic, "Oh, Poopsie," look like you might give a kid who's scraped his knee in a play lot.

Then she lifts her skirt just a few inches over her knee and flashes me some inner thigh. She's got a wickedly sly smile on her face now. And it is at that moment, or maybe a moment or two after I look at her face, then at her thigh, which is a little puffy but not bulging or sagging or anything like that, and I look back at her cunning, smiling face, and I realize "My Stupid Life Dot Com" has worked out pretty well after all, thank you very much.

SIDDHARTHA

WALKING THROUGH THE THICK Indiana forest, outfitted in a black canvas backpack, long Bowie knife and high leather hiking boots, Oliver Kline believed he was doing the right thing.

Oliver—he never liked the name but he liked his nicknames Ollie, Olive Oyl and Freak Face even less--stepped spritely over fallen tree trunks in his path and skipped with verve over little rivulets from a recent rain. The forest floor was dotted with Bluebells and yellow Coltsfoot, little sprouts coming out of the ground before the tulip poplars and silver maples fully leafed out above, but also rotting leaves leftover from fall and old pieces of peeled bark that added a smoky scent to the air, like walking through a charred and abandoned house after a fire.

"A lighting strike," Oliver said aloud as he stopped before one split tree trunk. He knew there was no one else about but he liked speaking into the lilting air that enveloped him as much as he'd loved swimming naked in Lake Monroe when he was younger. He looked at the burn marks where the fat Beech tree had been struck by the lightning bolt--a squirrel curled inside the ragged fractured tree trunk while munching on something good seemed impervious to all.

It was late afternoon on this, his third day out, Spring coming fast, and he had to think if he wanted to sleep under the stars on a palette of those mashed leaves or look for better shelter. The DNR had put up picnic tables and little shelters everywhere in the Hoosier National

Forest, he knew. It's where he had slept the past two nights since leaving home, leaving his young wife and their 3-year-old behind. He'd thought of taking the kid with him, but then she would have called the police, sicced the dogs on him, maybe stuck a Bowie knife herself into his back once and for all. Oliver stood and took time to think. A bald eagle circled above, its white crown and deeply curved beak prominent against the sky as it passed between swaying tree tops above. He walked deeper into the thick of it.

"OLIVER, PICK UP JEREMY from Day Care at 4," Chastity told him as she set off for work earlier in the week. "There's chocolate milk and raisin bread in the fridge. The laundry needs doin', too." Chastity worked at a nearby nursing home--she had recently completed a CNA course at Ivy Tech and was scheduled for a double shift that day. "Put him to bed by 9," she added. "And don't call me at the nursing home."

Oliver had picked up his son from the Day Care pretty regularly in the past. It was such a part of his routine that he didn't realize how much he'd looked forward to it. The Day Care, run by a small church on the poor side of town dotted with empty storefronts and shadowy workingmen's bars, just a small clapboard building across the street from a dusty, low-rise public housing project with broken swings out back, had staff that always greeted Oliver personally, treating him with a respect so rare it infused him. Oliver and Chastity purchased Jeremy's crib and baby clothes from a resale shop the church ran on the side, too, and more.

Oliver thought of the time he came early to the Day Care and saw his son playing in back. All the kids looked like action figures in a diorama-- some climbed a little wood fort or swung from a Jungle Gym, others sat in sand boxes and filled colorful plastic pails, while still others were off in a corner consulting conspiratorially. Maybe they'd found a dead mouse or, better, a live caterpillar. Jeremy squatted alone in the dirt building a mountain. He worked steadily, calmly, diligently, and Oliver didn't know how long he'd stood staring at his son from the other side of a low chain link fence that surrounded the yard. But after a bit, a tiny slice of his own history, Jeremy looked up and caught sight of his dad. The smile broke on his face like the dawn, only more readily. It shimmered. Jeremy rose from his haunches and ran to his dad.

"Let's walk home," Oliver suggested, pulling his son up over the fence by his arms. "It's a beautiful day."

Chastity and Oliver had grown up in the same trailer park, the one near the old RCA picture tube plant two miles west of the Indiana University campus, but had not known each other. They met in high school when each spontaneously joined a group of goths who walked out of assembly one morning--the topics had been diversity, global warming and "no means no," all preached by an IU football player doing community service after beating up his girlfriend. The school suspended all the kids who'd walked out after the vice-principal picked them out of a closed circuit video of the event. It was the most exciting thing that had happened to either Chastity or Oliver, but they didn't want to become goths any more than they'd wanted to be model citizens, so they became fast friends with each other.

"How come we never talked before?" Chastity asked on their first date.

"I thought you were going with Robert Pattinson," he replied with a wink. They did it the first time in her trailer while her mother sat watching TV in the next room with the sound turned up high.

Tall and gangly was bad enough--that's why he'd been dubbed Olive Oyl by some--but Oliver also suffered from terrible acne that left deep scars across his cheeks and temples and even down his back, sort of like barnacles on an old ship. His hair was dark, thick and straight, which he liked, but it could not be trained. He tried to comb it like Dillinger but it just wouldn't stay.

Chastity was short and had a small chin that seemed to recede into her jaw, not cap it. Her neck flared at the shoulders too, like something vaguely amphibian, so she wore her crunchy red hair long and full like Gloria Steinem, which she meant as a distraction, not a statement. Yet when Chastity cut it back severely after getting the job at the nursing home Oliver asked her why.

"It's because of who I am now," she'd answered. "I'm a mother and a nurse."

OLIVER PICKED UP THE BOY at 4, just as he'd been instructed, but took him instead to his mother-in-law, who was watching Maury Povich on an older 19-inch portable TV inside her trailer; he brought the boy over in his 1996 Dodge Neon with 135,000 miles on the clock and a rebuilt transmission, among other recent repairs. He could do minor mechanical work well enough, but mostly it was other men in the trailer park who would pitch in to help, maybe for a favor, maybe for twenty dollars.

"It's in black and white," Oliver noted after looking at the TV for a few seconds. "What happened?"

"Chastity says she's gonna buy me a flat screen," Mrs. McCarver replied. That's what his mother-in-law liked to be called, even though she and McCarver had never actually married. "What you got there?" she added, pointing to Jeremy. Jeremy was the kid.

"Oh, I gotta go to a job interview," Oliver replied. "Chastity said to bring him over to you. I got some cookies and milk for him."

"What kind of job?" Mrs. McCarver asked. "You goin' back to Mickey D's?"

Oliver had worked at McDonald's on South Walnut after dropping out of high school, and he'd worked at a Swifty gas station pumping gas for drivers willing to pay 1 cent extra per gallon for full service, which was the Swifty angle. Most drivers wanted to save the extra penny. He worked for a landscaping business one summer and he'd applied to the Job Corps, too, but was turned down because he was married.

"Why would you wanna run off and join the Job Corps when I'm pregnant?" Chastity had demanded to know at the time.

"You gotta go away for the Job Corps?" he'd responded.

Oliver never did pay much attention to details. He'd taken auto shop in school, which is where he learned his little something about servicing cars, but he had trouble with actually rebuilding motors or figuring final drive ratios and oil pressure and things like that. His teacher shunted him off to body work where he'd sandpaper rusting body panels down to the shiny metal, then patch holes with body filler, but he didn't want to be a body and paint man so he quit school.

Oliver looked at Mrs. McCarver on the tattered floral print sofa in the narrow living room of her 48-foot trailer and over at the old TV and rabbit ears antenna opposite and he wondered why she dressed like that in the afternoon--a sheer nightgown that showed her basset hound breasts and more below in pretty good detail. He inhaled the stale air inside the trailer, too, which he didn't think could be good for the kid, but he didn't want to object to that just then. "Oh, I just got an interview down at Kroger," he finally answered. "Stockin' shelves at night. That way maybe I can watch Jeremy days and we won't have to send him to Day Care no more."

Mrs. McCarver snorted but did not at first turn her attention from the TV screen. They were about to announce which of three anxious, even defiant men that a young mother had slept with prior to becoming pregnant was the real daddy of her child. "You don't have to put him in Day Care now," Mrs. McCarver said. "You ain't workin' yet."

Oliver wanted to defend himself--say something like, "I been lookin',"--but he was conflicted. He didn't know what he wanted, but he'd never wanted a steady job.

"Well, Chastity'll be by after 11," Oliver said. "She says to put the boy to bed by 9. Maybe you can just let him sleep on the couch, or he can sleep with you." Jeremy already was seated in front of the TV looking up at Maury Povich, then he began giggling nervously as the young mother threw herself on the studio floor and flailed wildly after the father of her child was identified.

"They can do that with DNA testing, you know, just like on the police shows," Mrs. McCarver told Oliver. "You ever been tested?" she added with a witch's cackling laugh after the words.

Oliver ignored the insult and started for the door, then he walked back to the kid and stooped beside him. "Here, lemme give you a kiss," he said. Jeremy wrapped his arms around his father and leaned his head against his father's thigh. "That's my boy," Oliver added. "You know I love you," he concluded.

"I know you do," Jeremy said.

As Oliver opened the flimsy front door to the trailer, maybe three-fourths the size of a real front door, Mrs. McCarver called to him. "Can you get me some cigarettes at the BP?" she asked. "I'll pay you back."

"I'll try," Oliver said, but he didn't turn to address his mother-in-law directly, and he didn't stop to buy her any cigarettes. Instead, he drove directly to the main lodge at Brown County State Park--peaked metal roof, stained cedar siding and fieldstone inlays-- about 30 minutes from Bloomington on State Route 46, and he backed into a parking space in a far corner of the front lot. Only a few people were about as it still was early spring; nobody would notice him. He took out his backpack, checked his knife again, and carefully bent low behind the car to remove the license plate. It would be a few days before anyone took note of the little Dodge, then an additional delay while they tracked the owner from the VIN. It would be enough.

THE CLOUDS BEGAN BILLOWING by 10 p.m. and Oliver had found no shelter for the night. He'd situated himself on the downside of a stout red oak on a gentle grade in the forest, covering himself in a plastic tarp from Lowe's, and he knew he'd get wet, very wet that night. The moon was nearly full and had risen early that evening so he could see the lumps and swells in the clouds like the folds of skin in a fat lady, like the misshapen globs of Pla-Doh his son would bring home from Day Care sometimes, and he reveled in the shades of gray and blue tinged vapors above he hadn't realized existed before. He saw diffuse flashes of lighting behind the clouds and he listened for the muffled thunder that followed. "Goodnight, Moon," he said aloud. He had read *Goodnight Moon* many times to his son, even noticing his wife once looking on lovingly and smiling at him, which she did not do often. *Goodnight Moon* always put his son to sleep.

Oliver Kline stood up and removed all his clothes, including his cotton brief underwear and well-worn wool socks, and stuffed everything into his backpack, then he lay down on the ground again and pulled the tarp tightly around his shoulders. It began to pour shortly.

The sky cleared by morning and Oliver didn't wake shivering at all. He had to pee--he just walked a few feet away from where he'd bedded down--then he pulled a thin towel from his backpack and dried his body as if he'd just showered. The towel had a coarse weave and felt hard to the touch; a blue stripe ran down the center of it lengthwise. It was just a cut-down, institutional-grade towel Chastity had taken from a health club when she'd worked in housekeeping there, before she studied to be a CNA. Oliver snapped the towel several times with his wrists after drying off, then folded it and put it back in his backpack. He reached for a Special K breakfast bar in a side pouch, ate it while leaning against the big tree he had slept under, then he dressed and reckoned where he'd go next.

He was headed toward Kentucky. That much was clear. He'd heard that's where his people were from so he'd decided to look for them there. He didn't know who his people were, but they were from Kentucky. He didn't remember who first told him that, either, but it's what he'd always tell people when they'd ask, and they'd ask quite a bit in the trailer parks in Indiana. Being from Kentucky had more status than being second or third generation trailer trash, which was like second or third generation welfare mother. He thought maybe he'd head to Bowling Green. How he liked that name, and it's where they made Corvettes, too. Or maybe he'd travel to the John James Audubon State Park--that was closer. Plus, he always liked the nice illustrations of birds he'd seen in a book when he was younger.

The day was clear and Oliver walked out of the woods and onto a county road in Southern Indiana, walked along it for a few miles against traffic, and he came upon a country store, one with two round-shouldered gas pumps on a small cement island outside, a white-enameled ice box inside with worms for sale, and a toilet with a sign that read, "Employees only." The clerk--maybe it was the owner, he looked South Asian--sat on a stool behind the counter and eyed Oliver suspiciously. The two men nodded at each other, and the South Asian couldn't help but notice the long Bowie knife in a sheath hanging on Oliver's hip.

"How much are those lottery tickets?" Oliver asked after walking up and down the aisles--there were only three in the small store, three aisles, with cracked and chipped linoleum tiles on the floor, and all the shelving was old, dented steel.

"One dollar," the man told him. "One dollar, like always."

Oliver understood it was a bad question, that it had alarmed the man. "I got a dollar," he replied defensively. "Give me one of them Megabucks. How much is the jackpot? That's what I meant to ask. What was I thinking, right?"

The South Asian hit a couple of keys on the lottery machine and handed Oliver a quick pick ticket. "Anything else?" he asked.

"Yeah, some jerky," Oliver said, and he reached behind to pull a package of beef jerky from a wire rack. "Hershey Bar, too. Here's five dollars. Will that do?"

The South Asian eyed Oliver disdainfully as he exited the small store. The items had totaled nearly six dollars, but he didn't want to say anything. Trouble had left, which was more important to him.

Oliver continued trekking into the rising warmth of day, reaching US 231 by mid-afternoon. That would take him to Jasper. He felt comfortable enough to stick out his thumb. Cars, pick-ups, a couple of flatbeds hauling logs all passed him by but Oliver wasn't upset. It was a long way to walk, though, and rescue finally came in the form of a matronly woman driving a Chrysler minivan.

"Thanks much," he told the woman as he climbed in the passenger side. "I'm Oliver."

"Mildred here," the woman said. "Where you headed? I'm going to see my son at Fort Campbell."

Oliver didn't respond at first, but dropped his head into the padded headrest and sighed. It seemed like years since he'd seen his own son, though it had only been days.

"Your son's in the Army?" he asked.

"Sure is," the woman said solidly, proudly. "The 101st Airborne. You heard of the Screaming Eagles?"

Oliver studied the woman in profile. She was in her early 40s, maybe, and he noticed that she wore carpenter jeans, the kind with pockets and straps to hold tools and tape measures and things, as well as a zippered grey twill jacket like bus driver Ralph Cramden would have worn on The Honeymooners, which he had seen many times in rerun. He looked down at her feet--she wore clunky Dr. Martens boots.

"Maybe I should sign up," Oliver said. Traffic on the two-lane was light and the woman turned down the blower so she could hear him better. "What's your son's name?" Oliver asked.

"Well, how nice of you to ask," the woman said, turning to him. "Jeremy."

Oliver was taken aback. "What about Jeremy?" he asked nervously.

The woman turned again toward Oliver, then back up the highway. "Jeremy," she repeated. "He's my son."

A smile crossed Oliver's face like the soothing relief that comes when you open a door to find nothing's behind it after all. "Jeremy's my son, too," he said. "I mean, I got a son named Jeremy. But he isn't in the Army. He's only three."

The woman nodded. "I read once that Jeremy was the third most popular name for boys in the country," she said. "I think it was in USA Today. Jeremy, Justin, Jason, Jacob, Jordan, you know, anything that starts with a J, really. I wonder why." She leaned a bit forward over the steering wheel and wrapped her arms on top; traffic still was light.

"Jeremy's a real smart boy," Oliver said. "I mean, my Jeremy. I'm sure your son is real smart, too."

"Not really," the woman quickly responded, "but I love him anyway." She turned her head once again to read Oliver's reaction. "It's a joke," she said, smiling. "He is, too, smart. Smart enough. He's an E-5."

They drove for a couple of hours, past Jasper and soon enough came upon the Ohio River. "The Ohio carries more water than the Mississippi," the woman announced. "Did you know that?"

Oliver stretched his head over the dashboard and strained to see the river that flowed beyond the tree tops, flowing almost above them as in a classic Japanese painting. He could barely make out the ripples along the surface, but he could see a barge and a couple of power boats creating long, v-shaped wakes behind them as they traveled up and down the river. "I did not know that," he said after a delay. "I didn't pay much attention in school, I guess."

The woman took one hand off the steering wheel and patted Oliver on the thigh. It was a motherly gesture but it made him feel sad. "Poor Ollie. It'll be all right, Ollie." That's what it reminded him of.

Oliver decided to get out in Owensboro, on the other side of the river, where the woman had stopped for gas. It already was getting dark. "You can come with me to Fort Campbell," she told him. "I know you don't got no money. You can sleep in the van, or maybe they got a homeless shelter in Clarksville."

Oliver grabbed his pack from behind and said that was kind of her, but he'd be leaving. "They probably got a shelter in Owensboro, too."

Before he could leave, though, the woman stuffed a $10 bill in his hand and squeezed it hard. "It's all I can give you. Go buy yourself a nice dinner. You've got a lot of decidin' to do," she said.

"EXCUSE ME, WHERE'S THE homeless shelter?" Oliver asked a suited man on Frederica Street, but the man ignored him and kept walking. He asked a couple of women for directions and they, too, disdained him. Finally a policeman pulled up in his black and white squad car, looked over Oliver closely, then told him where it was without even asking what he was looking for.

"Can I get a ride?" Oliver asked in a jocular vein. The policeman smiled and rolled away slowly.

The Jesus Saves John 3:16 Owensboro Homeless Shelter and Mission was housed in a square-faced former department store with standard brick façade and large picture windows in front. Once filled with fashionable mannequins dressed for the changing seasons, the windows now featured community art work from the nearby senior center hoisted onto cheap easels alongside AIDS-prevention and Well Baby posters from the county health department. The atrium-like main showroom that once displayed fine jewelry and imported woolens and the like now served as the day room. A sweeping stairway and balustrade in back led to the second floor--that regal feature remained, but led to the makeshift dormitory now. After registering, including submitting to a hair lice check and rolling up his sleeves so a worker could look for needle marks, Oliver was allowed in.

"Passin' through?" a man seated in a chair next to him in the day room asked. They both were waiting on dinner. The man was old, with few teeth and indifferent whiskers that grew out of his nose and ears like wood burrs. He was gaunt, too, dry and hollowed out like a felled, rotting tree trunk himself, and he sat leaning so far forward in his seat Orville thought maybe he had a curved spine.

"Yep, I'm visiting my buddy down in Fort Campbell," Oliver told him. "He's a Screaming Eagle, you know."

The gnarly, bent old man sighed. "I was in 'Nam myself," he said. "Rats as big as hedgehogs."

Dinner was fine--roast beef and mashed potatoes, whole milk and apple cobbler--and Orville had stood in silence with his head bowed in prayer with everyone else when asked to for the blessing. Some of the men talked while eating, including trying to engage Oliver in conversation, but he just smiled back, then looked down at his plate and cut more pieces of meat or spooned more potato into his mouth. Afterwards he went upstairs to shower, then he emptied his backpack in a washing machine and laundered everything together. But when he wanted to go to sleep all the bunk beds in the dormitory were taken so he had to sleep on a cot in the hallway.

"Don't take your boots off," a man in the cot next to him advised. "They won't be there in the morning if you do."

Breakfast the next day was hot, including bacon, eggs, biscuits and oatmeal, a really good breakfast, Oliver told himself, one that would keep him until evening. He was about to move on, but he wanted to check the computer first. He wanted to see if they were looking for him in Bloomington.

They were. *The Bloomington Herald-Times* displayed the story of the runaway dad who'd abandoned his young wife and their child at the top of the e-Edition, and they featured a photo of a stressed Chastity combing her fingers through little Jeremy's hair as both stood near a stream that ran through their trailer park. She held the sad-looking boy up high on her chest as he rested his head on her shoulder. An inset photo showed Oliver--it was a picture from a couple of years earlier taken at night while they all were at the Monroe County Fair. It had been shot with a cheap disposable film camera and the colored lights from the Midway attractions caused too much glare. Oliver remembered the shooting gallery and the ring toss in the background fondly, though. The picture was a bit out of focus, but at least that obscured his acne scars.

"What are you looking for, son?" a man asked from over Oliver's shoulder. It was Father Joe, which was how the homeless shelter manager had presented himself at dinner the evening before. Father Joe dressed in dark trousers and shirt and a white clergyman's collar. Oliver turned to look at him, but closed the Internet browser first.

"Oh, nothin'," he said. "I have some friends in Bloomington. Just checkin' the weather."

Father Joe put his hand on the younger man's shoulder. "You can't find anything out on the road that you don't already have at home, son," he said. Father Joe was older, maybe 50, with a linebacker's build and straight, crew-cut hair, mostly gray but still full and thick. His entire persona suggested he had been around.

"Well, I gotta go," Oliver said as he rose from the folding metal chair. Another guest at the shelter stood nearby waiting to take his place at the computer.

Oliver checked his backpack--he'd packed it tightly--and he headed out the door. The shelter had a free shoe store, so he'd picked up some Adidas running shoes in his size, still good tread on them, which he wore in place of his boots. His leather boots hung by their laces from a D-ring on the pack.

Oliver thumbed rides from Owensboro to Bowling Green--an independent trucker hauling gravel in a Tri-ax ("Stay 200 yards back, not responsible for damages," warnings that always made Oliver laugh when he'd see the trucks pass by on the highway); a traveling salesman in a Ford Taurus who called on locally-owned drug stores ("*We're still here*--that should be their motto," the salesman had said somewhat sardonically); and a man in an older yellow Camaro with the T-tops removed, even though a light drizzle fell across middle Kentucky for most of the day. The Camaro's driver had pulled up easily in front of Oliver as if he'd been expecting him and didn't say anything at first when Oliver climbed into the low passenger side seat. But as he spun his wheels on the shoulder and sped down the highway he asked Oliver if he liked loud music.

A blues-rock tune, *Train-Kept-a-Rollin'* was being heavily piped through the car's several speakers. The car had the optional, 500-watt Monsoon sound system GM used to sell. "Is that Aerosmith?" Oliver asked.

The man's face grew long and he turned to Oliver with a darker, more menacing expression now, then he slowed the car and pulled back onto the shoulder. "Get out," he said. "It's the Yardbirds."

Oliver reached the edge of Bowling Green a little before 3 pm and he walked all the way Downtown. He stepped into a small café that faced the town square, *Janet and Victoria's*, which was run by two waitresses who had purchased it from the previous owner, a retired United Auto Worker.

"We're closin' soon, Hon'," a woman told him when he entered. All the tables--all 8 or 10 of them—were covered with red gingham plastic tablecloths and the Formica on the old-style counter near one wall was worn on top from all the plates that been served over the years. A letter board up high announced prices--Tuna Melt for $2.50, Fries for $1.75, and so on—but some of the press fit letters were missing. Janet or Victoria reached for a switch along one wall and turned off the lights. "We can get you somethin' to go, that's all," she said. "You got any money?"

Back on the highway Oliver got lucky when a contract driver for the Postal Service quickly pulled over and offered him a lift. "I'm goin' to Clarksville," the driver said after Oliver stepped up on the cab.

"Well, hallelujah," Oliver said, but not too loudly. "That's just where I'm headed."

The driver turned up his radio--classic rockabilly from Johnny Burnette, a contemporary of Elvis, blared from a loose speaker that rested on the floor at Oliver's feet. The truck itself was a vintage Kenworth with a flat face and split front window, and driver and passenger sat ahead of the front wheels. After a while Oliver introduced himself.

"You from Indiana, huh?" the driver asked rhetorically. "I got relatives in Huntington. You been to Huntington? It's near Fort Wayne."

Oliver shook his head. "Never been north of Indianapolis, actually," he answered.

"I get runs through Indy all the time," the driver told him. He extended his right hand to Oliver while holding on to the hard plastic steering wheel with his left. "I'm Jeff," he said, "but everyone calls me Ranger. I was in 'Nam, but that was a long time ago, right?"

Ranger dropped off Oliver by Gate 7 at Fort Campbell, halfway between Hopkinsville and Clarksville right on busy US 41. Though it was night by now Oliver saw that the wide boulevard was denuded of trees; garish lights from the tattoo parlors and Korean seamstresses and used car lots lighted up the street, however. Lots of vehicles entered and exited the post, including many fast Japanese motorcycles, which Oliver took note of. He fitted his backpack more comfortably over his shoulders and strolled toward the gate.

"Got your I.D.?" one security guard asked. "Here, step to the side," he continued. "Where's your car?"

"Oh, I just took a bus in," Oliver said. "Indiana driver's license OK?"

The guard checked the license against pictures in a book and scanned it with a black light, too, before returning it. "What's your business here, fellla?" he asked. "You're not comin' from Basic like that, are you?"

Oliver chuckled. "No, I ain't in the Army," he said. "I'm just lookin' for a friend."

The guard shook his head and looked Oliver over more closely now. "What's your buddy's name?" he asked.

Oliver laughed again, then scratched his head. "You got me there," he said. "I don't rightly remember."

The guard scrutinized Oliver even more closely now. "You don't know your friend's name?" he said.

Oliver scratched at the pavement with his toes and licked his lips, too, before speaking further. "Well, you see, it's really my Dad," he said. "I think he was in this unit. The 101st? That's what everyone told me when I was growing up. He died in Desert Storm when I was just a baby. I figured maybe they got records here or something. That's why I'm here. His name was Kline, Oliver Kline. I'm Oliver Kline, Jr."

THE TV CAMERAS CAME late in the afternoon to Chastity and Jeremy's trailer in Bloomington, though one satellite van had parked outside all day, attracting other young mothers out strolling with their babies as well as old men on Social Security who lived in the park and, after school was out, plenty of kids on BMX bicycles with banana seats left over from the 1970s. When Chastity arrived home with her son she pushed through the barricade toward her trailer, wrapping one arm around Jeremy's head as if to protect him from projectiles and insults.

"Have you heard from your husband?" one television reporter called out, attempting to thrust a microphone in front of Chastity.

"Is the child in any danger?" asked another.

Chastity started to open the door at the top of the short wooden steps leading to her trailer, then she stopped, brushed her hair back, turned, and faced the clamoring crowd in front.

"Has your husband abused you?" a reporter demanded to know. "Have you filed a police report?"

"Did you know he was busted for possession once?" asked another.

"An Oliver Kline is wanted for manslaughter in New Mexico. Has your husband ever been to New Mexico? Is that where he's headed now?"

Chastity surveyed the 10 or 12 reporters pressing against her space and the dozens of neighbors who stood behind them. "You can all just go home," she told them, waving one arm at them as if she were trying to brush them aside. "Didn't some IU student get raped today? Isn't there a run on a bank somewhere? This is my life, mine and Oliver's and Jeremy's, not some TV show or gossip around town. Go home. It's where we all belong." She wiped Jeremy's face again, then opened the door to her trailer and stepped inside. Her mother, who had been baby-sitting the past few days, greeted her.

"Oliver called," she told Chastity. "He wants to come home."

Chastity went to the refrigerator and pulled out a carton of milk and poured Jeremy a drink, then she popped a slice of raisin bread in the toaster. "You want some raisin bread?" she asked her son. Jeremy nodded shyly.

"I got a number where you can reach him," Mrs. McCarver continued. "He's in Hopkinsville, Kentucky. He called collect and left a number. It's a pay phone at the restaurant."

"'The restaurant?'" Chastity repeated in a mocking tone. "They got but one restaurant in Hopkinsville, Kentucky?" She pushed off and went into her bedroom to change. Chastity had worked the 7 to 3 shift at the nursing home and didn't need to be back until 11 pm the next day.

Oliver came home two days later. A long haul driver from Sodrel Trucking in Jeffersonville picked him up on I-65 and dropped him off at the depot, then Oliver worked his way back to Brown County State Park where he retrieved his car. He walked through the front door of their trailer as if he'd just come back from shopping. He dropped his backpack on the floor and walked into the living room, where his mother-in-law sat watching TV. "Why don't you go home," he told her curtly while stretching to switch off the set. Her jaw dropped in response to his impertinence and she looked to her daughter for support.

"Come on, I'll take you home," Chastity told her mother. "Watch the boy," she told Oliver.

Mrs. McCarver grew huffy but had trouble pushing herself off of the sofa. "Don't do it. Don't take him back," Mrs. McCarver said. "Men are no good."

"I know," Chastity said. "Daddy left you because men are no good. And Oliver's daddy left him because he wasn't no good, either. But Jeremy will have a daddy. Come on, I'll take you home now."

When Chastity returned several minutes later she took Oliver by the shoulders and pushed him toward the bathroom. "Now you take a shower and get that road stink off you," she said. "There's mac and cheese in the fridge I can warm up. And I want you to read Jeremy a story tonight. I got some books from the library."

SACRIFICING ISAAC

THE YEAR WAS 1955 and the city Chicago when I decided to protest the Biblical account of the sacrifice of Isaac, which we were studying in Hebrew school at the time. What kind of God would order Abraham to kill his son, and what kind of man must Abraham have been to agree to this? Did Abraham take his son by the hand and smile at the boy, kiss him on the cheeks like any father would do? I wasn't the first person in history to contest this story, but then it was just me, the rabbi and the Torah.

The rabbi tried to calm me by saying God wasn't really going to let Abraham butcher his son. It was a test of faith, that's all. But to me that was the problem – God was playing this cruel hoax on Abraham and this man, the father of our people, really would have killed his son had God not stopped him. But such a man couldn't be my father - that's what I knew.

Rabbi Mordechai Fein was an old man with a big pot belly and buzz cut hair, sort of like Curly on The Three Stooges, which I could watch on TV after school at a neighbor's house sometimes, yet he dressed better than Curly, always wearing a light gray suit and dark tie and polished leather shoes on his feet. Rabbi Fein was nice to me in general, once whispering the answer to a question in my ear when it was my turn to say something and I didn't know the answer, but he grew impatient with me this time. I beat the top of my desk, the kind of old schoolhouse desk with cast iron legs and a wood top that opened like a lid, and I screamed, "No, no, no." I don't know if the rabbi charged me just then and dragged me away by the collar or if I tried to run away; I just remember being held by him in a head lock near the door to the room, his elbow folded under my right arm from the back while he pressed down on my neck with his forearm. I tried to stop him, to resist, as he wrestled me toward the principal's office. I can still see the look of horror on the other boys' faces but also empathy in the few who turned away in shame at this cruel reenactment of the sacrifice of Isaac.

MY FAMILY LIVED IN an apartment above a candy store on a commercial street on the Old Westside in those days, a neighborhood in transition from Augie March to urban slum. My mother worked as a cook at nearby Mount Sinai Hospital, which is why we were tethered there. I wasn't allowed my own key to our apartment but I could always find my way inside the stairwell because the lock on the door to the street outside had long since been broken; I usually waited at the top of the stairs for one of my brothers to arrive and let me in to the apartment.

My older brother Hillel, who attended the same school, came up the steps soon enough but didn't say anything as he walked around me. Once we both were inside, though, he said he'd heard what happened earlier that day. "God tested you today and you failed," he shouted in anger. "Do you know what that means?"

"God tested Abraham," I replied, brushing past him on the way to the kitchen to get a drink of water. "But Abraham didn't test God."

When our mother came home she wanted to know what I had done. If I was in trouble at school that meant I did something wrong. This was a normal and predictable interpretation for people who believe in authority, who trust it. But I could tell she wasn't going to pursue the matter further, at least not then. She'd had another bad day in the kitchen, making up for people who didn't show up for work, taking the blame for a dietician's menu error, or just listening on the phone to family members complain about the quality of food in general. She turned to the refrigerator and took out some celery stalks and carrots to chop and then she poured oil into a skillet for fish she would fry. At dinner Hillel sneaked looks at me, then at our mother, waiting for something to happen but nothing did. An older brother, Jacob, who came home late, said he ate already at a friend's house and he went straight into his room. Our mother got up from her seat and wrapped his plate in wax paper, then dropped it loudly onto a shelf in the refrigerator. It had been a very bad day at work, maybe a worse day for her than it had been for me.

My mother spoke with the principal the next morning by phone. "Yes, he's very sorry for what he did," she said. "I don't know what upset him. Yes, yes, I understand. Yes, yes, it won't happen again." My mother said all the normal and predictable things when she spoke to the principal. I stood with my arms folded petulantly across my chest as she continued speaking to the man. She listened to more jabber on the other end of the line while she fidgeted with buttons on her blouse. She had called the man and apologized. She had thought that would settle the matter. Now she had to get to work. "I'll talk to him!" she said with finality, and then she slammed the handset onto the receiver.

And as she hustled herself through the front door and down the stairs she said I better not make more trouble at school but her command didn't impress me; I wasn't going back to that school. I'd read books on my own, I'd get a job delivering newspapers and save up enough money to run away from home, I'd hole up like an outlaw in Old El Paso. But I wasn't going back to that school, and I didn't, at least not voluntarily.

After a few days of truancy the school sent someone in person to our home. Once more my mother apologized for me but I told this person what the problem was. God was a liar. He was crazy, too. My mother began crying when she heard me say that. I was threatened again and again by the representative. "They'll send you to a hospital, a hospital for children like you," she said. "They'll send you to the reform school on Foster Avenue," she continued. "You'll have to grow cabbages and potatoes in the field and scrub down the floors in the dormitory yourself. You'll live with *goyim*."

I took her at her word. It would be a new life. I'd work in the fields, which was great. I'd get to meet new kids. It was great.

The woman issued a parting shot to my mother. "They'll take him away from you if you don't make him go back to school." My mother tried to suppress her tears but couldn't. Then she hit me, slapped me across the face, and went off to work as usual.

I returned to the Hebrew day school after three weeks. No one carried out their threats against me, but I had become bored at home. It's like the immortality these people were always promising – eventually it would become boring. They put me in a different class.

"Why are we called the chosen people?" the new rabbi asked the students on my first day back. "Did God inspect all the peoples of Earth and decide we were the best, better than all the rest? Better than the Moabites? Better than the Idumeans? Better than the Egyptians, who were better than the Greeks and Persians combined? No, no. That's not what happened at all. God went to all the peoples of Earth, to 70 different nations and offered them the Torah, his law, his word. Anybody could have it. But all these other peoples, they wanted to know what they would get in return. They wanted to know what was in it for them before deciding."

I can see the rabbi bent forward over his old single-pedestal oak desk, an expansive chalkboard nailed to the wall behind him, and he's smiling warmly while scanning the room. He has intense eyes and a sharp little jaw with a trim goatee; he looks a bit like Lenin. "Only the Jewish people said without hesitation, 'We accept the Torah.' And God said, 'Yes, but what do you want in return?' and the Jews said, 'We don't want anything in return. We accept your law unconditionally.' That's why we are the chosen people."

MOTHER COOKED MEALS AT Mount Sinai during the day and after a while she took an additional, part-time job as a short order cook at a diner down the block from where we lived, working until closing time, which I think was 2 am, maybe even later. I had been to the hospital to visit her several times, but I never went into the diner. I decided to change that one afternoon. "Hi," I said to the man in a white paper hat who stood behind the counter at what I recall was named O'Reilly's Diner. I stared at the man's smudged apron and wondered if it was blood. The man, fleshy and ruddy, wiped his hands on a cloth and looked at me suspiciously.

"I'm Judith Silver's," I told the man. I didn't think to say son.

The man smiled. "Yeah, yeah, your mom said she had kids." The man cleaned his hands further and then stuck his right hand over the counter to shake mine. "She's comin' to work tonight, ain't she?" he asked.

I just shrugged. The diner was classic – round stools with chrome rings and shiny red vinyl seats lined the long Formica-topped counter, itself embedded with glitter, and you could hear the bacon and eggs sizzling and popping on the grill behind. I didn't know my mother served bacon and eggs, but I immediately intuited she was doing it for us. "She's not home from the hospital yet," I told the man. "I'm just out playing. That's all right, isn't it?"

"Sure, sure," the man answered. "Let me get you a Pepsi. You got any money? OK, your mom can pay me when she gets here."

I had watched the restaurant from across the street once before when I snuck out of the apartment after my mother put me to bed and I'd peered between the passing cars into this glowing hothouse of strange people who sat on stools in the evening and didn't go home themselves. I could make out my mother well enough behind the counter, moving her thick arms from pan to pan and pot to pot, flipping hamburgers with a spatula and serving up soup with a ladle. My mother had long, dark hair in those days but always wrapped in a bun and tucked under a hair net when she went out to work. I could see her chest heave as she flitted about and thrust her arms fore and aft, and I wondered what she was thinking when she wiped the sweat from her brow.

MY MOTHER, BORN IN 1917 in Zambrow, Poland, in the east-central part of the country, was a modern woman in her own way – she read romances in German and Polish and during a field trip to an art museum in Warsaw spent all her money on reprints of French impressionist art depicting dance halls and waterfronts and the like. Yet she also knew the standard prayer book as well as most men. She was a woman with her feet in two worlds. The eldest of 11 siblings, she was married off in 1935 – a teen bride - to a young *Hassid* she did not know and moved in with him and his family farther East, nearer the Soviet border. The Germans invaded Poland on September 1, 1939 and occupied most of the country, including Zambrow, but the Soviet Red Army quickly occupied the border region nearer their lands, including where my father and mother then lived. They, and a son born in Zambrow himself in 1936, were relatively safe because the Germans weren't ready to take on the Red Army just yet. The two other sons were born during the war, and I was born a year after it ended.

My oldest brother, Gerald, the one born in Poland in 1936, spoke only Yiddish upon arrival in America, but he was the *gaon* in the family and he was quickly enrolled in a full-time yeshiva in Cleveland. He was a great student, or so I was told, played the violin, too, yet he was expelled when he was 17 or 18. It was after he was kicked out that he came to live with us on the Northside of Chicago, where we had moved after my mother got a better job as food service director in a nursing home.

When Gerald came home from the yeshiva our mother ordered him to see a psychiatrist. Being kicked out of a yeshiva was a pretty bad thing, I surmised. "A Jewish doctor will know what's best," she said. Gerald had been through a lot in his short life. He clearly remembered Poland and he must have known his lost aunts and uncles, at least on our mother's side. He escaped when they had not. He must have remembered the long train ride across Russia to Vladivostok, then the refugee center in Shang

Hai, living on handouts and caution all the time. He remembered our father falling prey to a fever shortly after we settled in Chicago, making our mother a widow.

The psychiatrist worked at Mount Sinai Hospital. Gerald had to take the 'L' Downtown, then transfer to a bus, and then walk through a typical hospital hallway maze to find his doctor. I don't know what Gerald and the doctor talked about, but the psychiatrist told him to get a job and go to school nights like lots of American Jews had to do in the 1920s and 1930s, maybe like this doctor had to do himself when he was younger. That was the Jewish American success story when Gerald's success story was that he got out of Europe alive. Gerald took a job washing dishes at the nursing home where our mother now worked, and he went to school nights. He decided he wanted to be an architect.

"Here, help me set up this table," he said after our mother brought home a disassembled drafting table for him. We only had a pair of pliers and a butter knife for a screwdriver but Gerald proved to be handy. I thought we had made a mistake when we completed building the table because the surface was slanted, but Gerald explained that that was how one worked at a drafting table.

"I need a stool," he said. "Do we have a stool? Maybe somebody threw one out." He explained that you had to sit tall at a drafting table and get a good look at everything; you had to lean into the table top without falling into it lest you start to draw uneven lines. "It doesn't matter," he said. "I'll stand."

"Do you need to know algebra to be an architect?" I asked him one evening as I leafed through the inscrutable pages of a math book he had. He laughed. "It's calculus, not algebra," he replied. It's one of the few times I remember him laughing.

But it didn't last. He stopped going to classes and he stopped going to work, too. The doctor then advised him to join the Army. At least that's what was said around the dinner table. I didn't see that as a prescription or a punishment. I thought it was exciting. I still didn't fully understand that something was wrong, that what might look like opportunity to some really could be teetering on the edge. Gerald joined the Air Force and I still have a picture of him in uniform. He looks very thin and the oversized cap on his close-cropped hair lends a starkness to the image, perhaps exaggerating the effect. His wan, unhappy expression is unmistakable, though. Gerald lasted six months before getting a General Discharge. It was said he ridiculed the Godlessness in the barracks.

One day after this return he called me to the window in back of our third-floor apartment on Drake Avenue and asked me to look closely at a telephone pole in the alley below. "Don't stand so close," he said as he pulled me back from the window. "Do you see him now?" he continued. "The man hiding behind the pole? I don't want him to see you." It was the first time I cried for Gerald.

Gerald was committed to a state psychiatric hospital in Galesburg in western Illinois. My mother visited him on most weekends, taking a Greyhound bus from Downtown, then via a Studebaker Lark she eventually bought, in part to make it easier to see her son. She would always be agitated in the days and hours before she was to travel to Galesburg. One learned not to talk to her during these periods. After my mother died I found some old letters Gerald had written to her postmarked from Galesburg. "I promise to be good," he wrote in what seemed like a school boy's shaky cursive script though he must have been in his early 20s by then. "I don't want to be here. Please let me come home. I promise to be good."

This is how Gerald died: they were taking him back to the hospital, my mother and Jacob, who was driving by then, and Gerald did not want to go. I watched from our third-floor apartment as the drama unfolded on the street below. He would not get in the car, so my mother took off one of her shoes and began beating him about the head, which he covered with both arms and elbows.

"Mother, mother," he cried.

Then he broke free, turned and ran up the stairs of our apartment. He ran straight into the kitchen, grabbed a long, serrated knife, and stabbed himself through the heart; he died in the arms of a firefighter who came later to offer assistance. He did not die cleanly or instantly.

I should tell you that Gerald was not my oldest brother's real name. Nobody born in Poland was named Gerald, not Christian and not Jewish. When Gerald was born he was named Isaac after one of my mother's siblings. It was his father's family, which I guess is my father's family, a part of our father's family that had come to America years earlier, who changed his name to Gerald. What prophet was named Gerald? It's a name from a 19th century British romance. Yet it's still hard for me not to think of him as Gerald. Even his headstone says Gerald.

And my mother had only one wish when she lay dying in a nursing home many years later. Bury her not in Poland or in Jerusalem, but next to her oldest son in a sprawling, gothic cemetery in a western Chicago suburb, far away from and out of sight of all of God's creations.

THE SOUND TRANSIT 594

I WATCHED AS THE YOUNG MAN boarded the bus, swiped his travel card, and took his place at the head of the crush. Thin and bony, slack-shouldered, too, he wore a Nordic-style knit stocking cap on his head, the kind with tassels hanging from ear flaps, and his hair, though not overly long, stuck out like straw on a corn broom. He carried a chipped and nicked skateboard under one arm, which he stuck in an overhead bin, then he peeled a canvas rucksack from his back and tried to stuff it into the same storage bin, but it wouldn't go, even after several attempts. He gave up and tried to mount the rucksack on his back again but there barely was enough room on the bus to turn around, let alone hoist the heavy bag over his shoulders, so he impassively held it to his chest and steadied himself against the press of other passengers as the bus trundled on. I decided to get up and help the young man.

"Try this," I said as I pulled my old-style attaché case from one of the overhead bins, the kind of flat, stiff case all the ad agency types on "Mad Men" carry. I set it upright on its hinged bottom, and then I asked the young man for his rucksack, which I stuffed between it and a cardboard box nearby.

"There," I said proudly, turning to the young man. I tried to ignore the laconic, even fagged look on his face, a bleary, beat appearance that almost defined him. "You just have to analyze the situation, then come up with a plan. Big things or small, it's all the same in life."

The young man smiled wanly while balancing himself on the bounding bus, but I sensed a snarky, smirking sort of malevolent vapor frothing behind the façade. I wasn't going to challenge him. I just wanted to look at his emerald green eyes, bright even in this brooding, overcast Pacific Northwest sky, and at his wide, thin lips, raspberry red and smooth like melon, innocent, fresh and young. He said nothing; his head rolled on his shoulders like a ship moored at sea, waiting, a calculated delay more than at rest. I clenched my fist lightly and tapped him on his breastplate before turning away.

Once back in my seat on the Sound Transit 594, an afternoon intercity run from Seattle to all points south, I opened my tie at the neck and leaned across the woman in the seat next to me. I smiled curtly as I pinched the releases on the window so I could lift it high, then I smiled at her again as I dropped back into my seat. The bus was stuffy, yes, but breathing could be difficult for me at times like this.

"What was that all about?" the woman asked, looking up momentarily at the boy then back at me, concern in her eyes both for him and my own pallid appearance. "Who is he?"

I looked straight ahead without answering at first, then I took a deep breath and sighed. I suppressed a tear and told myself I had to be brave, and I answered her.

"That's my son," I told her. "He lives in Lakewood. I see him on the bus sometimes."

ANTOINE, WE CALL HIM ANDY, left home at 17. He didn't finish high school, had turned down early admission to Cal Tech, and wouldn't consider UW-Tacoma at all (we all lived together in Tacoma then). He just wanted to be on his own, he said.

"Fine," I told him, not squeezing him too hard for information, wanting to give him his space.

Andy had always been independent, even a bit edgy. When he was 14 he spent the night alone in the Olympic Mountains, climbed much of Mt. Rainier, too, organizing and planning the trips on his own.

"Lewis and Clark came all the way up the Missouri River and the Columbia River Gorge," I told Andy while he still was in middle school. "You could have been part of that expedition." I took him to the library and we borrowed a couple of books on the expedition. We read them together.

He was the little adventurer, someone who really did listen to the beat of a different drummer, but Melinda never saw anything positive in what he was doing, especially wanting to leave school early. "You've got to stop him," she harangued me when Andy first broached the possibility of dropping out. "He'll ruin his life. It's crazy talk. Stop him."

"*Stop him, stop him, stop him.*" That's how I remember her seeming then. She could be very shrewish.

I did ask, though, why he wanted to leave school, leave home, too. We were seated at our kitchen table, a round oak table my grandparents bought for their wedding that had been passed down, and only a single light was switched on. There was a soft, easy glow in the room.

Andy shrugged. "I don't know," he said somewhat haltingly. "I mean, why not, right?" He looked up at me hopefully, but as if he wasn't sure himself. "It's just, like, I know I don't want to go to college. Not really. I mean, if I go to college, then I'll have to get a job using my degree. Or I'll have to go to graduate school next. But eventually I'll have to get a job, buy a house, maybe marry and raise kids. Then it'll be all over. That's not living. That's dying." He was 17 at the time.

I reached across the table for his hand and clasped it firmly between my two. I remember how relieved I was that he didn't pull away. "Is it something at school we don't know about?" I asked. "You don't have to go to college. There are all kinds of post-secondary options out there. You like cars, don't you? And the military needs smart kids like you. You don't have to tote a gun."

"I just want to start with nothing," he said.

"You want to make your own way," I said. "I completely understand. But start with nothing? What does that even mean? Have you heard of John Donne?"

Melinda blew up when I agreed to help Andy find an apartment in Lakewood but it was a compromise, part of a plan. I didn't want him moving in with drifters, the kinds of kids who hang out at the Greyhound Bus Station or do Hare Krishna chants inside airport terminals. Living on your own could not mean living on the street. He'd have a warm, safe place of his own, and we'd know where to find him.

"You gave in?" she admonished me. "Just like that? What? You moving in with him? Is that it?"

Melinda had stayed home with Andy when he was younger, then she took jobs she thought were beneath her – check-out at Safeway, front desk at a day spa, even telephone newspaper subscription sales. They probably were beneath her – she was not stupid – and she blamed me for forcing her to stay home with Andy when he was younger, forcing her onto the Mommy track. She was so addicted to jealousy and resentment. She felt that if life were fair she wouldn't have had to take jobs like that in the first place. I secretly thought she should be more like Andy – if she really didn't like things, then make the change yourself. The world doesn't change for the person.

Melinda was 45 when we divorced. Andy leaving home was the excuse, and maybe she had stayed with me only because of him all along. She got the nice house and I moved into an apartment near Wright Park. We'd separated a month after Andy moved out.

ANDY LET ME VISIT HIM a few times. I helped him furnish his apartment – one bedroom with a kitchenette, maybe it should have been called a studio – and we went first to Salvation Army and Goodwill but there isn't much good stuff at those places anymore, all chipboard and veneer. We bought some knockdown furniture at Wal-Mart, imported pine pieces from Brazil, and that was much better, then a real chest of drawers and kitchen table from a consignment shop in Puyallup. It was fun helping him set up, and I thought Andy was proud of his place when he was finished furnishing it. For that I was proud of him.

"How's the job search?" I asked after a visit. I had staked him to some money, maybe Melinda had, too, but I didn't think this was welfare I was giving him. He'd worked some fast food jobs, even delivered phone books when he was still in high school, but he was in no hurry to find a regular job, he said.

"I'm looking for a life, not a job," he said.

"Can't argue with that, kid," I said.

But he had a job of sorts, volunteering at a bicycle action project near the University of Washington in Seattle. I worked in Seattle, too; that's why we would meet sometimes on the bus.

I wondered about his friends, what he did at night, why we did nothing more than go to a movie or dinner at a seafood restaurant together. "It's all good," is about all he would say. Or, "I'm getting close." I didn't know what he meant by the latter.

"How is Andy doing?" Melinda asked me over the phone one evening.

"Ask him," I suggested. I wasn't being facetious. I didn't say, "Ask him yourself," which would have been like throwing the question back in her face. I wasn't doing that at all. I just wanted Andy to know he had people who loved him, who cared. She needed to show more interest herself.

"I'm seeing someone," Melinda then said. "I haven't told him I have a son."

It was Melinda who had balked at having a child. That surprised me at first, but informed by the years I was able to look back at the past more critically. We'd met at a Presbyterian church's single mingle night, which is where I thought I'd find respectable, God-fearing, socially conservative people. I worked in the accounting department of a Fortune 500 company and was studying to be a CPA. I wore a suit and tie to work every day, polished brogues on my feet, Penny loafers on weekends.

Melinda had dark, salon-curled hair with maybe a bit too much mousse and she wore too much glossy red lipstick, as well, but it was a single mingle group and we all were trying to impress, right? She stood near the punch bowl holding a clear plastic cup to her mouth, gently swaying to a Harry Connick Jr. record when I approached her. She was a bit frumpish even then – her navy blue dress was cut high on her bosom, just straight across and ending in poufy shoulders at either end, and she wore maroon pumps on her feet that covered her toes and instep. She was not a style leader herself, but I kind of liked the traditional look. She had a wonderful smile – a smile can work wonders – and I thought she was genuinely happy to be asked to dance.

We did fun things on dates like trainspotting from a foot bridge over the Chambers Creek Properties, which is an old gravel pit on Puget Sound that has since been converted to a park. I still like the orange and dark green color scheme of the BNSF locomotives that pass through it on the way to California. In time, after we were married and after Andy was born, we'd all go trainspotting there. I thought Andy loved it, too. He always seemed to study the trains, to gaze at them, his eyes growing wider as they'd approach, sometimes eerily through the morning fog on the Sound. "Wave at the train," I'd tell him and I'd start waving frantically. Andy would wave, too, and sometimes the engineer would blow his whistle.

Basically, I'd wanted a job, a future, and a family growing up. I thought that's what I'd achieved, too. "Hon, I'm making enough money now that we can start a family," I told Melinda during our third year of marriage. We rented at the time. "We can buy a place of our own, maybe a nicer older home in the North End."

I'll always remember her look when I said those words. Dour. It was a dour look. *"Not interested,"* it said. Or, perhaps, *"Oh."* It was the kind of response that could make me think, *"Well, don't get too excited,"* that is, if I ever got facetious with people.

Melinda and I had family in the area so Andy did not want for doting grandparents and aunts and uncles, or cousins who would play with him just because he was their cousin. Hide-and-seek, building forts in the woods and searching for Indian artifacts – he seemed to enjoy it all.

But as he grew into his teen years the thrills needed to be bigger and scarier all the time, hence Mt. Rainier in the winter, hence bicycle rides in the direction of Spokane until we'd have to come get him.

I NEXT SAW ANDY on the Sound Transit 594 about two weeks after the day I'd helped him with his rucksack. I boarded at 2nd Street in Seattle, he closer to the architecturally calamitous football and baseball stadiums nearer the Amtrak station south of Downtown. He got on with another young man – this other one toted a guitar case and sported stubbly facial hair – and they seemed to be jovially engaged with each other as they stood at the front of the bus. A passenger had to snake around them to go down the aisle. The bus was not as crowded as the last time and they could have moved a bit closer to the rear themselves, but didn't. I was seated about halfway down the aisle.

What were they talking about? Was Andy really happy just then? Who was this other boy? Those were the thoughts that ran through my mind. I wanted to go up and approach them but I stifled myself. Andy no longer wanted to see me uninvited. He'd call when he wanted to see me. That was the contract. I had violated it when I helped him stow his gear and we both knew it, but he didn't make a stink. It was understood that I wouldn't do it again, though.

The inter-city bus pulled into my stop near the Tacoma Dome and I decided to exit via the back door; I didn't even turn my head for one last look at my son as I got off. I waited for the bus to pull away, and then I walked to my car in the parking garage and drove home.

There is a good side to Wright Park, one with a conservatory and young people throwing Frisbees, and there is the wrong side, one with men who drink cheap wine from plastic bottles and live in cheap apartments with broken door bells and ripped mailboxes. I lived in the latter, not because I was destitute, but because they gave me a month-to-month lease. I was still considering my options, even a year after the divorce.

When I entered my apartment I dropped my briefcase on the sofa and sat next to it, then I picked up the TV remote and turned on the news. This was much of my routine in the evenings. I'd watch the news, maybe

Jeopardy!, too, and only then would prepare a modest meal, fry a piece of fish on a skillet and open a can of corn, something like that. In the longer lighted summer evenings I'd take small walks in the park, or stroll along the waterfront at Commencement Bay.

"Why don't you move to Seattle?" a co-worker once asked. "You can afford it." I could. I'd thought about moving to Seattle, if for no other reason than all the time I'd save commuting. There was another reason to think about moving, too. I hadn't dated anyone since the divorce and all the available middle-age women at work were coming on to me. Word was out that I was available. I didn't know it was so easy. Either society had changed in 20 years, or it was getting near closing time at the bar, so to speak. I never was unfaithful to my wife, but I could see sleeping with other women in time. I wasn't against it. And it would certainly be easier to date women in Seattle if I lived in Seattle. So why didn't I move to Seattle?

I just wanted to see my son on the bus, the Sound Transit 594, where I knew I'd bump into him from time to time.

IT WAS A SATURDAY in May that Andy invited me to visit him in Lakewood and I was excited to come. I hadn't been invited over in weeks. Andy had touched up the place in detail ways – a black and white photo on the wall, correctly matted and framed, showing the 1940 collapse of the Tacoma Narrows Bridge, and a color movie poster from "East of Eden" – and he had a better table lamp and shade than I'd recalled. I liked the jute rug in the main room, too, a definite improvement over the unvarnished hardwood floor it now covered. I complimented him on all these things.

"How have you been, Andy?" I asked. I sat in an old Morris Chair I'd helped him pick out when he moved in.

"I'm doin' fine," he said. He sounded fine, too. His voice wasn't forced, not anxious in any way.

"So what are you up to?" I continued.

He didn't answer directly, instead apologizing for not offering me something to drink. "Would you like a Coke?" he asked. "I bought some Pomegranate soda at World Market. It's very tart. Would you like that?"

I chose the latter and Andy returned in a minute from the kitchen with two tall glasses filled with this new treat. It proved to be very refreshing and tart, just like Andy said.

"How's the insurance business?" Andy asked as he settled back into his chair. He sat casually but confidently and he peered into my eyes; we both peered into each other's eyes.

"Same old same old," I said. "I know that's not much of a description. I get a bonus this year. They used to give raises but now they just give bonuses. Raises are recurring, so companies don't like them."

"How's Mom?" Andy asked.

I was taken aback. "Have you spoken to her lately?" I countered. I didn't mean it as a challenge.

Andy leaned back in his chair. "She calls," he acknowledged, "but I tell her I'll contact her if I need to talk to anyone. She finally got the hint."

He was speaking pretty cavalierly about his mother and I have to admit I was somewhat gratified. Maybe he knew who the bad guy was in the split after all. I was feeling a bit vindictive, I suppose, but the main thing was for Andy not to blame himself for the divorce.

"So, what's new with you?" I asked, returning to my original query.

Andy told me he had done a lot of thinking about his future, that he was coming close to making some interesting choices. I was excited to hear this.

"That's good," I said. I thought I was speaking in good faith, but Andy admonished me for being patronizing. I wanted to deny the charge, defend myself, but I didn't want anything to become contentious. I told him, "All right. I'm listening."

"Good," he said, as if he'd won the battle, as if there had been the briefest of dust-ups between us.

I studied him in the light that filtered into the room, his face striped by bars of light streaking past the Venetian blinds in his windows, the lines of light on his face like war paint. *"He's a beautiful boy,"* I thought to myself. Did he remember the first time I took him to the Tacoma Center YMCA basketball camp and he didn't seem to know what to do with the ball when the counselor handed it to him, yet he made a basket in his first attempt? He'd looked down at his hands after the shot, then he turned slowly toward me and smiled. "I knew you could do it," I shouted then.

"So, tell me what you've decided," I said. "It's the story of your life. I think it's a pretty good read."

He chuckled at that, and I smiled in relief. He didn't think I was patronizing him now. "So?" I continued.

"Well, I've been thinking about college, for one thing," he said.

"Yes?" I interjected expectantly.

"Yes, well, I'm definitely not goin'," he said. He paused after that.

"All right," I said. "No one is making you."

"That's right," he said. "No one is making me."

"The military is out, too," he said. "There's a guy lives here, he's stationed at Lewis-McChord. It's not for me. 'Left, right. Left, right,' and all that."

"Well, that's not all they do, I don't think," I said, but I left it at that.

"I've been down to the carpenters' hall and they have classes. It's all paid for and then you get your union card. That's not so bad, I guess. I could learn to build my own house, you know?"

"Working with your hands is great," I said, "and it's working with your head, too. Fitting things, sourcing materials, bidding on jobs. Remember Charlie Wiggins? He was a union carpenter, took only high-end jobs, too."

"Then I went over to the train yard at BNSF. I asked if men still drove spikes into the ground with sledgehammers and one guy told me, 'Sure, we hire rail splitters the first Thursday of each month.'" Andy raised his elbow and pulled it down a couple of times, as if he was yanking a giant air horn. "He was joking. They weren't hiring rail splitters, only mechanics."

I yanked on the imaginary air horn, too, and we both laughed.

"Then there's the Philippine fishing industry," Andy said. "People still go to sea. I could go away for two years, ports of call in places I've only read about. Maybe that's why I was born on the sea."

Now I was concerned.

"And I've read about the diamond mines in South Africa, I've read all about them," he continued. "I could go down in the mines with all the natives and we'd dig with our hands for diamonds, and at night we'd plot rebellion against the slave masters. I'd go native, sort of like the guy in 'Dances With Wolves.' I'd live off of wild boar meat and dead zebra carcasses, you know, just rip the flesh from their bodies. Maybe that's what I'll do. Right now that's my favorite option."

I sighed deeply. I had thought he was being serious. Worse, maybe he thought he was being serious. I looked out the window. I looked for the sun that now fell behind a building on the other side of the street. I looked up toward the sky, still light blue beyond the trees. It was blue, baby blue the sky was. We used to fly a yellow kite against a sky like this, Andy and me. Even Melinda had cheered while seated on a blanket we'd spread on a grassy knoll in the park, reclining on her side, pushing down on her skirt if the wind whipped it up a bit, just a happy family then, me with a happy family and a beautiful boy, Edward Hopper contentedly painting us from behind his sturdy easel.

I HAD WANTED TO MEET the guitar player since I first saw him on the bus with Andy, but I always was afraid to bring up the prospect. Andy would know what I was thinking – *"What, you don't like it? You think something's wrong?"* – and so I waited. I waited.

I was visiting Andy about a month after the previous visit, sitting in his main room, when I heard the key turn in the lock. We were talking about a movie we'd both seen, albeit separately – "Mud," featuring Matthew McConaughey but starring the Mississippi River, which no one seemed to understand except us – and Andy jumped from his seat and trotted merrily toward the door. I saw the black guitar case but I could not make out the young man's face as his head was bowed and he wore a baseball cap with a Japanese motif or lettering on top, which obscured him further. But it was him, the guitar player, and he leaned his case against the wall next to the door, then he hung up his black motorcycle jacket in the nearby closet.

"I want you to meet Calvin," Andy said, turning with a flourish toward me. "Calvin is in a rock and roll band."

Calvin was about the same height as Andy but more broad-shouldered and muscular. His scruffy facial hair seemed more like a carefully crafted look, like all the GQ and Calvin Klein guys with that just-rolled-out-of-bed-and- didn't-have-time-to-shave look, a standard swaggering appearance for young men these days. But the black motorcycle jacket was cheap and thin, an even more egregious affectation, certainly not the thick leather that a serious rider would wear. I wondered if he could really play the guitar, or if he just strummed a few chords while banging his head in the air. I disliked him immediately.

"Hel-lo Andy's father," Calvin said as he walked over to me, extending his hand theatrically. "Andy has told me so much about you. Well, he's told me almost nothing, but at least he's told me nothing bad. That's good, isn't it?" His laughter at his own joke seemed forced and I chose not to join in, though maybe I just froze.

"Hello," I said rather formally. "Any friend of my son is a friend of mine." Calvin smiled curtly, then turned back to Andy.

"Do we have any whisky, Antoine, dear?" he asked while stepping into the kitchen. "I need a drink. Rehearsals were brutal today. I think we have to fire the bass player. We open in a week-and-a-half and we are in no way, shape or form ready. I cannot go on stage if we are not perfect. Would Jimmy Page? Hmm?"

Calvin already was deep in the kitchen as he continued to speak. I could hear a cabinet door open and slam shut, then I heard Calvin drop a couple of ice cubes into a tumbler. He returned with a short glass tumbler filled with what looked like whisky almost to the top.

Calvin and Andy had met after a show at a small bar in Spanaway. Andy had gone alone and they met after the set, which was a mix of Led Zeppelin covers and original progressive rock tunes Calvin had written. "We're going to be big," Andy assured me. "I'm the manager now, but sometimes I play the tambourine on stage."

I asked Calvin how long he'd been playing an instrument, where he studied and what might his day job might be, if he had one. He just made a face and continued drinking without answering me, but Andy interceded on his behalf.

"I think he's a genius," Andy said. "Well, maybe not. But you have to strive for perfection. That's something you taught me."

I was struck by that concession – "That's something you taught me." The years had not been in vain, yet what was he doing with someone like Calvin, I wondered. I looked closer at this young man. His skin was not that good, ruts and remnants of teen-age acne apparent even on his neck, and I sensed a sleeping malevolence just beneath the surface, a primeval predatory proclivity.

Calvin offered to play a song – it was a few bars from "Kashmir" on his acoustic – and I listened. He assumed the pose – head bowed, spine curved, the air surrounding him weepy with emotion – and he was pretty good, actually. I told him that, too, and added that this might make things tougher on him if his career failed to take off. "The closer you are, the harder it is to let go," I said.

I could see Calvin's head almost explode when I said that. His nostrils flared and his eyes rose up like two full moons and he took a deep breath, then he went into the kitchen and returned with his glass filled with more ice and whisky.

"I know you're right, Andy's dad, the sweet smell of success and all that, to smell it, almost taste it and then not have it, it has to be the hardest thing," he said, not looking at me as he spoke, but throwing his head back and downing half his drink in one gulp after he spoke.

"MELINDA, I THINK WE'VE LOST HIM," I told my wife a few days after the visit. We were at her lawyer's together to work out some details of our final divorce settlement, mainly how my retirement benefits at work would be divided. The new man in her life – he introduced himself in the outer lobby of the lawyer's office, he had driven Melinda there, he was quite a bit older – kissed her lightly on the cheek, then said he would wait downstairs in a nearby Starbucks. Melinda's lawyer asked if I wanted to consult with my own attorney before signing anything. I told him I'd read everything carefully, that I knew what the score was.

Melinda didn't react too strongly when I said, again, "I think we've lost him."

"Don't worry so much," she told me as she sat on the other side of the walnut conference table in the lawyer's office. Papers were spread out in front of us and the lawyer had his head buried in some of it, ignoring us like he must have ignored hundreds of other couples who were forced to use his services. "It's like you said yourself," she continued. "Everything will work out. And if it doesn't then there really was nothing we could have done about it anyway."

IT'S BEEN TWO YEARS since I last saw Andy. I'd gone one more time to his apartment in Lakewood, uninvited that time, and the building superintendent told me both boys had moved out, but separately. He didn't know where they went, but they'd left some furniture that he'd stored in the basement for a month, then he called Goodwill to come and collect it.

I didn't know Calvin's last name but I knew the bar where he sometimes played. "Oh, that band?" the bartender mused. "They broke up. Most do, you know." But the bartender gave me a phone number for the lead singer, a girl who lived in Seattle.

"No, I don't know where they are," the girl told me, "but Calvin likes to use people. He thinks he's all that. I used to date him." Andy had talked about signing up for the Columbia Gorge Job Corps, though, the girl told me. It was another lead and I checked it out, of course, but I came up empty again.

Now, I do little Internet searches for Andy, not just for his name, but for places and activities that I think he might have been drawn to. Maybe I'll see his face in a crowd shot, I tell myself. I just want to see him again; one more time would be enough.

On the other hand, I do see Andy sometimes. I see a young person who boards the Sound Transit 594 on my way home, I can never leave Tacoma now, just anyone who is tall and lanky and relaxed, more so if he's wearing a backpack and carrying a skateboard, and I see Andy. I remember him, I love him, I see him. It's almost like dying a peaceful death and hoping to be reunited in that place called Heaven with a lost loved one and there he is, we're all together again, all is forgiven and forgotten and we're together for ever and ever and ever, all the pain gone now, worth the wait and whatever else it may have been, too.

BEST JEWTOWN HOT DOGS

SOMETIMES I WANT A MEAL, and sometimes I just want a hot dog.

Being in Chicago I have choices. I can go to any gas station and grab something off the roller grill for 99 cents with beef as the third or fourth ingredient, or I can walk up to a corner stand in most neighborhoods and get a better quality Vienna hot dog, all the sauerkraut and pickles and onions I want, for about $3.50. That's actually what people think of when they think of a Chicago hot dog.

I always got my franks at Best Jewtown Hot Dogs, which was the name of a little, one man stand in the old Maxwell Street Market just southwest of the Loop. Don't let the name distract you. There's a Chinatown in lots of cities; there's often a Little Saigon and a Moscow on the Hudson and the Barrio, too. Here we have Jewtown, or at least did, once upon a time in Chicago.

I'm a newspaper reporter by profession. Some people might call me a hack, a fear-monger, a paparazzo, maybe even a shill for corporate interests and the current white male power structure. But I like to think of myself as a journalist on the go who gets hungry sometimes.

Early in my career I worked the cop shop, which is where they always start cub reporters, though no one uses the term "cub reporter" anymore and, in fact, I never heard anyone use it from the time I got my first job at the Sun-Times back in 1989, the year the Cubs won the National League East title, if you can believe that. On a typical shift I might be listening to the police scanner while playing Solitaire at my desk and some body had been found shot up pretty good in an alley near 79th and Drexel – not somebody, but some *body* – and it's 3 a.m. so I put on my nice jacket and run down there to cover the story. Or it would be a big arson fire and they were still pulling out bodies, or there was a hostage situation and the SWAT team had been called in. If it was really late I'd tell the night editor to hold six inches for me – OK, she was a babe and it was a running joke between us, but Becky was a good sport – and after the first few months I'd written so many homicide stories I could almost file my copy ahead of time, just fill in the names and addresses later.

I don't cover crime anymore. Like I said, they just make newbies do that, and as soon as they hire another fresh-faced kid out of college they put that person in the cop shop and you're free to go, which in my case meant covering high school sports, at least for a time. I remember being told to insert as many names as possible into my stories because that way parents would buy extra copies of the paper – they told the photographers to do lots of crowd shots and team photos for the same reason – yet management took me off that beat after less than a year. See, the editors always wanted me to be enthusiastic in my copy and tout the next Michael Jordan or Mike Ditka and the importance of good grades and all that but after I wrote in one game story that a running back from Morton Grove couldn't find a hole if he was standing on the edge of the Grand Canyon I was transferred. I thought it was a pretty good line for a sportswriter, actually, the most successful sports writers always being assholes anyway, but we issued a written apology to the young man and his school two days after the story appeared. Lately I've been covering zoning board hearings and garbage strikes and Tax Increment Financing for the Metro section, which at least allows me to get out of the office a lot.

Now, before giving you the full scoop on Best Jewtown Hot Dogs, I want to assure Abraham Foxman that I am, like him, Jewish. I don't say "member of the tribe" because I hate the smug, insular nature of that expression, but I don't deny my heritage like some Jews do, either. Basically, I'm a native Chicagoan. I grew up in Albany Park, right next to the Ravenswood 'L,' they call it the Brown Line now but that's got no character, and I graduated from Theodore Roosevelt High School on Wilson Avenue before studying journalism at the University of Missouri-Columbia, "*Go, Tigers*," like I really give a shit about that.

Anyway, now that you know a little about me, I have to tell you more about Best Jewtown Hot Dogs.

I discovered the place while still on the police beat – some guy was cut up pretty good and thrown in the river nearby with a heavy chain wrapped around his ankles so that he would sink to the bottom (like that trick ever works) and the police pulled out the corpse easily enough, but they had some scuba divers go in once dawn broke and I had to hang around to see what forensic evidence they could turn up, *like the shiv!* They weren't making any progress at all – they found lots of guns and broken glass bottles and tire irons but no knives of the right size – and suddenly I noticed the sweetly organic scent of fresh onions hot on a grill, the tangy, juicy smell of really good all-beef hot dogs, too. "Oh, that's Best Jewtown Hot Dogs," Sgt. Sean Flannery told me. I worked a lot of cases Downtown with Flannery. "Come on, I'm hungry, too," he said. It wasn't even 10 in the morning but I loved every scrumptious, mouth-watering bite and when I finished the first dog I bought another.

Best Jewtown Hot Dogs was just a shack built up from two-by-fours and plywood with hand-painted signage, a cross between something you might see at a county fair and a vegetable stand out in the country. There was a front counter as well as a roof that tilted up in front a bit, plus a long shingle with the name, "Best Jewtown Hot Dogs," emblazoned in red, blue and yellow, basically the Vienna brand hot dog colors. None of it looked permanent but that was part of the charm. A few pictures of famous people who'd eaten there hung from hooks – Mike Royko, Bob Newhart, "The Big Hurt," which is how baseball player Frank Thomas always signed his autograph – plus a faded newspaper feature story about Maxwell Street sealed in plastic that had mentioned the place.

Willie Williams – he was the owner – was a traditional black Chicagoan, hence the name, Willie, not Abdullah, not Ja'quan or Jay-Z or Snoop Dog, either. He wore his hair in a short Afro like it was 1962 and had a big gold chain around his neck like he was starring in a Blaxploitation flick from the '70s, but when it was really hot and muggy like it often is in summer here he dressed in a kind of skin tight blue polyester shirt that made no sense at all to me.

Willie and I became pretty good friends over the years. We'd go to White Sox games together and we'd get good seats, too, box seats along the first base line and we enjoyed the overpriced beer and salted-in-the-shell peanuts, and sometimes Frank Thomas or Paul Konerko would really smash the ball and the home team would win. Several people over the years recognized Willie and would come up and tell him how much they liked his dogs, but I was only recognized once. *"Aren't you the asshole who wrote that an expansion at Midway Airport would add 3,000 jobs and $200 million a year to the economy, but didn't mention that the contractor who won the bid was the county commissioner's son-in-law?"* some guy demanded to know. I guess he got pretty drunk on the 3.2 beer they sell in ball parks. I told him that the guys with the juice paid the managing editor

$5,000 to keep that detail out of the story but it wasn't me who'd written the story anyway. That was David Warshawsky, I said. There was no David Warshawsky at the paper, he was just some kid I remembered from Sunday school, and I had no idea what story the drunk was talking about.

The great thing about Best Jewtown Hot Dogs, what made their dogs great, was that they had the right amount of sizzle. "It's all about time and temperature," Willie once told me. "You start with an all-beef hot dog, the best cuts from the cow, not too much filler although you do need some. You can't make a great meat loaf without filler, right? Then you put it on the grill for just so long, and you turn it over just so many times. That's the main thing."

Willie liked to jabber when I would come by, which was one of the reasons I always stopped by, over and above the food. I'm sure he talked to all his regulars, knew most of them by name, too. Willie always would ask me about crime in the city, even years after I'd been off the police beat, and I would make up all kinds of shit, like me once tailing all the Italian gangsters from Oak Park for three weeks.

"They still got the mafia out there, don't they?" Willie said when I told him of my escapades.

I shook my head as if to say, "Yep."

"And you weren't never scared to write about those people?" Willie said.

I just shook my head.

"Well, you sho' is full of shit, Mr. Rosen," Willie finally said. Rosen – that's me.

"But, Willie, why do you keep asking me about the crime beat all the time?" I asked him. "You know I write about landfills and illegal dumping now."

"Cause no one is a better bullshitter than you are, Mr. Rosen," he said.

It was all part of a larger game between Willie and me. He would ask me about all the beats in the newspaper, about the world outside his little two-by-four shack and beyond the imaginary walls of the Maxwell Street Market. "How's the Mayor?" he might ask one day, or, "Did you get to interview Mick Jagger when he was at the United Center?" Then I'd make up some incredible shit about actually jammin' with The Stones on my harmonica and Willie would say, "I sho' wish I had yo' job, Mr. Rosen" and I would say something like, "Yeah, I'm doin' Uma Thurman next week, I mean, I'm doing an interview with her."

Before you call me a racist, maybe you think I'm portraying Willie like he just stepped out of a Stepin Fetchit movie, you should know that Willie was a very individualistic person. He liked to play the fool with me just because he was making a commentary on the stereotype, not conforming to it. Anyway, it meant we were friends, that we trusted each other.

I liked Willie and his business so much that I often took my girlfriends down to Best Jewtown Hot Dogs. "Hey, this is my good friend Willie," I'd tell the ladies, then I'd tell Willie, "This is Bobbi Jo or this is Angela or this is Olga." Willie would always wink at me when I introduced a new woman and he didn't try to hide it and I didn't want him to hide it, either. It made the women feel special, like they were hot. I get laid pretty regularly, no complaints there, but I never stay with one woman for more than 12 or 18 months or a couple of years at the outside.

"Willie, do you know what day it is today?" I asked him once. It was August 25.

"Wednesday?" he replied.

"No, Willie," I said. "It was 10 years ago on this date that I first encountered your hot dog stand. Remember that body they pulled out of the river? Me and a fat cop came over for a bite to eat while they were still diving. He was the guy who told me about this place. You gave him a dog for free but you charged me."

"Yeah, yeah, yeah, Sgt. Flannery," Willie said. "I remember him. Nobody gave me trouble when he was around. Didn't he get killed in a shoot-out a couple of years later?"

"Yeah, well, that, too," I said, "but the important thing is he introduced me to your dogs."

Over the years a few people complained about the name of Willie's establishment. One time it was a gaggle of Chabadniks who carried signs, "The Messiah is coming" in Hebrew and another time someone painted a swastika on the side of the stand. I asked Willie once if he knew the real story behind Best Jewtown Hot Dogs and he said he only knew about the place from the time he bought it to the present so I filled him in. See, I'd made a point of researching the history of Jewtown and the hot dog stand. This is more or less what I found.

The origins go back to the Old Westside of Chicago, as it was called by all the Jewish people who'd lived there when they were younger, but it was Jewtown to most everyone else, particularly black folk. In those days the area around Madison and Pulaski or anywhere near the giant, terra cotta covered Goldblatt's Department Store at the same intersection was the heart of Jewtown. The streets were rife with Jewish bakeries and kosher butcher shops and Jewish-owned candy stores and card shops and clear vinyl upholstery businesses and more, the kinds of businesses that middle-income Jews ran so they could send their kids to Harvard or the University of Chicago and what not. One place in particular sold hot dogs and polish sausages; the business operated out of a little shack right on the sidewalk, but it really was the adjunct of a delicatessen right behind it, Manny's or Marty's, I don't exactly remember which. The proprietors lived in an apartment on top of the actual store, which was common for any Mom and Pop business in those days.

On a Friday afternoon everyone would stop into the deli. They sold cold cuts like salami and pastrami and cured corned beef and all sorts of freshly ground sausages and hot dogs tied together in long strings, not packed and wrapped in plastic, and they bought fresh bread and bagels and especially *Challah* at a bakery next door. Both the deli and bakery were happening places on Sundays after church, too, as a lot of Christians and Greek Orthodox stopped in to buy pretty much the same stuff.

Then, one day, just like that, snap your fingers and it was all gone, the stores and the bakery and the deli and almost everything else on the Old Westside, otherwise known as Jewtown all gone. Even Goldblatt's was shuttered, later to become offices for the public aid department or some state agency like that, though the store's memory lived on in a Jimmy Reed song, "I Ain't Got You," the dude boasting that he had an Eldorado Cadillac with a "fat tire on the back" and a "charge account at Goldblatt's," too, meaning he'd really made it.

But the hot dog stand survived. Not the original owners, perhaps, but it was just that somebody opened up this little hot dog stand in the Maxwell Street Market and named it Best Jewtown Hot Dogs. Everyone would have understood the reference, at least in the beginning. When that proprietor died Willie came along and bought the place. Best Jewtown Hot Dogs continued.

I KNOW I COME OFF as a pretty streetwise guy, but really I'm a pussycat. I mean, I never laid a hand on one of my girlfriends in anger, I never tried to embarrass anyone in print, and if I caught a couple of married reporters making whoopee on the side I never spread it around. I always drove American-made cars, too – a Second Generation gold Camaro just like James Garner on the Rockford Files, I was going to restore it but gave up, then a Mustang GT convertible with the old pushrod motor, it was OK, and currently an extended cab Dodge Ram pick-up, why not. I'm now The Newspaper Guild vice-president at the Sun-Times and I work five or six disciplinary hearings for errant reporters each year, maybe they'd come to work drunk, maybe they'd paid a source, or maybe they'd spat in the face of a copy editor who changed their lead, and I get most of them off, or at least nothing worse than a suspension. And I did flip the bird to a corporate lawyer during contract negotiations one year when the company said it was going to unilaterally cut wages, which was my way of telling him to go fuck himself and I think he got the message but we ended up with a shitty contract anyway.

And I've even opened up my house to a new girlfriend, Theresa, and her two kids. See, they were homeless when I took them in, but only technically so because they were living with Theresa's mother on the far-northwest side at the time. Theresa was a woman I'd met a few years earlier. It was at a police ball they were having at the Blackstone Renaissance Hotel on South Michigan and I'd been invited because everyone remembered how I would cover up for police misconduct when I worked the cop shop (the real reason I was transferred to the women's pages, I suppose) and, truly, cops never forget a favor. This was well before Theresa was homeless. She was working the bar at the event and she gave me the eye each time I asked for another Scotch and Soda and, well, to make a long story short, she's a Size 38 D cup, even if the rest of her is a little large, and though we stayed in touch, just occasional phone calls and text messages, we never got together in that sense. But we did after her divorce. She's in her early 40s now, just like me.

I live in a nice house in Evanston, a four-bedroom Colonial in brick that I got cheap because it was a murder house, that is, a murder-suicide had been reported to have occurred on the premises and there was yellow police tape all around the property for at least a week after the bodies were discovered. The house was badly stigmatized, a word Realtors use among themselves but never publicly, meaning if people knew something terrible had happened in the house they'd never buy it yet everyone knew anyway as it was in all the media. I wasn't working cops at the time so I didn't cover the story but I asked the guy who did if the house still looked OK on the inside and he said it did. I figured the stigma would go away after a while, as it always does, and I bought the house cheap.

I explained to Theresa when she moved in that I was really doing it just for the kids and the arrangement was only temporary until she got a place of her own. She said, "Uh, huh," and unzipped me right then and there and got undressed herself and we made love on the big L-shaped sofa in the living room. The kids, age 8 and 10, were in Girl Scouts at the time.

Theresa and the kids have now stayed with me for six months. Their dad gets the kids every other weekend and there's been no trouble with the guy when he comes by to pick them up other than he's real snarky and he drives a Chevrolet Cavalier. I'd become so used to the arrangement that one recent weekend I had the brilliant idea to take Theresa, the kids, and him – the ex, I mean it – all of us, let's go down to Best Jewtown Hot Dogs. I had the Dodge Ram parked in the garage and although the kids wanted to ride in the bed of the truck I got everybody inside the cab well enough. It was that or take the Cavalier and I was not going to let Hank – that was the ex – drive me around in a 12-year-old Chevy Cavalier, even if it wasn't rusting too badly yet.

Oddly, none of us thought it was strange that we would all go out together. The kids wouldn't have thought it was strange in any case – kids are like that, they just like large families and for everybody to get along, even if they do pout and fight among themselves sometime - and Theresa was a very tough babe, actually, so I wouldn't have expected her to care but, I mean, did Hank have no self-respect? I wouldn't let my ex-wife's lover take me along on a date anywhere, ever, that is, if I had a wife.

It was a Sunday and of course Willie was working the trade; Sunday was the busiest day for everyone on Maxwell Street. "Hey, Willie, how many dogs you serve on a good Sunday," I asked him once.

"I don't know," he answered.

"Yes, you do," I said. "For inventory, for tax purposes. You gotta know how many you sell."

That was when he told me he had one cash register where he'd ring up sales while at work, and another cash register at home where he'd ring up the fake sales, like keeping two sets of books. He'd jimmied the time of day stamp at the home cash register to randomly add between five and 30 minutes to each successive sale.

"What you got there, Chief?" Willie asked me when I showed up with Theresa and the clan.

"Yeah, yeah, I bought some friends with me," I told him. "This is my friend Theresa, this is her husband, what's his name, and these are their kids. I told 'em all about your dogs and they insisted on coming."

"They want the special dogs or the regular dogs?" Willie asked. He was wearing a heavily stained white apron at the time, mostly from sweat and relish and mustard. I didn't know anything about "special dogs" but I figured Willie was just saying that for the kids' sake. If so, it worked, as the girls clamored for the "special dogs" with "everything on 'em."

I paid for the dogs and Cokes all around and we went for a little tour of the Maxwell Street Market. We passed the usual electronics stands with old boom boxes and Walkmans and myriad old DC converters, past the used tire displays, past the cardboard boxes packed with original vinyl LP records, past the crappy used clothing racks, though one showed a little style, specializing in second hand high school and college varsity jackets. I especially liked a clean Lane Technical High School jacket – all wool, chenille Indian head logo on the back – but I didn't go to Lane Tech so I passed.

And then there was a guy with a gazillion new Parker Jotter ball point pens, still in blister packs, on a folding card table at one corner. I had to stop there.

"Where you get these, man?" I asked. It was a hot Sunday afternoon and it was almost time to head back to the truck. The kids had been surprisingly compliant and I didn't want to push my luck with them too far, but I figured I could use a new pen on the job with a spare in my desk. I never liked the Bic pens the newspaper provided.

"Don't worry where I get pens," the man in an ill-fitting suit speaking in a thick Russian accent said.

"Do they work?" I asked.

"Pick one, anyone," he said. "All work good, *ochen xorosho.*"

I tested his hypothesis and he was right. I looked closer at the clicker on top and noted that the Parker logo was stamped incorrectly so I figured they were factory seconds, but the sample wrote fine. I bought a dozen – the man wanted a dollar for each but I gave him a $10 bill and when he protested I retrieved the bill and wiped it across my crotch and handed it again to him and even though he sneered heavily I knew we had a deal. I was only surprised that the girls didn't think this behavior was abnormal at all. I gave one pen to each person in my company at the time, even Hank, and when we walked past Best Jewtown Hot Dogs I gave one to Willie. "That's for when the state auditors come by," I told him.

It was a great afternoon with Theresa and Hank and the kids but when we got back to my house I told Hank to get lost. I wasn't that liberal after all. "But I get the kids for two weeks every summer," he protested. "This is the time. I just went along to that hot dog place with you to keep you happy. Aren't they packed yet?" I looked at Theresa and she made a face. Oh, yeah, what was I thinking? We all went inside and helped the girls pack – the My Little Pony, the chapter books, the frilly underwear and the bathing suits and sandals and it got to be so much I just gave them an old duffle bag to use.

"Make sure you launder it before you give it back," I told Lisbeth, who was the older girl.

"I do not do windows, either," she said while batting her eyes. She was a good kid.

Actually, they were both good kids. Unfortunately, too many kids think it's normal to be shuttled like this between schools and between families and between neighborhoods. That's another story, I guess. Thank goodness they were resilient kids.

Theresa lit up some weed immediately after Hank and the girls left. I was a bit surprised because I did not keep marijuana in the house, not counting the guy who once sold stuff to me out of the evidence room at police headquarters but that was years ago, and she had never offered me any before, either. This was the first time the kids would be away for an extended period, of course. "Where did you get that shit?" I asked Theresa.

"From the caterers," she said. Theresa still worked galas and balls and conventions and all that. In fact, our best sexual fantasy was when she'd dress up in full black and white hostess attire and put on these very clunky, almost Nun-like black leather shoes, but with no underwear underneath whatsoever, and I'd put on my best suit and tie and a nice felt fedora and play the role of out-of-town conventioneer. I'd say I was from Des Moines and she'd ask me how was the corn crop this year and then she'd pull me down on the bed by my tie while she straddled me and slapped me around a bit, but not too hard.

Well, we got really wasted that evening and by the time we were finished it was past 8 p.m. and I didn't know what I wanted to do next but I was hungry. "You know something," I said. "I think I need a hot dog. Come on. I bet Willie is still there."

That was a long-shot, actually. The tourists and day trippers would be well on their way home by 8 pm, or they'd go over to Grant Park to catch the light show at Buckingham Fountain, but I thought Willie might still be closing up. Any leftover hot dogs – the ones that maybe had been on the grill for hours like at a gas station – they had their own charm, too. We rushed down to Maxwell Street in my truck.

Shit. Best Jewtown Hot Dogs had burned down, plus a couple of stands on either side of it. A fire department pumper had doused the blaze with a high-pressure water cannon, which pushed over the charred remains of all three simply constructed and nailed together shacks and blew out several windows in an old warehouse behind the stands, too, where they stored used auto parts.

"Move along," a policeman said to us. "You have to move. We're setting up a perimeter."

I recognized the cop – I'd interviewed him once in years past, I think he was a detective then, but I forget the story – and he didn't seem to recognize me, or maybe he was embarrassed that he was doing shit like this now, basically security work.

"What happened?" I asked. I didn't identify myself. He pointed to what looked like an oversized sack of potatoes lying on the pavement just a few feet from us, which I hadn't noticed at first. Except it wasn't a sack of potatoes. It was Willie all bent and twisted, blackened and crispy with white ash at the tips like a burnt, spent log in a fireplace. It was Willie and he wasn't moving. Two EMTs stood just beyond the body – one was on a cell phone, the other leaned against the outer panel of an ambulance. I looked at the second man – I didn't know him at all, but he read my mind perfectly, he shook his head and looked away after spotting me – and I knew Willie was dead.

Willie was dead.

"How did it happen?" I asked the cop.

"Gas grill blew up, or the LP tank did," he said. "They'll do an investigation but it's pretty obvious. Hey, don't I know you from somewhere?" he asked.

I told him I didn't think so, then I said I wanted to look at the victim, that he was an old friend of mine, and the cop looked around to see who was looking at him and then he said, "Sure, why not?"

It was Willie.

A full moon rose in the east. Normally you cannot see a moon rise in Downtown Chicago unless you're standing right on the lakefront or it's already well over the skyline, but then it'll be small again in the sky. Yet, at certain points and from certain angles, you can draw a bead on it as it rises between the buildings, looming large and prescient, worthy of a primitive people's worship for sure. I could see the moon rising from where we stood next to Willie.

"Bad moon rising," I whispered. Theresa turned and looked at the moon, then asked me what I meant.

"It's just Credence Clearwater Revival," I said. "It was on the radio as we drove down. Don't you remember? Willie was dying then."

It's hard to tell with black people sometimes just how old they are – yeah, I know, that's another racist stereotype of mine, sure, sure – but I think Willie was well past 60, past 70, maybe even 80 when he died. Now he was gone. What happens when bad things happen to black people? They just disappear. Maybe the paper would do a real story on the man and his business, something more substantial than the standard small obit the funeral parlor operator would be willing to buy. Then I looked around and realized that this would never go beyond a one paragraph entry in the police blotter. I saw no satellite TV trucks, no night public safety reporter, which was the new name for the police beat, not even a gawker or rubber-necker slowly driving by. Willie Williams' passing was an inconsequential event in the life of contemporary Chicago chronology that almost no one would remember. Just like Best Jewtown Hot Dogs.

KHALED

THE FIRST DAY OF CLASS, August 1982, about 18 students had registered for "The Israel-Palestine Conflict: A 100 Years War," and Professor William Hardenberg was quite apologetic in announcing that he'd been recruited to teach the course only at the last minute.

"I've taught international relations for many years," he said as he stood in front of what was a slate chalkboard still in use in the old classroom. Hardenberg was a tall and full man, not quite bearish in his aspect, and his Princeton-cut hair had been thinned by the years – perhaps "gentle giant" would be the best way to describe him. He was dressed in a ruffled suit jacket and wrinkled trousers, all wool in spite of the always torrid temps in Carbondale that summer.

"I guess the department thinks I know everything from the Boxer Rebellion in China to the Falklands War in the South Atlantic and everything in between," he continued, "but I don't."

A few of the students laughed weakly at the joke, a courtesy, no doubt, but not Khaled or I. Khaled simply sat stone-faced and four-square in his classroom seat, his hands clasped on the chair's tablet arm, and he studied this curious American professor intently. I sat under one of the large double-hung windows, the paper roller shade all the way up, the glare from the blinding summer light behind affording me a certain anonymity as I studied Khaled.

Hardenberg went around the room, asking everyone to share a little about themselves, quite normal for the first day of class, and Khaled reported that he'd studied at Birzeit University on the West Bank and, before that, at a madrasa in Hama in northern Syria. Most notable of all, though, was the revelation that three of his uncles had been killed years earlier during an Israeli raid at Qibya.

"I'm wanted by the authorities in two countries," he told us. The Arab students laughed loudly and knowingly at this remark while Hardenberg and the other students looked quizzically at the young man. Not I, though. I knew all about the massacre at Qibya in 1953; it was how a young Ariel Sharon earned his bona fides in the Israeli Army, and I knew all about the even bigger, more recent slaughter of Muslim Brotherhood activists and sympathizers in Hama in February 1982. It had taken little more than two hours for the Israelis to kill 70 Palestinians at Qibya, but Hafez al-Assad required a full month to annihilate 10,000 Arab men and women at Hama. Some say the toll was more like 20,000 men, maybe even 25,000.

Khaled appeared to be about 25 years old, and he looked more Greek or even Sicilian than Arab. I think it was his round face and olive-toned skin and, well, ancient Palestine had been occupied by plenty of peoples passing through over the eons. Yet it was the beard that gave him away, that is, if being a fundamentalist was something you might not want to alert other people to. He wore no keffiyeh.

"I'm truly embarrassed," Hardenberg said, speaking in a deep but affable voice after Khaled had introduced himself. "I think our young Palestinian friend will know more about the situation over there than I ever will." He looked pointedly, expectantly at Khaled.

"Yes," Khaled replied, speaking in a perfectly dry and even tone. He wasn't smiling at all.

I told everyone I was from Chicago but more recently had been a volunteer on an Israeli kibbutz (helping make children's high chairs and other baby furniture in a cooperatively-owned factory there, nothing to do with oranges or dates at all), then I'd kicked around for a while working for some English-language media including the AP and *The Jerusalem Post*.

Hardenberg seemed impressed by my resume, too, and he told the other students how lucky they were to have not one but *two* authentic "participants in history," his expression, in the same class. "Maybe these two should teach the course," he offered. Then he asked if I'd known Khaled while abroad as if someone might meet the Queen during a visit to England, but which also provoked not a little suspicion in me, too.

"Yes," I said, "I think he was the one we beat up for ogling girls on the Tel Aviv beach. I think he ran back to Jaffa when we finished with him."

That brought a smile to Khaled. "Yes, you should always make sure the person is dead when you try to kill someone," he said, turning to look at me. "I tell this to the Jews all the time."

EVERGREEN TERRACE WAS MY encampment in Carbondale, as well as that for a couple of hundred other graduate students, many of whom came from foreign lands, often with small families in tow. It was about two miles from the heart of campus, but only if you cut through nearby woods and ran across a corner of the posted and fenced President's House and grounds. That was the scenic route; most students drove home after a day of study, the international students typically in cars they'd purchased for cash at Ike's Premium Used Car Lot, cars that had been bought and sold there by other international students before them. That trip required traversing three long sides of a rural rectangle, the last being a two-lane blacktop with no yellow median strip that led to the wooden arched gate of the compound itself (the gate reminded me of the entrance to a small ranch in Montana or Texas, just three thin logs braced together, two sides and a top). I sometimes rode a red 3-speed Schwinn along these narrow rural roads, and in time I bought a second-hand VW Sirocco from an undergraduate who said she had to return to Taiwan immediately, but oftentimes I'd find myself walking home through the dense woods because I liked the frontier-feel of the afternoon light streaking between the tree trunks, I liked stepping over rotting fallen logs and even having to walk around the little mud flaps of marshy wetland here and there, deep in the forest. It was a personal space I found and, besides, Supertramp's "Take the Long Way Home" was often on my mind in those days.

Evergreen Terrace looked a lot like public housing, not the high-rise kind in a Chicago ghetto, just squat two-story apartment buildings with eight units each, artless red brick facades and 12-inch linoleum tile throughout, the kind of floor covering they always put in automobile showrooms in case the engines dripped oil. Carbondale lay midway between the Mississippi and Ohio river valleys – I think the evaporation from each waterway met up there and presented itself as steam – and most of the air conditioning units didn't work, which meant everyone used box fans, but propped up on chairs or step ladders as none would fit in the casement windows, some of which had screens, some not.

Being in a river valley again: the university provided exterminators every other Tuesday, or on request, and recommended spreading boric acid powder everywhere, unless you had children. The roaches were as big as thumbs, the flies fat as if devouring a dead horse.

My immediate neighbor to the left was Jon Hall, from Uganda, and his pretty young wife and two toddlers. I say "pretty young wife" because Jon Hall was at least 40, maybe 50, he had a thick neck like a Beech tree and rubbery skin and his eye sockets were eerily the same texture and color as the rest of his face, and his pretty young wife was just that. He introduced himself shortly after I'd moved in. "You have any soap?" he asked while standing at my door. "In Uganda we have no soap. No toilet paper, either. Nothing. It comes in and everything is stolen." I invited him in, offered him a Coke (he accepted, but it was Kroger brand cola), and I fetched a bar of Dial soap.

"Thank you, man," he said as he sat on a bench by my little kitchen table, one of the things I'd had delivered from a used furniture store, a place that might as well have been called Ike's, too, or Ike's 2. Jon was sweating heavily, the beads of sweat along the folds of skin on his neck like pinkish jelly beans, and his knit shirt was dark and stained and sticking everywhere to his skin.

"Do you have a fan in your apartment?" I asked. He finished his cola and shook his head. "No fans. No fans in Uganda. We have nothing in Uganda." With that he rose and retreated to the door, but he stopped and turned before leaving, holding up the yellow bar of Dial soap I had given him. "Thank you, man," he said again.

On the other side of my unit lived Bob and Julianne, an eager young couple from Rockford. Bob was studying civil engineering – they had a good program for that in Carbondale – and Julianne was in my Israel and Palestine class. She was, in fact, pursuing an advanced degree in international relations. She'd interned with Republican Senator Chuck Percy the summer between her junior and senior years while an undergraduate at Wheaton College, and he'd encouraged her, she later told me; she told me this one night when her husband was studying late in the library and she and I were in bed together, which was when she always found it most comforting to talk to me, she said. Percy had been relatively outspoken on the need for America and Israel to negotiate with Yasser Arafat and the PLO; some say he lost his re-election bid in 1984 over the issue.

Khaled lived across the way, on the other side of the parking lot our two buildings shared. "Hey, that's a nice car you have there," I said to him later on the day we were formally introduced in Bill Hardenberg's class. The late model Chevrolet Caprice was painted an ice blue metallic, a very popular color in the 1980s. Khaled parked right in front of his unit.

"Abdulraheem gave me the use of it," he said. "I have friends everywhere, you see." Abdulraheem also was one of the students in our Israel and Palestine class; he was from Riyadh.

Khaled spoke perfect English. I don't know where he learned to speak English so purely, so correctly, with such a deep and nuanced vocabulary, though that would only become apparent in serious discourse, not casual conversation. It certainly wasn't at any madrasa or from watching badly dubbed shows on Jordanian and Israeli television. Khaled was later to tell me that his hero was Edward Said – he wanted to teach at Columbia, too, though he really wanted to write op-eds for The Washington Post, he said. "On a host of topics," he said. People said he spoke perfect French, as well.

PROFESSOR HARDENBERG HAD ASKED to speak with us after that first day of class and was quite adamant that he wasn't the man to teach this course. "Would you two consider coming up with something?" he'd asked. Khaled and I accepted immediately, Khaled saying the offer was "generous, indeed" (his words) while I'd shrugged and simply said, "Sure." Hardenberg handed us his syllabus, which wasn't bad, it included Michael Grant's "The Jews in the Roman Empire," (they were 10 percent of the population at the height of empire); Walter Laqueur's "The Israel-Arab Reader," which included copies of the Balfour Declaration, Sykes-Picot agreement, and various British "white papers"; and George Antonius' "The Arab Awakening," among other titles. Khaled and I decided to meet in my kitchen later in the evening to complete the syllabus – he was to add Edward Said's "The Question of Palestine," some essays by Maxime Rodinson (the French-Jewish-Stalinist), and Amos Oz's "Israel, Palestine and Peace."

For my part I objected to sections of the PLO charter, which was in Laqueur's book. I wasn't thinking at all of the part that called for the Jewish state's destruction.

"The part that says Jews are citizens of whatever country they reside in?" Khaled challenged.

I understood the retort. Jews had often argued that they were citizens of the country in which they lived, not outsiders or "the other" or whatever it was they were presumed to be, and what Khaled said was exactly what the PLO Charter declared. But I objected.

"It's not unusual for people to advance arguments that serve their interests at the time, and then contradict themselves later," I said. "The problem in history is that the Jews are always the wrong thing so they're forced to change their story." We were drinking Wissotzky Tea that I had left over from my stay in Israel.

CLASS TIME WAS NEVER CONTENTIOUS, though in one discussion with an Iranian student, no doubt Shi'ite, Khaled asked how the Ayatollah Khomeini could claim to speak for Allah.

"He interprets law for us, that's all," the Iranian said. "It's no different than the Catholic Pope."

Then Khaled turned to me. "Who decides what is and is not law in Judaism?" he asked. I told him that my religious education stopped in the eighth grade and that I was completely secular, but I added that he, Khaled, had asked me the easiest question of all.

"The community decides," I answered. Khaled was very satisfied with the answer for it was just so in Sunni Islam, as well.

Other times people might debate who really started the Arab-Israel conflict or who was the real enemy of peace – "The Syrian Army routinely fired down on Jewish farmers from the Golan Heights" one young Jewish woman from Skokie, I believe, proclaimed, which was followed by a Malaysian student's retort, "The Israelis sent in armored vehicles disguised as tractors for the sole purpose of drawing fire," and so on – yet no students overtly called for continuing the war. It was Abdulraheem who one day said, "The problem with trying to kill people is that they will have to defend themselves." He said this out of the blue, we were discussing water rights at the time, and I couldn't tell which side of the conflict he meant to address.

It was Julianne's sweet innocence in class that first caught my attention – years before Rodney King she was asking why Jews and Arabs couldn't all get along. Some of the students just rolled their eyes at such naiveté but I thought, "How comely," I really did. Plus, she stood out in the class. She almost was the only "white" person present, not counting Hardenberg, her pale skin as smooth as polished stone, her thin lips ripe without added color, and her long hair almost as fine as golden threads. And then there was the way she'd touched me on the forearm after class one day early in the semester, and especially the look she gave at the Labor Day picnic we jointly hosted on my back patio in Evergreen Terrace.

"I told you to buy ground round," Julianne chided her husband. The coals in the small hibachi I'd found abandoned on the patio when I moved in still smoked a bit but the tips were turning a nice powdery white and it almost was time to throw the meat on.

"But chuck was on sale," Bob replied. He had popped open two beers, Milwaukee's Finest (the brand name, not the truth), and had handed me one. Julianne and I hadn't begun sleeping together yet.

"Eighty percent lean?" Julianne said.

"Uh, 70 percent, I think." Julianne pretended to throw one of the unused coals at her husband.

We had lots of meat, actually, and corn on the cob and I invited Jon Hall and his family to join us.

I would have invited Khaled over, too, but I'd seen that the blue Caprice was not parked out front just then and, besides, it would be awkward for us to be eating beef that was not Halal and drinking alcohol that was forbidden.

Jon Hall's wife was called Miriam and their two young children, boys, also had Biblical names. The wife was very shy – her dark skin highlighted her ivory-like teeth and piercing eyes – but it was her moon-shaped face and small chin that made her stand out the most. She looked to be very young, I mean, very, very young, with budding breasts seemingly as firm as tennis balls and buttocks as round as melons. She went about barefoot, like her two young boys.

Jon Hall was working toward a Ph.D. in "agricultural management in sharing economies," then he hoped to get a job at an American university and never go back home. He'd tell this to anyone he met.

"Then I'll bring the rest of my family over," he told me once. "No point sending money home. Everything is stolen."

Wavy ribbons of smoke floated in the air and Bob wrapped the corn in aluminum foil and put the ears on the hibachi in between and around the hamburger patties, and I retrieved small sticks of wood like prongs to hold the slices of Mary Jane white bread instead of proper buns that we'd toast several inches above the grill.

Bob complained of how far behind he already was in his work – besides four tough engineering and math classes he had to take, there were the two sections of a large lecture hall class for undergraduates he had to teach, including grading all the papers by himself. "Money is tight, but I guess that's true of all graduate students," he said while flipping our burgers, while looking deeply into the glowing hot coals as if it were a cauldron of exploding stars. "Julianne says she doesn't think she'll go further than a Master's Degree, then she might apply for a teacher's license somewhere. But she can get a teacher's license right now, if she really wanted to."

Hmmm, I thought.

The next day, after our Israel and Palestine class, Julianne asked me to join her in the cafeteria for coffee.

"Bob really works hard, you know," she said. She'd ordered a latte; I'd drawn a soda from the fountain tap. "He wants to teach at Stanford or Cornell. He's so focused on getting a Ph.D. he doesn't have time for anything else." She slowly stirred her coffee with a little wooden stick as she spoke; very demure she was. "I mean, he doesn't have time for *anything* else," she added, looking up preciously into my eyes.

I'd never considered myself a lover, someone with swagger, or Adonis in any way. I was tall enough (5-feet-11) and fit (I swam and jogged, but I'd never played on varsity teams in high school and I didn't compete in triathlons). I was a bit sensitive about my looks, actually – I liked to think that my thick, black, short hair made me look more like someone from Asia Minor, one of those darker converts to Judaism in the early Middle Ages, than some Ashkenazi from Poland. But I suppose it was the aura of international intrigue I brought with me that engaged Julianne – I'd been a foreign correspondent, sort of, even been up to Lebanon earlier that summer to survey damage at the Al Rashidiya refugee camp, all rubble and graffiti inside bombed buildings and wrecked Peugeot 504 sedans and kids who could still play among anything.

("Mister, mister, take our picture." Four kids line up against a broken wall, all dressed in shorts and American T-shirts. "Mister, take our picture." I do, they are happy, I have no idea how I'll send the image back to them.)

Fooling around with a married woman should have been off limits. I'd had a girlfriend for a time after I left the kibbutz – Irit, a soldier, she started talking about how she *could* get a Green Card and come to America, but *should* she - and I'd later done it once with a middle-aged married woman who hated her real estate developer husband (we'd met while I worked on a story about the time-share and condo boom in Israel). Somehow that was all right because the woman was old enough to know what she wanted – a veteran of the gender wars, you might say – and I didn't like the developer anyway.

Cuckolding a man behind his back while pretending to be his friend, or at least a good neighbor, disturbed me more than my complicity with Julianne's infidelity but I concluded that if she wanted to cheat that was her decision, and if Bob found out and had a problem then he'd have to work it out with her, not me. Besides, I didn't have to pretend she was mine by right; I didn't have to take her by force.

THE "ISRAEL AND PALESTINE" class met three days a week, following the usual MWF schedule. I didn't have any other classes with Khaled, but we both were studying journalism (the study of which at the graduate level having nothing to do with the actual practice of journalism, of course) and he'd spoken to me about a couple of his professors so I knew his schedule, more or less. This was useful information as I had no trouble tracking him down on the afternoon of Thursday, September 16, 1982, when something big was about to happen at two Palestinian refugee camps in suburban Beirut known as Sabra and Shatila.

I didn't bother to knock on the heavy wood door to the classroom in the Communications Building; I just peered through the small glass panel at eye level and twisted my neck until I saw Khaled, then I barged in. The teacher – a young white guy, my age, probably junior faculty, was startled by my audacity, I suppose. And I was struck by his appearance – stiff blue jeans, black T-shirt rolled up a bit at the sleeves like John Travolta in "Grease," and wide leather belt with a large silver buckle like a Peterbilt truck driver. I wanted to say, "Hello, Tex," but I didn't. I just beckoned Khaled with my index finger, curling it in once, that's all that was required, and he looked at me curiously for a second, then the color suddenly drained from his face. A couple of other Arab students seated nearby looked at him, then at me, and back to Khaled before they, too, straightened up in their chairs. They knew something bad had happened. The summer's Israeli invasion of Lebanon (fill in the blank space as to who started that war, who was to blame, and where will it all end on your own) was in its mopping up stages, but that was the most dangerous period for those willing to make a last stand. Or in hiding.

"Sabra and Shatila," I said. "Ariel Sharon just announced that the Phalange would police the camps."

They say history is written by the victors. What happens when no one is winning, though? You get different versions. Years later, years after the bodies and body parts have been buried or merely disintegrated, years after a separate 1985 invasion and massacre in the camps by a Shiite militia group, what happened at Sabra and Shatila on September 16 and 17, 1982 still is contested. Namely whether it was 350 people killed, or up to 3,500? And just how many were women and children – a handful, or half? Let's assume the worst, though – 3,500 people killed in 36 hours, about one every six minutes, a rate somewhere between Qibya and Hama.

There was nothing for the Arab and Muslim students to do about the slaughter from their safe harbor in Carbondale other than hold a protest rally, which they did on the waterfront at a local reservoir. This occurred on the following Sunday, in the morning, a time I thought was chosen because the Christians would be booked into their churches then. I was in the scrubby yard in front of my unit at Evergreen Terrace when I saw Khaled drive slowly out of his parking space the morning of the 19th in his blue Caprice, rolling slowly up the little feeder street toward the main road, and he looked out his open window at me silently with an implacable expression that I tried to gauge but couldn't.

The reservoir was not so far away and I decided to bicycle there; the trees still were full and I was in shade most of the way. More cars than I would have expected out in the country at that time of day passed me as I came closer to the venue and I could tell that most were headed to the same place as I – swarthy men with beards, women in hijabs, kids bouncing in back seats like any kids. Once on the scene I stayed back nearer the road or, rather, just inside a stand of tulip trees and maples. The gathering was held on the east side of the little artificial lake and the morning sun created a haze, a dreamy ethereal vintage scene and though I stood back from the crowd I could make out Khaled well enough, the center of attention as expected.

Now here is where I could summarize all the defiant and nationalistic speeches by several of the speakers – most were in Arabic or Malay (Southern Illinois University always attracted a large number of Malaysian students, mostly due to its aviation program) and I didn't always know what they were saying except for the easily recognizable taunts of *yahud* (Jew) and *al-kayan al-Sahyūnī* (Zionist entity), but some folks spoke in English, or switched back and forth, including Khaled, who received the most applause when he was introduced, who was interrupted by shouts of support more often than any other. It's hard for me to distinguish what he said on that morning from what he'd said to me before or what he'd written in any of several essays that he'd asked me to critique but one cry stood out, which was the obligation of every Muslim to help the Palestinians.

"The usurping regime is engaged in extreme brutality and oppression and it has proven that it is prepared to commit any crime in order to reach its expansionist and dangerous goals," he declared in English, then he quoted a line from the Quran, which is not to be confused with anything Muhammad *said*, but is the voice of God himself: "Verily, you are one Ummah. I am your Lord, worship me."

My assistantship was in the university's marketing department located in an old clapboard house that the expanding university had encroached upon, surrounded and finally absorbed after World War II and my main function was to write for the weekly faculty newsletter. Normally I interviewed professors who'd recently published a book, or quoted an expert on nutrition or climate change for a "news you can use" article, or I introduced a new administration appointee to the academic community at large. Sometimes I reported on actual campus events.

"Are we going to write anything about yesterday's demonstration?" I asked the news director, Paul Brown, a wily backwoods character who often sat with a corn cob pipe plugged in his mouth and who walked around with a frayed straw hat on the crown of his head. Paul sat in a big office on the first floor of the old house, what clearly had been the parlor once upon a time with its nicely sized fireplace, since converted to gas, and I and another graduate assistant, a fellow from South Korea, worked upstairs in what had once been a bedroom.

"What demonstration?" Brown replied. He didn't look up at me as he spoke; he was sorting through some paper files on his desk at the time.

"Over the massacre in Lebanon," I said. "A few hundred students were gathered out by the reservoir yesterday. People are talking."

"Oh, really," he said, feigning mock interest, again without looking up. "Are we *The New York Times* here?"

The student newspaper didn't report on the event, either. The local newspaper ran a Letter to the Editor from one of the Muslim professors on campus a few days later, but that's all.

KHALED'S SPEECH WAS NOT met with indifference inside other circles. By late September rumors had it that two FBI agents had driven down from Chicago to ask about a "suspected terror cell" on campus – well, I'd overheard Paul Brown on the phone talking about it, and I'd called the university provost on my own to ask what he knew about all this. It wasn't rumor, in other words, any more than the G11 license plates on a grey Plymouth Grand Fury I'd seen parked in front of Woody Hall was an illusion. Woody Hall hosted international student admissions and records.

"So, what's going on?" I asked Khaled. I'd been peeking out my sliding glass double doors at home waiting for him to walk to his car; when I saw him I hurried to intercept him. He stood before me as he often did, very formal, hands behind his back, chin out. Khaled was a bit overweight and not tall, maybe 5-foot-7, and on this day he wore a white crocheted *taqiyah*, or Muslim skullcap.

I knew what was up, of course. I'd stopped Abdulraheem after class a couple of days earlier to ask about a relief effort being organized on campus to help the displaced and the injured in the Lebanon war. That effort was covered by campus and local media and had wide support, though I didn't think that canned peaches and the like or second-hand clothing was what the people in the Middle East needed just then. He told me that a few students had returned to Lebanon - both Muslim and Christian, though presumably not to the same neighborhoods – and others had collected money, which was being routed through "channels" to the proper relief efforts. I had read about the intricacies of informal Arab banking and didn't ask for details, which would not have been provided in any case. Was Khaled's recent speech the impetus, I asked? I knew he also spoke regularly at Friday prayers held in an empty storefront on West Grand Avenue that had been rented for the purpose. Abdulraheem just said everyone agreed on what had to be done.

Khaled told me that, yes, he'd heard about the FBI coming to town. What did *I* know about it, though, he asked. I didn't think he was accusing me of being an agent or a snitch. He'd often ask me about things *Americana*, from the odd infield fly rule in baseball to why we let our women parade half naked in public, and why was it that only international students plied the aisles in Morris Library after 10 pm. (One afternoon I'd spied Khaled standing near the patio at a tavern on Main Street as several revelers, male and female, poured beer into their glasses from a large pitcher. I don't know that he was contemning them with his eyes; it was more like he was wondering how people could sin like that on their own.)

I told him it was unusual for the FBI to come to campus, and that I didn't think it was because Leonid Brezhnev might be sending Soviet agents to gather intelligence in Carbondale. "They'd spy on Fermilab or the Tennessee Valley Authority before us, I'd think," I said. Khaled seemed puzzled by the references at first, perhaps it was oblique, and then he said, "Nuclear power, of course. Perhaps I'm studying the wrong subject."

I wanted to ask him about everything he'd said at the reservoir, or during those Friday prayers, that might have attracted the attention of the feds. Fiery people usually know what fuss they're making. But I told him that no one had come to interrogate me.

"What would you tell them if they did?" he asked.

I shrugged. "Whatever I know, I guess."

"And that is what?"

I smiled wryly and harrumphed. "Nothing, I guess," I said.

KHALED HAD GROWN UP IN HEBRON, about 30 miles south-southwest of Jerusalem. Like many places in the West Bank and Israel, streetscapes there were narrow and teeming with life, little outdoor cafes and businesses you'd duck into, steel shutters that came down at night like overhead garage doors, and the housing typically was built with natural stone facades, sometimes cinder block and stucco. Only rooftop antennas and cylindrical solar water heaters marred the view. Oh, and there were minarets everywhere.

Yasser Arafat once said Hebron was more important to the Jews than Jerusalem, and he was right. By tradition, foundational figures including Abraham and Sarah, as well as Isaac and Rebecca, and Jacob and Leah, all were buried in the Cave of the Patriarchs in the Old City there. The Muslims give more prominence to Abraham, or Ibrahim, their foundational figure. The first Jewish settlers after the 1967 Six Day War were led by Jerusalem-born rabbi Moshe Levinger, ultimately establishing a home just outside Hebron they called Kiryat Arba after a Biblical reference to the place. Hebron was later to be the site of a horrific massacre by American-born zealot Baruch Goldstein, who killed 30 Muslim worshippers in the shared Mosque of Ibrahim in 1994. None of this is to be confused with the massacre of sixty-plus Jews in Hebron in 1929, during the British Mandate period in Palestine.

I knew Hebron because of a young Canadian volunteer, Troy Rosenfeld, whom I'd met on the kibbutz. I'd thought him one of the lucky ones because he got to work outside, actually picking fruit and olives and things, the idyllic image of the happy, hearty Jewish pioneer. Troy was a tall, even gangly young man with big lips and a perennial smile on his face; he also liked to walk in the nearby Judean Hills which largely buttressed Hebron (well, everything is close in that part of the world). One day when Troy hadn't returned by dark the kibbutzniks became concerned, then we remaining volunteers started to worry, and when the Army patrols on Jeeps rumbled by we knew something terrible must have happened. Troy was found the next morning, his neck slashed and heart pierced, his torso overall cut to ribbons. He was found lying on a rock like so much garbage that had been dumped there. Three Arab men from Hebron were later arrested and charged with the crime. The news was all over all Israeli and Palestinian media.

"Did you know any of the perpetrators?" I asked Khaled. We were having tea again, this time in his apartment; he also had a box of Wissotzky Tea at hand.

"Did you know the victim?" he replied. I told him I did, which seemed to take him aback.

"All right, I'll tell you," he said after a few seconds. "I was helping work my cousin's spice shop in the market and we were closing up, then while I walked the short distance to my parents' house afterward, as I turned the corner, I saw three men running toward me. They were running very fast, looking over their shoulders, all breathing very hard. I could hear them from some distance, actually. They almost were like thundering horses. They ran right by me and their eyes were big, they seemed crazed, and I turned to look briefly at them after they passed me. Then one slowly stopped and turned and walked calmly back to me. As he came close he looked me straight in the eyes and shook his finger. He didn't have to say anything. I didn't know then what they had done but I knew I would have to dismiss this vision from my mind as if it were little more than a bad dream. The man backed away from me, shook his finger again, and then turned and ran after his friends. I truly didn't know what they had done but I suspected it had something to do with the Israelis. When we heard they were arrested the next morning, even when the Israeli soldiers first swarmed the town, we knew what it was. By then we'd heard that a Jew had been killed nearby."

Khaled shrugged, scrunched his mouth, and reached for his glass of tea.

"Were you sorry they killed someone, or sorry they were captured?" I asked. Khaled looked at me, sighed, and sipped from his tea yet again.

IT'S BACK TO NORMAL in Carbondale, headlines in the local media and on TV now more about upcoming off-year elections and the first snow of the season. I'm eyeing a short Thanksgiving holiday and then the end of term. Grad students with teaching assistantships could take the entire winter break off, but I'd only get the week between Christmas and New Year's because I worked with "staff," not faculty. Still, it would be a relief. Though I had no close relatives there any more I think I might visit Chicago – the train still goes there (the famous City of New Orleans route, in fact), or I might head south. I've never been to Memphis, which is on the same train route. Or New Orleans itself – why not? I wouldn't want to go on an actual vacation alone, but I couldn't very well invite Julianne. Anyway, things had cooled between us.

"I shouldn't really be doing this, should I?" she'd said the last time we slept together.

"It has to end sometime," I'd replied. "That's why it's called a fling." What an asshole I could be sometimes.

"So, maybe we should stop?"

I still saw Julianne in class but we were very professional with each other. She and her husband stopped coming over for brewskis or just to shoot the shit of an evening, though – I don't know if that was Julianne's doing, or if Bob was pulling away just in case – and, all in all, I had to accept that the affair was nothing more than a brief detour in our respective lives. There were other fields to plow.

Helping lead the "Israel and Palestine" class had been satisfying, even instructive. One Arab student had challenged why more Jews don't move to Israel, that is, if it really were the Jewish homeland, and another, a journalist from Kuwait who was attending school on a government-funded exchange program, said Islam should welcome the "return of the exiles," as David Ben-Gurion had termed it, but that a Jewish *state* would never be accepted in Dar-al-Islam, that is, in the domain of Islam.

"Some people say all Jews after 1948 have to leave," Khaled said on the day the Kuwaiti had spoken. "Others say those who came after 1917 will have to leave, or even after 1881." It was his way of beginning a conversation- "This scholar teaches," or "Some have argued," and so on, and in fact all of the dates he mentioned were milestones – the most recent date marked the official founding of the State of Israel, and 1917 recorded the Balfour Declaration in which His Majesty's government viewed with favor the establishment in Palestine of a Jewish national home. The earliest year, 1881, saw the first substantial migration of mostly Russian Jews to Palestine, a period that even Mark Twain had written about, largely in the context of "the Jewish question" that was debated even then.

"The problem with the Jews is that they're no better than anyone else," Twain wrote. And Maxime Rodinson had written that Europe had no special obligation to help the Jews after World War II.   "What is your position?" I asked Khaled. "Should the Jews stay or should they go?" It was colder now, and he'd begun wearing a surplus Israeli Army field jacket, colloquially known in Hebrew as a *"Dubon"*, or Teddy bear. Khaled was criticized by fellow Arabs for doing this, but he brushed them off.

"It's not about punishing the Jews," he'd said once. "I just want my rights."

Khaled didn't answer my question straightaway; he continued his sometimes way of looking far off into some imagined place, perhaps a remembered place. But I didn't think he had settled on an answer. I think he wasn't any more certain of what tack to take than anyone else. Hamas and Hezbollah were not yet fully formed in 1982; they would make the choice for him in time.

TOSSED

I LOOK OUT THE WINDOW of my tiny room to see a moon lurking behind a tree line to the East; it is full and rising, a tincture of old gold on its scarred face from the setting sun opposite it. The moon is indifferent to me, but I am not indifferent to it. Please, pull on the seas inside me, lift me up with your high tide. I turn my head and look at the weak shadows on the far wall; my room is bare, not of things, but of significance.

Reaching for my cigarettes on a side table I find that the pack is as empty as the ash tray is full, and I look at my watch, something I bought at Goodwill for $2 because no one wears watches anymore unless they're Rolex or heart monitors or perhaps holographic devices. The nearest liquor store, which is where I occasionally buy cigarettes, especially if I'm out of whiskey at the same time, closes in 20 minutes. I could jump in my car, an old Chevy Cobalt, but it's not running, or play 'beat the clock' and go on foot. The moon, with its sublime, unfathomable light, soon will top the trees and I want it, I want it bad, my drug of choice, as it were, so I am happy to walk underneath its domain.

I live in a kind of transitional neighborhood in Seattle, lots of young singles moving into their own apartments and newlywed couples purchasing small frame houses they're going to fix up. The house flippers, too, of course. It's not gentrification per se, but a new generation is replacing the older, white working-class folks who've lived here 40 years and more and are now dying off. Most American cities had neighborhoods like this in the past, all anchored by a busy commercial intersection, dissected by a kind of High Street lined with its own jewelers and insurance agents and small bakeries, maybe a locally owned hardware store and card shop, too, and always an independent Rexall pharmacy. It's mostly bars and coffee shops now, and I'm the exception among my youthful peers, too. I don't have a great job or a cool car or a 401K and I live in one room in an older Queen Anne-style home that was subdivided into smaller rental units years ago, something that was done before the recent upswing in real estate values. I enter and exit via a spiral staircase on the side and I sleep in an old, steel hospital bed I also bought used at Goodwill. I cook on an electric hot plate and the shared bathroom is down the hall.

On my way to the liquor store I pass a new bar with garage doors that fully open to the street – it's a former auto repair shop that's been converted. The people inside are as noisy and gay as in any Toulouse-Lautrec painting, if not as lavish or colorful, and I take note of all the pretty girls and their body language, who's leaning far forward with her chin resting on her hand and which guys are staring at the women with moist eyes and hard dicks. I don't have a chance, not in my current situation.

I wait for a traffic signal to change to "Walk," to show the little walking man with the spritely gait, the world's original GIF, before continuing. In the old days I would have passed a pool hall by now, maybe a few young toughs standing under a lamp pole on a street corner shooting the breeze and I could just bum a cigarette from one of them instead on continuing on, but that's not the scene anymore. I have about five minutes to get to the liquor store but it's just around the corner and I think I'll make it.

I'm surprised to see Big Rick when I enter – I hadn't seen him in a month and I know the turnover is high at places like this so I really am surprised. I know the man by name because we'd struck up a conversation the last time I was in here – he'd asked if I'd ever tried Dunhill cigarettes in the blue box, which they'd recently started carrying, and I told him I hadn't, just Camel Filters, and then he asked me which whiskey I preferred and I told him J&B Rare, but that I wasn't out yet.

"So, you live around here?" he'd asked as he rang me up that first time. Big Rick was tall and well-built, not fat but sturdy, like a linebacker on a football team, and he had orangey-red hair and a thick, wiry beard of the same color.

"Just a few blocks away," I told him then. "And you?"

"Oh, I just moved to town," he'd said. "I'm staying at one of those motels where you can pay by the week."

"You don't have your own pad? Furniture? Friends you can turn to?" I asked. I stopped feeling sorry for myself, at least for a few moments.

He shook his head. "No, I just got out of the Big House after doing time. Then I got this job and they gave me credit the first week at the motel. When I save up a little I'll get a real apartment, maybe even a car. You know anyone with a car for sale?"

Well, the Cobalt still was running then, then something very loud and bad happened to the transmission and I wasn't going to bring it up with Rick this time.

Rick remembered me, too, when I made my entrance on this evening. "The usual?" he asked. He pulled a pack of Camel Filters from the rack behind him, and he informed me that Dewar's White Label was on sale for $18.99, which really was a good price. "*Yeah, all right,*" I mumbled or something like that, and I purchased a fifth of whisky that night, too.

SO, HERE'S THE DEAL. I have three days to make the rent or else the landlord, who lives in a luxury condo in the city center and owns several properties all over town, would start eviction proceedings. He'd threatened to do this the previous month and when I didn't come up with the "bread," his word, not mine, he's an aging hippie, he gave me an extension, but added that he would have to charge me "interest." He never said how much interest I'd have to pay and I didn't ask; all I knew was that I had another month to live here. In the meantime, I finally began looking for a job.

It's not hard landing work in America. I mean, everywhere you look, they're hiring. I could work at an Amazon distribution center that's only 20 miles away. I could be an "assistant manager" at Burger King, much nearer. I could even apply at Big Rick's liquor store – I noticed the hand-printed sign in the plate glass window there saying, "Help Wanted, Inquire Within." It had been up so long the paper was curling at the edges and yellowing.

Then there was the Sherwin-Williams paint store a few blocks from me – they're always hiring there, too. I decided to check that one out. When I entered the store, an electronic beep triggered by my arrival, I was immediately struck by the nice displays – wood-handled paint brushes hanging from hooks, white painters' pants neatly folded and stacked inside cubbies, and color charts featuring a *plethora* of paint samples.

"Howdy," a guy behind the counter called out. He looked to be about

50, thinning brown hair on top, and he wore a white, short-sleeved shirt with a necktie, *that* look. "What can we help you with?"

I turned a little and pointed with my thumb to the sign in the window – "Help Wanted, Inquire Within." He lit up at my words, I mean, High Gloss Enamel bright.

We got to talking, and he asked if I'd worked in a paint store before – "No? That's all right. We train," he said – and if I had any references. On the latter question I told him that I did, but none that were positive. He gave out a nervous laughter, and I reassured him by saying it was a joke, and he seemed relieved. But then he leaned forward over the counter and looked me square in the eye. "You ever been arrested?" he asked. "Won't matter as long as you completed your sentence. It wasn't for assault, was it?" He scrunched his nose and screwed his eyes even more tightly. Right then, he reminded me of Long John Silver in "Treasure Island," my favorite movie on DVD when I was growing up.

"No, I've never been arrested," I told him. "Not even finger-printed." That was true.

The man seemed relieved by my innocence, but then he took a deep breath and lunged back over the counter with his head. "Can you pass a drug screen? Most of you young ones coming in here wanting a job can't even pass a drug screen. What is it you take? Mary Jane? Uppers?"

"No, but I am an alcoholic. When I can afford it, that is."

He seemed relieved to hear this. The man straightened up again and seemed to pull on up his pants. "Well, that's all right. I'm a drunk, too," he said. "Been in 12-Step groups, even 30 days in one of those phony rehab places the insurance will pay for. But never on the job, understand. I've never come to work drunk one day in my life. Sure, there were days I couldn't come to work because I was too drunk, but the point is, I never came to work drunk. You know what I'm saying?"

I had no idea what the man was saying, what he was *really* saying, but I grabbed an application – he said I could fill it out right there but I said I wanted to think about it – and I went on my wary way. I ate lunch at a nearby Wendy's – walked right past the placard announcing a "Hiring Event, Today, 4-6 p.m.," and ordered a Junior Hamburger, extra tomato, and a Chocolate Frosty. Maybe I wasn't serious about finding work after all.

IT WASN'T LONG BEFORE I was tossed out of my apartment – my scant furniture dumped on the front lawn, my credit rating ruined, and my prospects dimmer than a blind mole rat who shows himself at High

Noon. Alas, I was not homeless for long. I quickly found new digs in an old paint factory that had been liberated and occupied by the people, as we like to say. There was a working toilet on the third floor and a water tap but no shower, though you could do a sponge bath. No electricity, either. Some people had flashlights or Atomic Beam gear they'd stolen from the "As Seen on TV' end cap at Bartell or Walgreens – that Atomic Beam crap works pretty well, actually – but somebody was always telling someone else to turn off the fucking lanterns because the cops might see the light. I don't know why the water was still working if the electricity had been shut off.

There were, like, 30 or 40 of us who stayed there at any one time, and you got to know a few of the other people, or at least learn what they were willing to let on. We scrounged food as best we could and people shared stuff, too. There was a grill on the rear fire escape and we would burn bits of wood ripped from old pallets or crates to cook meals or boil water. Mostly, though, we ate corn flakes straight out of the box or canned meats or Snickers bars and stuff. Every once in a while a woman would show up with a child, or two or three, and they'd get a lot of attention, and there was one girl who lived in the factory, Wendy she called herself, admitted she'd appropriated the name from the "Peter Pan" stories, who would help feed or clean the youngest of the children. The weirdest people were the Chinese exchange students who sometimes stayed with us. They never spoke to anyone, wouldn't even look you straight in the eye when they'd hurriedly pass you on the stairs. They would disappear at dawn and return only late at night, presumably when the libraries on campus closed. I thought all Chinese exchange students were the sons and daughters of billionaire real estate moguls and import-export tycoons, or else high-ranking Communist Party officials, so I was surprised to see them staying with us. Maybe they gambled a lot, or they were saving their money for when they got their Ph.D.'s, then they were going to defect.

Theft was uncommon, but not unheard of. It was at the paint factory that I learned to sleep with my boots on, and cash was always kept on the person, as well. But all in all, people were friendly. I learned where to get hot lunches on certain days, any clothes I might need, too, and which were the cleanest shelters when it came time to move on. It was understood that everyone would move on eventually. Think of the paint factory as a halfway house, except you were transitioning to the margins, not the mainstream.

Sometimes the cops – if they stopped by without a warrant – said they were looking for witnesses because there'd been a robbery or stabbing in the neighborhood, or someone had been seen taking a dump in the alley and the trail led them here. Mostly, though, they were just making the rounds, like cops on a beat peering through storefront windows after hours, trying to see that all was well, *"Good night, Irene, I'll see you in my dreams,"* before moving on.

It was a great fire that chased us all out. Perhaps you read about it. Twelve people died and I wasn't one of them. It was that night I learned what a blast furnace must feel like. People speak of heat from a fire as being intense but this was mighty and strong, global warming in a crucible strong; it was Chicago fire strong. The flames shot in and out of the thick smoke like popups in a haunted house attraction, like sparklers so close to your face they could blind you. I heard groans that sounded like a giant oak tree bending in a strong wind before snapping; I heard the screams and sobs of people who were fully aware of their fate and knew there was nothing they could do about it. One child huddled in a corner with her My Little Pony; I looked for her mother, then I grabbed the girl by the arm and led her down the stairs. Others, those who hadn't escaped yet, were all behind the wall of fire. They were being roasted on a spigot. After I ran from the building with the little girl I moved to safety on the other side of the street, the fire raging and relentless and remorseless, and I just couldn't believe I'd actually escaped from *that*.

The Seattle Fire Department soon arrived and took control of the situation, establishing a perimeter to keep everyone away. I walked up to their line with the little girl and caught the attention of a female firefighter, who turned to me, and I pushed the little girl into her arms. "Who's this?" she asked.

"A little girl," I answered. "I never got her name."

The woman looked down at the crying babe and ran her fingers through the girl's hair. "Where's her mother?" she asked.

I turned my head toward the conflagration and motioned with my chin. I didn't have to say more.

I lost some of my belongings that night but still had my backpack, as well as my good boots. I was sorry for all the dead and dying but I had to think about my next place to stay. That's when I moved to Pioneer Square, which is where panhandling comes into play. On lots of days now I set up shop in Red Square at the University of Washington, which is not named for what you think, but only its red brick pavers. Usually, depending on the weather, I'm wearing a Tilley hat I stole from REI the previous winter and I hold it upside down so the kids will know I want their money. Once, I found a clipboard on a bench and I started asking the students to sign my petition and most of them would agree even though I just had the back of a McDonald's wrapper clipped to the board, then I told them the petition was to help fund the homeless, which was true, of course. Some of the kids looked at me funny, others told me to fuck off, and a few wanted to interview me.

"Oh, you study sociology here?" I asked one collegian.

"Yes. We learned all about you people," he replied.

"'You people?' What, you think we're not like other people? Not as good as you? Is that it?"

"No, no, I didn't mean that at all. It's just that we're studying multinational corporations and the need to raise the minimum wage. By the way, do you identify as white, Latinx or Black?"

Foot traffic in the square is steady, if not heavy, and there's a bit of a crush every time classes change, yet the revenue stream is weak. I blame this trend on credit cards. Not many people carry change anymore, and I don't accept Apple Pay. There also is the competition. A busker who's pretty good is juggling tenpins – Dad always said learn a trade and you'll never want for work and I guess he was right about that – and Joan Baez is strumming a guitar and singing in a scratchy cat voice in the center of the square. She's dressed only in a long, black knit dress, sleeveless at that, and I think she's shivering. If I haven't seen her in Pioneer Square before, I will soon. There are some other young homeless people about but they don't seem to be panhandling on this day, and a dude with a really long beard like Walt Whitman, only still black, is carrying a real petition for people to sign. I approach him and ask, "What's it about, Bro?" and he gives me the once over but doesn't answer right away.

"What, you don't think I'm a registered voter?" I say. I act like I'm offended because I am; I think he should have asked for my signature. No, I'm not a registered voter but he doesn't know that, does he? I don't like that he's profiling me. Finally, he says it's a petition to raise the minimum age for purchasing assault rifles in the State of Washington from 18 years of age to 21.

"Whoa," I say. "You mean, I could have bought an AR-15 as soon as I turned 18, just like drinking beer legally? That's fucked up, man."

"Damn right, it's fucked up," he says, and he gives me the clipboard, but not before asking if I'm a registered voter. I tell him I'm not, but at least he's asking me now, and I walk on.

SOMETIMES, DURING EITHER THE MORNING or afternoon rush hour, I'll work the highway exit ramps, preferably one with a stop light so my prey will be captive.

You've all seen panhandlers and beggars at highway exit ramps, the armless veterans and toothless grandmas, as well as people who can twist their feet and ankles 180 degrees backward. You turned your head away as you rolled to a stop; you hoped your car wouldn't land immediately opposite such people; you looked at the driver two or three cars up who'd lowered his window to hand over some ashtray change and you resented the fact that you would probably miss the green light or left turn signal because of it, then you watched with fear and loathing as the beggar worked his way down the line to your car while you were stuck in traffic gridlock.

"Who are these people? Why don't they get a job? Is this even legal?"

You felt superior. And, maybe, just maybe, you figured out their secret: it's a business. Most of these beggars are independent contractors who must pay their handlers upfront for a ride to their street corners and highway exits, a "nut" just like taxicab drivers have to pay if they don't own their vehicles, keeping only the receipts they take in over and above that fee. Sometimes, though, these people really are the injured and insulted, as my good friend Fyodor Dostoevsky once wrote – it's not always a fake amputee, an alcoholic masquerading as a former Navy Seal, a crack-addled woman claiming to have three hungry children at home. Usually it is a fake narrative, but not always. For these truly pure and innocent, every street corner and park bench and food pantry is another station of the cross.

SOMETIMES, THOUGH, IT'S SOMEONE like me, more than a fish out of water, a person on the border of time and space.

ONE OF THE GREAT INCONVENIENCES of working a highway exit is needing to pee, not to mention take a crap. I'll go up against a wall in an alley any time but I don't know about whipping out my dick in front of a line of cars and impatient, frustrated drivers, and turning my back to them is even more humiliating because I should not have to be ashamed of needing to pee and not having a better place to do it. On this particular day, the area near my station is reasonably prosperous and alive and after a couple of hours working the morning rush I walk toward a busy intersection nearby, the first four-way stop after the highway exit. There's a small group of demonstrators standing under the marquee demanding an end to the occupation in Palestine. I go up to one gaunt-looking old man who's holding a placard on a stick, "Free Gaza," and ask where a guy can go take a dump around here. He looks at me incredulously and exclaims, "What?"

"You're Daniel Berrigan, aren't you?" I say in a good deadpan. "The Chicago 8, right?" I respected what he was doing well enough, but I don't like the way some people look at me.

"What do you want?" the old man demanded. Momentarily, a couple of his assistants – a trim, young woman in a puffy Under Armour jacket and a guy in a Fidel cap – came over to see what was happening, or perhaps to protect Mr. Berrigan.

"I'm working the exit ramp up by the Interstate," I say. "I just need to know where I can go to take a shit." I almost threaten to drop my pants right there and then. But the guy in the Fidel cap turns out to be a decent enough chap, or means to be, and he tells me I can use the facilities at a Trader Joe's a couple of blocks away.

"If you want to join us when you're finished, you're welcome to," Fidel says. "You don't have to beg for money." I nod appreciatively to him, offer Daniel Berrigan a snippy, insincere smile, and confirm with hand signals the right direction to head, then head there. I'm fuming as I walk away.

"I beg for money? I beg for food?" That's what I'm saying to myself. Yet, as I wait to cross the street, crowded on both sides by people of all races, classes and genders, I know it's true. I am now begging for money. For lunch, I think I'll steal some fruit from Trader Joe's after I'm finished in the crapper.

I DO NOT RETURN TO MY STATION after eating. I've got a crunchy apple in my hand, a couple of plums in a jacket pocket and a granola bar in my hip pocket. I'd drunk a half-liter bottle of fizz, some kind of flavored, zero calorie mountain water, while still in the store and so was set for the afternoon. The air around me is breezy and mild – an air bath, I think they call it in Japan, or so I'd once read in *National Geographic* – and I think I might nap on a grassy knoll in a nearby park. Once I arrive I discover that the geese are a real nuisance on the trail that wends its way around a small lagoon, yet all the signs say they're an endangered species or protected or something like that. *Pick up after your dog, but don't touch the geese.* You could feed a lot of homeless people with these fat geese, I'm thinking. At least the air is still fresh, even as the smell of weed wafts by occasionally, and a couple of girls, having removed their tops, are sunning face-down on a berm. Some biker dudes are revving engines on old shovelhead Harleys in one of the parking lots and other homeless people are congregating outside a public toilet at the opposite end of the lake when I pass by. I sneak a peek in and think I'd rather remain dirty. *Pick up after your dog, but don't touch the humans.*

I decide to park myself on a bench and light up – a cigarette, that is. And this is where I meet another freak who's taking a cigarette break of his own.

"Big Kahuna," he announces after he turns to me.

"Say what?" I reply.

"Cliff Robertson in one of those Gidget Goes Crazy movies from the '60s," he explains. "He played a surfer and all the chicks were wild for him. He was the Big Kahuna. My Grandpapa had it on VHS."

I remembered Sally Field from the old TV reruns of "Gidget," or was that "The Flying Nun," can you dig it, but who the fuck is Cliff Robertson, I think.

"Come on, he played JFK in 'PT109.' You know, our martyred president? He was a war hero, not like the draft dodgers we elect today."

Okay, I say, I'd read about the Kennedys, and next Big Kahuna asks me which shelter I'm staying at. Ho-ly shit. Do I look I stay at a homeless shelter? Of course, I do. I was staying at a homeless shelter, but I didn't want to *look* like I was. Well, I hadn't bothered to shave in a few days and I'd slept in my street clothes the night before so, from his point of view, it would have to be true. "Where do you stay," I ask, trying to divert attention from me.

"I stay with my old lady," Big Kahuna says.

"Your mother or your girlfriend?" I ask, then I tap him lightly on the shoulder and say I was only kidding about his mother.

"My girlfriend," he clarifies. "She works at the KFC. I take care of the kids on Tuesdays and Thursdays but they go to a church day care on the other days."

"Your kids?" I ask. Big Kahuna looks down and shakes his head. "No. They're from a previous relationship, you might say. The dude's in prison so I help out where I can."

"What'd he do?"

"Oh, robbed the gas station over there." Big Kahuna turns and points in the direction of a small stand of trees. "Just past there, that Exxon Mobil.

Really stupid. Everybody knew who he was. At least nobody was shot."

"And then you moved in with the woman? What happens when he gets out?"

"Oh, it'll be all right. We all lived together before. I was taking care of the kids before. Maurice was in no condition to take responsibility for them."

"So, the woman from the KFC, she's not really your old lady?" Kahuna shrugs and slouches against the bench's back rails.

"Well, we get it on sometimes, you might say. Maybe we've been drinking or whatever. Maurice, he doesn't like it too much, but really, Chelsea is the boss, not him and not me." Then he laughed weirdly. "He's got to wait his turn. I got to wait my turn, too. Sometimes Chelsea brings another guy home with her and we both gotta wait our turns."

Big Kahuna next asks me for a cigarette because he's out – I knew that was coming and I can't deny him a smoke, but I gratuitously add that I won't give him any money. The man seems startled, then he shakes his head and looks off into the distance for a few moments before telling me to go fuck myself, and he ambles off without even taking the cigarette I've extended to him with my hand.

This guy has more pride than me? Then I've really got a problem.

I NEVER THOUGHT I'D END UP in a homeless shelter, but who does? I'm standing outside one of these John 3:16 Jesus Saves places, standing in a sad little line of hunchbacked people waiting to get a bed for the night. The mission is not open yet and the line is growing, but I've arrived early enough that I think a spot is assured. These are the new rules in my life.

"Welcome, good person. Have you thought about what will happen to your soul after you die?" This is what the Peters and Pauls inside will say to me and I'll express surprise, then joy, accepting that there is hope after all, and these acolytes of Christ will all smile at me sublimely. They'll speak reverentially, their hands clasped and pressed against their chests, and they'll have a beatific affect on their faces. They've seen the light and they want me to join them on the other side when God calls in the chips. They have the patience of a Buddha. But not always. Sometimes they snap at us – "*Stand over there! What do you have in your pocket? Have we seen you here before?*" – cold words like a driving rain at those times.

The line eventually starts moving and the apostles check us one by one behind the door. One guy frisks me and checks my pockets, and then I take off my jacket, which is an older green Army field jacket I bought used somewhere, and I roll up my shirt sleeves so he can check my arms. It's all about needle tracks but I'm clean. Really, you're supposed to learn all the rules on the street, like tramps in the 1930s sitting around a campfire and talking about the places where the police will lean on you and where they'll look the other way, and which farmers nearby are hiring or at least will let you sleep in their barn and drink from their well. I learn fast.

A lot of the men here, they were tossed from their homes by their parents when they were younger, or their old ladies threw them out, or they couldn't make the child support payments so they went into hiding. Some lost jobs when the factories shut down and have been on the road a long time. Some of the more militant young homeless dudes, they call themselves Crusties because of the way they look and smell and dress, what they believe in, too, like to make speeches. "You read about the tax breaks they're giving the rich? What kind of tax break are you getting?" they preach. It's the black guys who are the most normal people at shelters like this. They don't act like they're in shock to have ended up here and they're rarely the ones to start fights. I don't know if that's a 'roll with the punches' attitude or if they're accustomed to being screwed in life, always expecting the other shoe to drop, or if their perspective is different because they've been on the outside since birth.

AFTER DINNER WE'RE ALL INVITED to Chapel, which is how they refer to the service, not just the room. They call it Chapel, as in, "Are you going to Chapel, brother?" and "It's time for Chapel." I don't like to go to Chapel and it's only mandatory on Sundays, so I retire to the TV room. They don't have cable at John 3:16 but there are all these free rerun channels that show old programs such as "The Rockford Files" and "Magnum, P.I.," basically any stud who drives a hot car and tracks down thieves and murderers. That's what most of the older men here like to watch and they always cheer when the bad guys get caught, as if they truly believe in the criminal justice system! Plus, there are the cars.

"Damn, you shoulda seen my 308 GTS after I wrecked it. Doin' 165 on the Interstate before I went airborne."

"Shut the fuck up. I saw you on a Schwinn 3-speed last week."

"Who said that?"

That's when the staff walk up and down the rows pointing their flashlights at us.

After dinner, I retire to the small library and pick up a James Patterson spy novel – it must be one of his early efforts because we're still fighting the Soviets in East Berlin – and I find a seat. Some guy tells me to move my legs and I wonder if he's angling for a fight but then I realize my legs are splayed and blocking the aisle, so I reel them in but don't apologize because, basically, you never apologize. It's a sign of weakness and even if you fend off the immediate threat, word will still get around that you're weak. After reading the first few chapters of the James Patterson book, though, there are so many tells as to what's going to happen I figure I know how the book will end and so put it down, safe in the knowledge that democracy will prevail. It's time to go to bed.

The bunks are arranged in neat rows. Some are singles, others are double-deckers, and they're all narrow, as you might expect. The double-deckers have little ladders that lead to the top bunk, and everyone has to make up his own bed with linen and a camp blanket they hand you as you file into the dorm. It's very crowded and will get warmer through the night; being on the second floor doesn't help, either. There are a few windows in the old factory walls – the building once housed a company that made men's shirts – but staff will be loath to open any wide as it's raining again outside. The blankets feel like something akin to the coarse moving pads they loan you at U-Haul if you rent one of their trucks, but seemingly with even more horsehair and thistle reinforcement. The narrow beds have no box springs, just a wire mesh under a very thin mattress for support. I always check my sheets for stains – there usually are some – and though I undress for bed I sleep with my leather boots on. You can place your valuables in a room that's guarded by a guy who sits behind a Dutch door and places your stuff in a wire basket, but I won't turn over my boots. If you have nice shoes or boots they might be gone the next morning. Good boots and shoes are among the most important possessions a homeless man can have.

I have a bunk near a window and I'm glad of it, even if it is shut. I can hear the drizzle tapping the glass pane and I listen for the gentle slap of tires as cars drive by on the wet pavement below. I'm at ease. This is my safe place. I'm a kid again and I know nothing will happen between now and the morning, when the great adventure will begin again. That's what I tell myself. What do you tell yourself?

NIETZSCHE'S DOG

A FULL MOON RISES over the city, dry leaves spin in all the alcoves, it's a Halloween kind of night. Elastic shadows stretch under gaslit lamp posts as frightened men hurry down the streets, their hard heels clicking on the cobblestones before they turn and disappear around a corner in every direction.

Now you are alone in this dollhouse village square. You long for the sound of young girls laughing gaily from behind shuttered windows but it is not forthcoming. You cup your ear in favor of distant bells, but they are faint. You went out to meet someone this evening but you don't know whom, or where it is you were to gather. Your barely remember the leaving. You pull up your jacket collar and hurry down the street, only to turn a corner and disappear yourself.

BACK IN MY TENT NOW, having failed to find my focus yet again, I tell myself it was a night well spent, the search being the thing, the reward in the risk. My shelter is a tarp hung over rope that is strung between two poles; this homemade pup tent itself sits in a viaduct beneath an abandoned railroad bridge on the edge of town. It is an encampment I share with my fellow American castoffs, our own little Hooverville, a real Boy Scout Jamboree. Besides me, who I will introduce later, there is Angela, a 38-year-old German-American woman from St. Louis who

Abraham Aamidor

says she's fled from a convent. She wears tailored men's shirts in summer, albeit wrinkled, and covers herself with animal hides in winter, and when she goes off to pee behind a silver maple that grows just beyond the viaduct she laughs hysterically and shouts, "Don't peek, now!" I think she's schizophrenic but who am I to say.

Then there's Harold, a 52-year-old divorced man who lost his job when the paper mill shut down somewhere, or did he work in the textile industry in North Carolina or make cathode ray TV tubes in Bloomington, Indiana, I don't really know, but he says his wife left him for a cop who still had a job and a good pension and she got the deed to the house, too. He opines for the days when one would hear a freight train trundling past in the middle of the night, maybe even hop in an empty boxcar and try your luck elsewhere. But the train doesn't come this way anymore.

And there are others, Roadrunner and Big Willie and Little Debbie and, well, you get the picture. No one reveals their real name here, their true back pages, and no one stays for long, either, other than maybe Angela and me and a couple of others. They've all got plans, they got big plans, and they were dumped here only because of some weird ripple in the cosmic undertaking, sure, don't you know, and when each and every one of them gets back on their feet, it's inevitable, just a matter of time, they'll walk out of this echo chamber of bad humor and into the bright sunshine of their intended promised lives. Well, they will disappear, but they don't see that.

Nonetheless, some of the hoboes who come and go may argue with each other well into the night over the most trivial of matters, "*Those are my shoe laces you stole,*" or, "*You never been in the Army, asshole,*" just spit and beat on each other but rarely really put the hurt on anyone because they don't have the strength, not anymore. They lost that with their spirit. They are derailed. And when the bickering stops they go back to their normal. They remind me of animals in the wild that immediately return to foraging and grazing or shitting a big pile after butting heads for an hour or maybe fucking a cow, no memory at all.

How can there be humanity without memory? There can't.

I wonder what a sweep of these homeless headless chickens would look like. The world would be a better place without them, wouldn't it, you *normal* people think.

My story? I got here by dropping out of college, part of the new breed of homeless in America, middle class youth who reject it all, even if we actually have a shot at all of it, whatever *it* is. It's the new nihilism –

fuck all of you, not just Trump – but I'm not Antifa or violent or the stranger your parents warned you about when you were growing up. It was just that I couldn't wait for class to be over in the courses I took, a good liberal arts education in a good undergraduate program, but the drip, drip, drip of futility nonetheless. On the other hand, I got to read both Herman Hesse and Friedrich Nietzsche and discovered that, of course, you shouldn't expect to learn anything in school. Either you go on the road and learn for yourself, or you take the show on the road and try to teach others, pilgrim or prophet, two sides of the same coin. You must do it on your own, out on the road, feel the pain before you can appreciate the joy.

Birds fly the coop, Ishmael goes off to sea, and women bleed. No direction known, yet I still go forward.

"YOU WRITIN' A BOOK about us, Tommy? Is that it? You studyin' us like specimens in a bottle, like bacteria in a Petri dish? That's it, isn't it, you little cocksucker. That's what you are. A cocksucker, you fucking cocksucker."

That was Maurice speaking – pronounced like Morris, the English way, because Maurice is English, came to America for his Ph.D. in Social Anthropology and dropped out; he's schizophrenic eight beats to the bar for sure. Maurice is short and skinny with a wispy beard like Ho Chi Minh, and his teeth are bad like a lot of English people have, and I do not argue with him, either.

No, I am not living under an abandoned train trestle just so I can write a book about these people, these *other* people. I say "other" because I have not yet accepted that I am one of them even though I am living *among* them. I have a purpose, but it is not to write books. I am Siddhartha on the path of righteousness. I am Mao on his long march. I am Zarathustra *going down*, a mighty roar is stirring inside me.

Am I not noble, then?

Yea, as I wearily make my way through these seasons of loss and expired dreams, as I come to terms with the face in the mirror, I still hold out hope against hope. It's not over until it's over. It's always darkest before the dawn. Use the Force, Luke!

"*Komm lass uns Lieben heut Nacht,*" whispers Angela in my ear. She bends deeply; it is the middle of the night when I have come back early, when everyone else seems asleep though liars some of them are, and her breasts are exposed behind the deep scoop of her blouse. She is motioning with her index finger for me to come with her; she sends a soft breeze my way.

Angela is not so bad looking, not when I've become accustomed to sleeping in mud and I haven't been with a woman in years. She is not yet so old or dry or hunchbacked; her hair is not weed-like, her skin is not barnacled. And her eyes, they are hypnotic. They are deep and shimmering, wet like liquor, and I want to dive in.

"Can you get pregnant?" I ask.

"No-o-o," she warbles, and we go off behind the maple tree and make love.

I had a girlfriend, call her Nina, and she was a better student than I. We made love on our third or fourth date – real dates, too, with appointed hour and place and an agenda for the evening like a dance card – but I didn't want to marry her. And I didn't want her just for the sex, ergo, there was no reason to continue the relationship.

"It's not you," I wrote her. I wrote her an actual letter, on paper, neatly folded and with a nice commemorative stamp I personally selected from several sheets of offerings at the post office, something from a famous female artist. "It's not another woman, or man (not that there's anything wrong with that, *ha ha*). I need to find myself, that's all. No, that's not the truth, either. It's just that, I feel something is out there and I must find *it*. Can you understand?"

That's what I wrote her, and I'm sure she was relieved to discover the truth about me so early in our relationship. Why would she want to bother with anyone who could write such claptrap?

I am not really homeless. I'm not in the same predicament as my compatriots under the abandoned railroad trestle. They were kicked out of their homes; they couldn't meet the child support payments; their factories closed for good and they don't speak Chinese or Vietnamese or Hindi. I have unconditional love to fall back on. I can picture my mother saying, "I was so worried, Tommy," upon seeing me after so long a time. Or, better yet, welcoming me back with a joyful smile and outstretched arms, warm smells wafting in from the kitchen and an incandescent glow from a 60-watt Soft White light bulb under a fabric lamp shade in the corner of the living room, real Norman Rockwell stuff, and there is nothing wrong with that. Yep, a home-cooked meal sure is fine, but then what? What comes next? And after that? That's what I wanted to know. I was feeling boxed in, all four walls closing in on me like some diabolical torture chamber, which is what I thought of life when I left it. Escape was the only answer. Can't you see that? Anyone?

Sometimes I take stupid jobs out by the strip mall to make a few bucks. Tax season is always best – they'll dress me in a Statue of Liberty hat and paint my face silver, or outfit me to look like Abraham Lincoln with a tall stovepipe hat and gnarly beard made of black Brillo pads, and I'll wave people into the parking lot where they can get an immediate cash loan against their W-2 statements, interest starts *now*. Subway sandwich shops are good, too, and they'll even throw in a free 6-inch when your shift is over. I never panhandle, though. I still have my pride.

Maybe I'm schizophrenic, too. The first step in getting help, they say, is to admit you've got a problem. But I don't know that I've got a problem. I'm on the road less travelled, that's all. I've read *Siddhartha* and *Thus Spoke Zarathustra*. I've even listened to Bob Dylan on vinyl! I must do this! That's what I tell myself. And that nothing will matter in the long run, anyway. How old is the universe? Snap your fingers – that's how old it is. How long are you dead for when you die? Snap your fingers – it's the same thing.

YOU THROW OFF THE GRAVE blanket you fashioned from tree moss and pine needles because it is time to meet your interlocutor even though you still don't know who he is, what he looks like, or where the hunt will end. You only know that it's time again, if not since the initial leaving, at least since you last lost the scent.

A new moon has risen above the tallest trees, the wind is so strong shutters flap against their siding, and grit stings your skin when it strikes your face. Dogs howl and dig deep in the yards for their bones, not to chew them, but to lie down beside them. It is the kind of night when even dogs believe in ghosts.

You find yourself in the center of the village square again, the gaslights are dim, and the cobblestone streets are rain-slickened even though it is not raining. It's a trick you've seen in the movies many times. But now, faintly, you hear someone cough, then clear his throat, and you snap your head sharply to see a man in a long cassock standing against a strong backlight – behind him is sunlight in a box.

Is the man beckoning you? There is no one else in the street; they have all fled around corners or closed their windows, per usual. Maybe it is he whom they always feared, not you. You straighten up, take a deep breath, and approach the man. As you come nearer, you can better discern the features of his face, the prominent bumps on his forehead and the regular shape of his nose, the strong but not overly long jaw. He is a sculpture by Rodin. You proceed cautiously and stop just shy of his presence; you look him in the eye, the wormhole to his history, and he looks at you in the eye as well, and then he stands aside to bid you enter his home. You pass through the heavy door jambs, thick as railroad ties, and you find yourself inside a small, low room, more cabin than apartment, and as you look over your shoulder for another glimpse of the streetscape you are leaving behind, you now think it does look like a movie set, maybe a sound stage secured for the night. The man tugs on your arm but not forcibly; you notice his crooked, arthritic hand, his splotchy red skin, and veins as thick as jungle vines.

As you stand on the wide plank pine flooring, unvarnished but swept clean, as you admire the oak beams that support the ceiling and roof, you realize that this is a villager's cottage. Copper pots hang near the burning hearth, that source of light that awed you earlier, and a small basin with water sits on a three-legged stool. You notice the Grandfather clock that stands against one wall ticking regularly, yet there are no hands on the clock face. It just ticks.

"I don't need to know *exactly* what time it is, beyond light and dark," the man says. "I just like to be reminded that time is flowing, one moment follows another, that things happen and then they *have* happened."

"But all is erased in time," you protest. "What does it matter what *once* was real?"

The man sits opposite you and raises a long knife, a long, serrated bread knife, as if he is about to strike you, then asks if you would like bread and jam with tea. You take a seat at his table and inhale the soft steam from the welcoming beverage.

"I could have opened my door and bid you come in anytime," he says, "but it was up to you to make the first move. Maybe I did act to draw your attention, though. How long should the master wait for the pupil?"

His words sting but you are accustomed to such. "Yes, yes," you mutter while staring into your cup. "I've been walking in circles, yet the answer was here all along."

"I didn't say I had any answers. I just said if you were looking for me, I was here the entire time."

The man questions you about your youth – *suburban; divorced parents; was not the homecoming king* – and your life lying down with snakes. He asks if you're making progress in your quest, but does not define progress, and you answer truthfully – you don't know, you tell him.

"But tell me this," you add. "Am I on the right path?"

"You found me, didn't you?"

TOMMY DIDN'T KNOW if the encounter was a dream or not. He hadn't been sleeping well lately, and he hadn't been diligent in pursuing this ghost each and every night. When it became routine for the police to stop him on the street after dark, ask him to put his hands up on the patrol car while they searched him, he couldn't help but think it was all a recurring dream, including dreaming that it was all a dream, a vicious infinite regression into the present.

"You're not gonna plant drugs on me just so you can take me in, are you?" he'd asked a cop the last time he was stopped; it was a female officer he knew from a previous stop-and-frisk, and they both laughed.

"I'd be doing you a favor," the officer replied before telling him he could put his hands down and stand up straight. "You have to get off the streets. You got a family you can go back to?"

One time, Tommy had been beaten and left for dead while on his nightly trek. He'd been walking diagonally across a city park, and he stopped to see his reflection in a small, still pond when he was jumped from behind by two assailants of unknown gender and heritage. When they turned his pockets inside out and didn't find a wallet or even a dime they beat him viciously, beat him as somehow *he* had betrayed *them*.

When Tommy recovered, he started off to the police station to report the crime but a passing patrol car saw him first. The driver and his partner shined a spotlight on him but did not immediately get out of their car; when they did, they walked slowly toward Tommy, pulling on their gun belts but not drawing their weapons. Tommy knew he looked pathetic; he would have been more proud had the policemen thought he was a menace.

"You look like you just got rolled," the burlier of the two men asked. "You wanna report it?"

Tommy shook them off. "I don't think it's all their fault," he replied enigmatically. "I shouldn't have been out at night, cutting across the park like this. I make poor choices, that's all."

I DIDN'T KNOW WHAT was in the tea the man served me, but when I awoke I was lying in a narrow bed, just a sisal robe web that crisscrossed a wood frame on short legs. A light blanket had been thrown over my body. The man was sitting in a chair near me, breathing calmly. I'd awakened with a start and could feel my heart race, yet he remained calm, smiling at me with a wry yet confident expression, or was he slightly amused at the sight of me? He spoke first.

"So, you think nothing matters, not in the long run? All is erased, as you say? Even the present doesn't exist? Oh, well, some people do believe that."

Still groggy, I needed several moments to recall our earlier conversation. I sat up and combed my fingers through my hair, then I wiped the accumulated scum from the edges of my mouth onto trouser legs. Snap your fingers and all is gone – yes, I'd said that. Snap your fingers and all *will* be gone – I'd said that, as well. Irrevocably so, being in the moment the same as the end of time. Yet, he was dangling another option over my head.

"Friend, if you were to live your life again, would you want to live it exactly as you have lived it?" he asked. "For, in infinite time and space, the choices you make today will be repeated over and over again. It's only logical."

I considered more carefully what he was saying, that to which he had alluded. *Ah*, the recurring universe, which I'd heard about before, maybe many times, maybe an *infinite* number of times! I didn't believe it, of course, yet, I put my finger to my lips in thought, in further consideration of what the man was supposing. Most people would think being reborn offers a second chance, but this man was saying something different. The life you commit to *now* will be replayed over and over. You will not be able to correct anything in the future.

"But, tell me, good sir, if everything that happens must happen again and again, then everything that's happening has already happened," I replied. "If so, I don't have a choice at all."

My interlocutor was nonplussed. "Not if this is the first time around."

"But how can you know if that is so?" I asked.

The man raised his long bread knife again, but the bread was all gone; only crumbs of its past existence remained.

"You're mad," I told him.

"Yet you are here," he replied.

Yes, it stung. I was just another person who wanted someone to tell me what to do, neither a Siddhartha nor a Zarathustra. All the faults in our stars are in us, not vice versa, just as Shakespeare had written.

I thanked the man for his hospitality – a wind could pass through him without disturbance – and I walked out the door into a new dawn. I saw many people coming and going on the streets then, and a dog leapt from its haunches and nestled against my leg. We hurried back to the encampment only to find it abandoned, save for a single note from Angela pinned to a tree.

"*Ich gehe nach hause*," she'd written. "*Und du?*"

IN THE GRAVEYARD OF PAST EXPERIENCE,

(A Novella)

THE FURNITURE WAS DATED – brown velour sofa, floral print drapes, and machine-made Oriental-style rug, all wool yet with a well-worn path from the inner office door to the saggy sofa like a shortcut across the lawn. Even the gold-tone table lamps were pitted and tarnished and their fringed shades frayed as well, everything wearing its neglect like a played-out hotel room. Maybe Dr. Tobias Silver's patients never noticed the accommodations because he liked to keep the curtains closed, the room analgesically dark, or else they were so fixated on their own problems, so intent on receiving solace and absolution, that they only saw in the veteran psychiatrist a safe harbor, a father figure who would welcome them with open arms like coming home, Jesus.

Yet the decay and delinquency evident in the office belied the exclusive Michigan Avenue address where Silver had practiced for nearly 40 years. Eleventh floor of the historic Monroe Building and lakefront exposure to boot, the early Chicago high-rise was esteemed for its colorful terra cotta exterior and boxed gable roof. When he'd signed his initial lease the young doctor was full of promise and expectation, buoyant like a new sailor embarking on his first ocean voyage. Business being what it was in more recent years, though, he should have relocated to lower-priced digs, something in the suburbs or even the end unit of a strip shopping mall somewhere, but Tobias Silver was keen on keeping up appearances, a good address being like old gold, or so he believed.

"How's the practice?" a colleague might ask.

"As good as ever," he would reply chirpily.

It wasn't true. Depth psychiatry had been squeezed for years by insurance plans that pushed patients into group therapy and as mental health consumers were seduced by ads for Zoloft and Xanax, Paxil and Zyprexa, all names concocted by Madison Avenue ad agencies or even computer-generated because they *sounded* like wellness and hence should sell well. What did any of these insurance underwriters and Big Pharma multinationals know about mental health, Silver would fume. "I've held bereft mothers to my bosom like babes in swaddling after losing a child," he'd tell himself. And he had done so, but not in many, many years. Now, he would turn a deaf ear to bored housewives who didn't want to have sex with their fat, hairy husbands while smiling patronizingly at them; he'd peer through a slit in his window curtains and out toward the little skiffs in the lake and wonder if it wasn't time to trade in his Mercedes E-class, it's getting on six-years-old now.

"Oh, Dr. Silver, I just don't want to get up in the morning. I mean, what's the use, right?"

"Doctor, I think I was raped as a child. That's what I've been keeping from you all this time."

"No one likes me at school."

Silver barely listened to his patients anymore. "I can tell what they're like the moment they come through the door, whether they'll be difficult or quite malleable, even what their problem is," he'd once boasted, speaking like a slick car salesman who sizes up customers immediately, the young couple with two small children that's going to buy a minivan, the technical school graduate in engineer boots and a curled baseball cap who will want to sit behind the wheel of a Dodge Challenger.

Not many people went in for depth psychiatry anymore, what the pop psychologists on TV would casually refer to as "talk therapy," a term that outraged Silver. Talk therapy was for social workers and 12-step groups; he'd immersed himself in Freud and Jung and Adler. He knew *theory*, not tips for a healthier, happier life. But all the European gurus had lost their mystique, their exotic appeal, and old tropes and once taboo topics had become commonplace. *You want to fuck your mother?* But everyone does! Politically, the New Left and Post-Marxism had won over the intellectuals. Even the feminists, generally more attuned to emotions and subliminal thoughts, had turned on Freud because of his suffocating view of women. Psychiatry, psychology and sociology all had been invented to undermine the church and take human behavior out of the realm of sin, to stop blaming people just for being what they were. Fair enough, Silver had once thought, but everything that came after was invented to pin the blame on someone else altogether. He knew better.

Tobias Silver only saw four or five patients a day in recent years, if that. In between breaks in his appointment calendar he would take long walks through nearby Grant Park, see the saffron-rich crocuses and richly pigmented tulips erupt in early spring, or shop the aisles at the former Marshall Field & Co. and especially its Store for Men, maybe look over the latest wrist watches of just pick out a new tie. Or, he'd stop into the Art Institute, go directly to the room with the Monet waterlilies and be annoyed at all the school teachers already present who would proclaim to their young charges, "Look at how the light plays on the water," as if that was all there was to Monet, or he'd find himself watching with bemusement the office girls on their own lunch breaks who'd turn and twist their heads at the balloon-like breasts and white rhino thighs in Max Beckmann's "Reclining Nude."

Then he'd return to his office to prepare for his 2 o'clock appointment.

"Doctor, I finally told my wife I was leaving her last night and ... ."

CHAPTER 2

TOBIAS SILVER HAD GROWN UP in Skokie, an insular Chicago suburb made famous when neo-Nazis marched through but which the ACLU defended as free speech. His parents were not particularly ethnocentric or even sentimental – no hackneyed art of a bearded Rabbi deep in prayer hanging from the wall, no Mezuzah on the front door jamb, yet they had built a small collection of quality memorabilia reflecting at least not a distaste for their heritage – a silver wine cup from Belarus, a ram's horn from 19th century Palestine, and their prized possession, a 17th century Passover Haggadah printed in Warsaw. Tobias first became aware of his own Jewishness not by his surroundings – if everyone on his street and around the corner in Skokie was Jewish then he hardly could have seen himself as "the other" – but it was when he met kids who were not Jewish that he first sensed a difference. What was it about them, and about him? That they prayed on Sunday, not Saturday? Their parents were carpenters and auto mechanics, not accountants or doctors? That they were better at sports than him? Yes, that's what bothered Tobias Silver the most when he was young. He'd go to a park on a long summer's evening and ask to join a pick-up ball game, and he would be slotted into the lineup, the other kids perhaps staring at him but only because they didn't know him, not because he was one of *them*, and when he muffed a couple of fly balls in the outfield, then struck out at the plate, he felt humiliated and didn't want to play with these other boys anymore. He turned to music instead, taking up the clarinet for a while, which his parents thought was grand, and he applied himself even more energetically to his studies. He could excel at something! Yet by the time of his Bar Mitzvah he still was short, pudgy, coarse-haired and bad at sports – it killed him to be like that, to be one of them after all, which is how he looked at himself. He balked at having a Bar Mitzvah, even at the loose, liberal Reform synagogue his parents had begun attending, submitting only when his parents accepted that he would choose his own path immediately after ceremonially becoming a man.

AS MUCH AS TOBIAS didn't like being pigeon-holed or channeled, wearing a yellow Star of David imprinted on his brain if not sewed to the breastplate of a jacket, by high school he accepted that he belonged in all the advanced placement courses available, which bestowed on him a kind of peerage. Dating was feasible if problematic – the only girls interested in him were also short, brilliant and Jewish-looking, but as king of the pigeons in his cohort he found he could seduce the ones who were as impatient to have sex as he was. When he came down with syphilis his mother cried and his father apologized for never having had "the talk" with him when it would have done some good, but the antibiotics worked and Tobias did not change his behavior.

"You know this is my first time," a girl said to him after the junior prom. They had gone to an independent motel on Lincoln Avenue, the kind that was little more than a configuration of small units in a row with a gravel parking lot in front. Tobias had only recently gotten his driver's license and his parents said he could have the car for the evening on condition that he was back by 1 a.m. It was well past midnight when he and his date checked into the motel, paying cash and signing phony names in the register. When the night clerk demanded identification he just said to the man, "Are you shitting me?" and the man rang them up.

Once embedded in Room 8, which was a cottage with low-wattage bulbs, thin blankets over the twin beds and a vinyl-printed pine theme covering the walls, the young lady hesitated. "Oh, come now," Tobias demanded. "You've let lots of guys feel you up. Now show me your pussy."

"Well, did you bring the rubbers?"

The girl had ridiculously shellacked hair piled high on her head, red lipstick thick and dark, too, and wooly eyebrows that had been filled in with too much mascara. Her body was soft and round, and her diffidence hardly hid her desire. She turned her back to Tobias as she disrobed, then slowly turned to reveal all of herself.

"You've done this before, right?" the girl asked.

"Please," he replied, "you want to fuck as much as I do."

CHAPTER 3

THE UNIVERSITY OF CHICAGO, where Tobias was destined after high school, had been good to people like Tobias Silver over the years and had paid a price for its principled stance, earning the sniggering sobriquet, "Jew U," along with a few other leading colleges and universities, most notably Columbia in New York City and, to a certain extent, Harvard. Tobias was always aware of this, as were some of his classmates. Fellow students and his professors typically were correct when greeting him or addressing him, "Oh, Silver, will you be in class Thursday?" if it was the day before the High Holidays, or just a cordial but de rigueur "Well done, Silver. Yes, very good," for a paper or presentation he'd tendered. Their body language occasionally said something different, however – a suppressed titter, a tilt of the head away from him when he was standing too close – and there often was a palpable silence when it would be expected that he move along after, say, joining a conversation already in progress.

"Europe's Jews?" he'd once said to a friend. "They should ask us about getting into a good college or medical school."

Silver had taken a variety of prerequisites and electives during his undergraduate career, including several courses in philosophy and psychology. He enjoyed the course on Freud best. It's not that he was taken in by the hysteria over the Oedipus Complex, but he did fancy the seasoned wisdom of "The Future of an Illusion," which sought to put God and his believers in their place. In it Freud suggested that the Supreme Being was merely what a father figure would look like to a very young child – all powerful, providing all – a very plausible memory for a child but an illusion if projected onto the sky. Tobias did not realize it at the time, but the authority figure and its impersonation was to become a major feature of his own life.

Another key work, "Moses and Monotheism," had gotten Silver thinking about religion, too. In this tract Freud argued that there were two men named Moses and that the man who'd led the ancient Hebrews out of bondage had simply created himself in the image of the original Moses, who *might* have been a Prince of Egypt. Who were the Hebrews to argue – they just wanted out.

"Isn't it interesting that all of monotheism is based on schizophrenia," he intoned in a rich basso voice in seminar one day. "One man named Moses, but they're two men. And one of them heard a voice in the wilderness, no less. Saul of Tarsus had a conversion experience on the road to Damascus and discovered that he was really Paul. Jesus was the Son of Man and the Son of God; he could give you eternal life, but he dies, yet he is resurrected and you die. Mohammed was a trader on camelback and the Seal of the Prophets – who knew! And was that really God's voice coming out of his mouth, or was he hearing voices in his head?"

The options for graduates of the University of Chicago were well delineated – half of graduates from the College typically would go on to earn a Ph.D. somewhere and get a job teaching, doing research, publishing a little (or a lot) and, in general, enjoy good status in life and reasonable comfort in retirement. That was one option. Some of the rest would go on to become lawyers, and a subset of them would work for the ACLU or other non-profits, become warriors in the fight for social justice, less money but greater prestige. The best bet for many because it offered both good status and good money was to go to medical school. Silver hated the stereotype, "My son, the doctor," that gentle jab at the Jewish American success story. Yet, medical school it was, but he would not cut people up or wear a stethoscope. He would explore their minds; he would become Sigmund Freud redux, maybe even better than Freud. What he wanted to do was interrogate theory; what he wanted to discover was meaning. That's why he chose psychiatry, he told himself. The sentient human experience was to be found in the activity of the mind, nowhere else.

TOBIAS'S GREAT ACHIEVEMENT in medical school was a kind of internship with Bruno Bettelheim, a man who'd managed to escape Europe during the Holocaust and land in the United States with the help of the University of Chicago, and wound up leading the university's Orthogenic School for Disturbed Children from 1944. Though he was long considered one of these "pioneering researchers" into child psychology, his reputation suffered over the years as it slowly emerged that he had faked some of his early academic credentials, and then had been abusive with some of the children in his charge, a kind of "tough love" for the mostly autistic charges that was heavy on discipline and light on tenderness.

Tobias always remembered the day he first met the great man – balding, smiling, adorned with horn-rimmed eyeglasses. Tobias had rehearsed his greeting, the way he would thrust his jaw out confidently, just walk up to the great man and shake his hand, even grab his arm by the elbow to show they were true compatriots, or could be one day. Bettelheim had personally escorted Tobias across the corridors and into the remotest anterooms of the Orthogenic School and introduced him to a few of the residential children – two boys deeply involved in a chess game, another who was building a house of cards, literally, from a poker deck, and a girl who dressed and undressed a doll with both great intensity and urgency, seemingly never satisfied with the result. Tobias had heard all the rumors about the director even then, that he had earned an advanced degree from a university in Czechoslovakia, but in art history or something like that, not psychiatry; that he was married twice but had abandoned his first wife on his way to America; and whether he really knew Freud well or perhaps they had just met in passing at a conference or lecture.

"So, why do you want to work with traumatized children?" Bettelheim had asked over a cup of tea; a kitchen aide had brought out the fine china on a silver platter reserved only for special guests. They sat in a large office; Bettelheim sat behind a double-pedestal walnut desk and Tobias in an upholstered armchair on the other side. The draperies were pulled open wide and a strong side light flooded the room.

"I want to learn from you," Tobias had replied.

"Are you seeking to butter me up?"

"I would if I thought it were possible. But you have an inventive mind and are independent, not a follower, and I admire people like you."

Tobias later related that he'd worked with one child closely that summer. Twelve at the time, a boy named Robbie would bite himself when he got angry, say he was hungry, and then throw his food on the floor when served. He'd pee in his bed at night, then find an attendant and order him to change the linen. Tobias was certain the boy knew exactly what he was doing and so set himself a goal to not only outsmart the child, but make him accept that he couldn't win. He would do this without corporal punishment, restraints or drugs, however.

It was on a mild and airy spring day that he and Robbie had gone for a walk on the Midway, which stretched from the Museum of Science and Industry in Jackson Park to Washington Park at the other end; they walked toward the Washington Park side that terminated in a massive Lorado Taft sculpture. The boy was exuberant, perhaps overstimulated by all the trees that lined the Midway and the cars passing on either side of it. Man and boy would hold hands for a bit, then Robbie would say, "No," without saying to what, and he'd pull his hand free and run ahead and turn around and laugh at Tobias, then jog back and take his hand again. He did this several times before they reached the sculpture.

"This is it," Tobias said when they arrived at their destination. "It's big, isn't it?"

"It is so big," Robbie said. "Are the people real?"

The wide sculpture, "The Fountain of Time," featured dozens of figures of all sorts, workers and farmers and mothers all cast together in one examination of humanity. Tobias again asked Robbie what he saw but the boy didn't respond further. "Okay, it's big," Tobias said. "And no, they're not real people frozen in time there. Sculptures like this are based on models. The models are real but the sculpture is not. Models pose for the artists."

"Oh," Robbie said, but Tobias wasn't sure he really understood.

"Would you like to be a model?" he asked the young boy.

"Would I be in this sculpture then?"

Robbie ran up to the piece and tried to wrap his arms around one of the figures but it was hard to get a grip. He looked back at Tobias to see if it was all right to do this, if he would get in trouble, and Tobias let him play. Then the boy stopped moving much; he turned his back to the sculpture and squeezed in between two of the figures. "I'm not coming back with you," he declared. "I'm staying here with my friends."

A few college students walked by and they marveled at how imaginative the young boy was and they smiled at Tobias but he wasn't interested in their attention. He just wanted to know what worlds churned inside the boy's head.

"How long will you stay up there?" Tobias asked.

The boy pouted and put a finger to his lips and looked off into the distance thoughtfully. "Oh, forever, I guess," he said.

"And how long is that?"

"Forever is tomorrow and tomorrow and tomorrow and tomorrow until there are no more tomorrows. You run out of tomorrows and that's forever."

CHAPTER 4

TOBIAS SILVER HAD CHOICES after graduating from medical school. He could latch on as a staff psychiatrist at a state hospital – they were always hiring – or apply for a job with a private group as a kind of junior member. Instead, he wanted to try something more creative, to carve out a path for himself. He applied for a position with the Joliet Correctional Prison in Downstate Illinois where, he told himself, he would become a pioneer in studying the criminal mind.

"Very impressive," the prison's Chief Medical Officer said from behind his grey-painted steel desk; Tobias had made the shortlist of candidates and was called down to Joliet for an interview. "You could have gone anywhere," the man added. "So, why here?"

The congenial chief was setting a trap – would the job candidate in any way agree with the sly innuendo that this posting might be beneath him? Would Tobias confess that he'd tried and failed to go elsewhere? Or, claim that he'd always wanted to work with the write-offs of the world? He'd have to be careful not to sound too much like an Albert Schweitzer or Mother Theresa, like a martyr intent on sacrificing his personal well-being to help save the wretched of the earth. He must not appear arrogant or superior in any way, he knew, but not too modest, either.

Tobias gave the correct answer, which was to say that he believed all people deserved good mental health care. "Had they received treatment at an early age they might not have ended up here," he said. "As the old saying goes, an ounce of prevention is worth a pound of cure."

Tobias was struck by how substantial if uncoordinated the prison complex was – high walls on the outside, of course, but with castle-like guard towers that looked like they belonged in a Disneyland annex; interior flooring in some of the great rooms that was made of natural stone but elsewhere that ranged from terrazzo to linoleum; and a roundhouse with a huge domed roof for the prisoners instead of the usual square or rectangular cell block. There was even a modern church addition that had won a national award for public architecture.

Tobias was eager to get started. He'd brought only two large suitcases filled with clothing and personal effects, and he could have moved into town but instead chose to live in a furnished apartment within the prison walls provided by the state. He checked that the phone worked, opened and shut all the windows, and looked for signs of rodents or cockroaches in all the cabinets and along the walls. He'd brought a small selection of books with him and most would go in his office but he put some on a mantle in his front room, and though he'd brought no photographs with him he hung a Picasso lithograph, "Carnaval," in a prominent place on one wall. It reminded him that he had to laugh at humanity sometimes. After his inspection he felt confirmed in his choice to live on campus – the place was clean, the furniture new if cheap, and he'd have stories to tell when he was older, how he was forced to live in half of a "double" out in a prison yard when he'd begun his career. Collecting good stories could be even better than collecting art.

SILVER'S FIRST OFFICE was in a trailer. Doctors always were assigned real office space but an entire wing was being rehabbed and this was where he'd have to greet his patients for many months. The stifling summer heat was everywhere when he arrived and a window air conditioner, supported only by sheet metal screws and a wood stud underneath, droned loudly. A guard would rap on the thin front door to announce every new patient; Jackson L. Jackson was one of the first. A tall, sturdy-looking black man of about 40 with a neat Afro showing grey at the temples, Jackson was doing life for two second-degree murders in Chicago in 1977. The guard asked if the doctor would be all right alone with the new patient and announced that he'd be standing just outside the door in case there was a need. Silver motioned with his hand for Jackson to take a seat on a narrow sofa along the wall opposite him. Though he was a murderer – he was that – Jackson had not been a career criminal or drug dealer or gang banger of any kind before his arrest. In fact, the murders were the only items on his criminal record. He'd graduated from high school in the inner city and immediately had gone to work nights at the Main Post Office in downtown Chicago sorting letters and flats, pushing carts and dollies filled with boxed merchandise, and generally keeping his nose clean. Payday came Thursday evenings for all the second shift employees, and he, like most of his colleagues, would head over to the storefront currency exchanges on Canal Street, all of which stayed open late for them, to cash his check. The nearby bars did, too, and the celebrations, raucous behavior and general buffoonery could be heard for several blocks in all directions on those nights. Police tried not to interfere but would assemble farther up and down the street, their headlights off, waiting patiently in their patrol cars in case there was trouble. Jackson L. Jackson was one of the dependable people who would stand in line patiently at the currency exchange until it was his turn at the gated teller position, then he'd count his money out a second time before placing the cash in his wallet and stuffing everything deep inside his front pants pocket. Then he'd head home. Jackson didn't usually expect trouble on the commute back to his apartment because he was a healthy-looking, well-built person who walked tall and straight. One night, though, as he was walking up Harrison Street behind the post office, a zone less well-lit than the front entrance but not entirely deserted, two men with pistols in their hands jumped out of an alley and demanded his money.

"It's in my pocket," he calmly told them.

"Then get it," said one of the men, waving the gun nervously at Jackson's face while turning his head left and right to see if anyone unwelcome was watching.

"I'm just reaching for my money, all right?" Jackson said as he carefully pulled out his wallet. He stretched out his arm out and one of the thieves grabbed the wallet, then both men turned and fled on foot toward the bridge over the Chicago River. That's when Jackson L. Jackson calmly pulled up his left pants leg and snatched his own gun from a holster strapped to his calf. He smartly, almost mechanically, aimed the gun at the fleeing thieves and squeezed the trigger. One man fell with the first shot; Jackson fired several more rounds before the second man went down. Each gunshot sounded like a short thunderclap and several people working on nearby docks ran to see what was happening; a lone car traveling across the bridge from the opposite direction slowed, then the driver doused his headlamps before throwing his transmission in reverse and backing up quickly. Jackson stuffed the gun under his belt and impassively walked toward the two assailants, checking the first to see if he had his money, then moving a little closer to the second man to find his wallet, which had been propelled several feet forward when the man fell. Waiting patiently for the police to arrive, he went voluntarily to the station to file an attempted robbery complaint only to find himself charged the next day with two counts of second-degree murder.

"But why? Why did you have to shoot them?" Tobias asked after Jackson related the story.

"They took my money. That's what I told the police. And they did. They took my money. How else was I gonna get it back?"

"And what did the police say to that? The State's Attorney filed charges anyway?"

"They said my life wasn't in no danger at that point. I didn't have a right to kill those people, they said. It was in all the papers."

The state was not merciless; they'd offered Jackson L. Jackson a deal. Plead guilty to manslaughter and you'll get five-to-ten, but you won't even serve that with time off for good behavior.

"And you didn't take the deal?"

"I told you what I told them. They took my money."

Jackson was not an agitator or a threat in prison but he didn't always follow orders, and he wouldn't work in any of the prison jobs. The warden gave him his own cell and allowed him a personal library, mostly histories of different peoples and travel guides, and Jackson seemed to meditate a lot, though not according to any discipline or recognized method. He'd just sit on the hard, concrete floor in his cell with his legs folded, taking deep, measured breaths. That was when he was referred for psychiatric evaluation.

Jackson's medical file listed his place of birth, which was Leland, Mississippi, a former cotton town in the Delta, and Tobias went to work probing his patient's psyche, connecting dots, always looking for root causes. "We was four kids," Jackson said, "kinda small for that community, and my father picked cotton, *yessah!* Me and the boys, that is my three brothers and me, we weren't gonna have none of that shit. When Pa got busted for somethin' – they said it was gamblin', or he'd beaten someone at a pea shake or somethin', maybe he'd looked too close at a white girl, I don't remember – our Mama packed us up and said 'We goin' North.' We stuffed our clothes in a single cardboard suitcase and a few neckerchiefs we tied to long sticks just like in the old cartoons and we put our pennies together and bought tickets at the Central Station in Memphis. I remember going up the stairs under that lighted Checker Taxi sign but we didn't take no taxi to get there. We didn't have enough money, actually, but a stranger gave us a few dollars. A white man, too. I haven't forgotten that. Well, we was in Chicago by dawn the next morning. Chicago was somethin' then. You from Chicago? You probably are. You look like someone from Chicago. You say hello to all my friends up there, you hear?"

Jackson L. Jackson had made a poor, poor choice in shooting the men who robbed him, but he had stood up for his rights, Tobias understood. He'd proven his manhood. Teddy Roosevelt was famous for saying, "Walk softly and carry a big stick," yet here was a man who did it. Teddy was up on a stallion cast in bronze recreating his charge up San Juan Hill while this man was in the Joliet prison for life. Who would memorialize him?

SURPRISINGLY, THEY HAD A *MINYAN* on Saturdays at the prison and Tobias was invited to attend a prayer service early on. "You're Jewish, aren't you?" the warden had asked. This was very early in Tobias's tenure in Joliet, and he hadn't yet confronted any Jewish prisoners. Tobias asked what sort of inmate prayed on the Sabbath. "It's a different crowd," the warden said. "Some guy kills his business partner who was skimming off the top or hires someone to do it. Or a doctor overbills on Medicare or Medicaid, I mean by a lot, and he gets caught. It's often major financial crimes. I don't mean anything by saying that. I hope you're not offended. There are a couple of Black Hebrews from Chicago, you know, the breakaway sect from Elijah

Muhammad. I'm surprised you haven't treated any yet. And there are the child molesters. That perversion knows no national, ethnic, racial or religious boundaries. They're just people who can't help themselves, as I'm sure you know, but we must keep them in relative isolation. The other inmates, even the lowest among them, like to tell themselves that at least they're not as low as that. Having at least a modicum of status is everything to people. That's what I've figured out. Have you? Anyway, we've had a couple or three murders in here over the years. It's usually the child molester that gets a shank in his back."

Tobias agreed to attend one Saturday morning service, but only as an observer. He sat quietly in the back of a square little room where the *minyan* assembled. He knew it wouldn't be in the church but he was surprised at the meagerness, even meanness of the venue provided, just a former office with one window and electrical outlets in the floor, not the wall. Apparently, it had once hosted the secretarial pool or something like that. About a dozen men had presented themselves and instead of pews they sat on folding metal chairs, the cheap kind with no padding in the seats, and in place of a *bima* there was a folding banquet table covered by a white sheet at the front of the room. A large picture of the Ten Commandments was taped to the wall behind the folding table. There wouldn't be a rabbi, nor did religious law require one, but someone would have to lead the call to prayer. That task fell to Irving Horowitz, an erstwhile jeweler with stereotypically thick lenses in his dark, round eyeglass frames and a curved spine from years bent over a work bench analyzing precious gems with his loupe. He was a very short man, maybe 5-feet-4, and completely bald on top with heavy signs of rosacea on his face and nose. Standing at the head of the little group, a tasseled prayer shawl draped over his shoulders, he announced a special guest in the "auditorium" – an ironic word for the tiny venue and not said facetiously – and the gathered turned in their seats and acknowledged the doctor, who said nothing in response but only nodded his head once while sitting with his arms folded and legs crossed.

"Will you be joining us in prayer?" Horowitz asked aloud. "We would like you to make *aliyah*, to come up and read the Torah with us."

"No, thank you," Tobias said in a clear voice, not in a loud or disapproving way but firmly enough that he would not be asked again.

The little congregation had *siddurim*, or prayer books, printed with English and Hebrew text side-by-side. Horowitz read select prayers for his congregation in both languages, sometimes in a singsong voice and with the traditional *shuckeling*, or swaying front-to-back during prayer, and two or three men followed in Hebrew, the rest in English only. When it was time to say the *Kaddish*, the prayer for the dead, several of the men stood. Tobias had long thought of prayer as no better than throwing bones in the desert, and he wondered what these men, incarcerated for long terms, some for life, could possibly find in it. Hope for the future, if not in this life then in the next? Or merely a salve on their wounds, respite for an hour or two before they were squeezed back in their holes, a taste of normalcy away from the bitterness of their fate?

The Bible portion for the week was *"Lech L'cha,"* or "Go forth." As the prison had no true Torah scroll nor a proper cabinet to store one in, Horowitz could only read from a well-worn printed copy of the Old Testament he'd long owned and kept. He read a bit in Hebrew, then summarized the content in his own words in English. "There's lots of interesting stuff in here," he said. Even though it already was October it was warm inside the poorly ventilated room, and he wiped his forehead with the palm of his hand, then he wiped his hand on his shirt, looking somewhat self-consciously at the other men but they all remained attentive. "It's like a TV mini-series, you know? First, there's the tale of Abram – that was Abraham before God changed his name – and his wife, Sarai, which was her name before God said to call her Sarah – and they're going down to Egypt because of a famine. I love that expression, 'Going down to Egypt.' Don't you? So, upon arriving in Egypt Abram tells Sarai to act like she's his sister, not his wife, because he thinks he'll be killed otherwise. She does as she's told, and he is spared. Commentators have struggled to understand why it was safer to call Sarai his sister instead of his wife but to me it's obvious. You couldn't ethically seduce someone else's wife so you might have to make the woman a widow first, that is, kill the bugger who was in your way, which was Abram, and then seduce the widow. But if she were unmarried, well, you see where I'm going. That still leaves open whether Abram was resigned to his wife being seduced in the first place. I don't have an answer for that. Well, there's a lot of other stuff in this week's portion of the Bible – the birth of Ishmael to Hagar, a promise to Sarai that she will have her own child one day, and the commandment to practice circumcision. We men can't forget that one! There's more about Abram and his cousin Lot agreeing to split up the Promised Land between them, too. Well, I think you see why I say it's bit like a TV mini-series, like "Dallas" with Larry Hagman, maybe. But to me the whole point is to tell us Jews how we became Jews. This is where it all begins, you might say."

The service was limited to an hour or so, then the men would have to march back to their cells. Before dismissing the group, however, Horowitz said he wanted to deliver a sermon, partly in honor of their guest that morning. "Pretty funny, I know," he said. "We Jews don't really give sermons. Often, we're the subject of sermons, someone else's sermons, and that's never a good thing. It's more like a lecture then and we're being lectured to. But I have something to say so here it is. We're all part of this big picture called crime and punishment. We commit the crime, we do the time, just as the saying goes. We know what crimes we were accused of and we all heard the judge read out our sentences. But did you know that the Old Testament provides a way out of sin, a path to redemption even after a crime has been committed? Yes, there are punishments in the Old Testament, usually of the stone them until they're dead variety. That's why people think our Hebrew God is cruel and unforgiving. Barbaric, even. If only the ancient Hebrews had nice prisons with comfortable beds like we do here in Joliet, right? OK, OK, stop snickering. Yes, you had to be punished for your crimes but there was repentance, too. You could repent for your crimes. The Christians think of that as one of their innovations but it's right there in Judaism. It's already there. More in the Talmud than in the Old Testament but it's there, nonetheless. 'In the place where the repentant stand, even the wholly righteous cannot stand,' it is written. And this. 'The repentant receives a great reward because he has tasted the taste of sin and yet separated himself from it and has conquered his evil inclination.' We're not such a bad people."

Afterward, as the small crowd quietly departed – Tobias turned in his chair and watched the men parade single file through the door as a guard stood back a little way down the hallway – Irving Horowitz approached him directly.

"Thank you again for coming," Horowitz said. "The warden honored us with his presence once, too. He had many questions but he also knew some things. Very impressive. You've met him, of course, so I'm not telling you anything new. I just want everyone to know that you can be in jail, in jail for terrible crimes, there's no point in denying things, but you can still improve. What alternative is there, really? All we have left in here is our dignity. If we lose that we have nothing."

"Sit, sit," Tobias told him. "I'd like to speak with you."

"You would? Oh, well, I must then, mustn't I?" Horowitz gripped the back of a chair and swiveled it around, then sat facing the doctor squarely.

"How long have you been in here?" Tobias asked.

"Ten years, maybe 12. I've stopped counting. I really have."

"What were you convicted of?"

"Stolen merchandise, you might say."

"And where are you from, originally, I mean?"

"Originally? Oh, originally, you say. They tell me the Land of Israel. But Gary, Indiana is all I remember. Then we moved to Chicago. You could see the skyline from the beaches near Gary, at least on a clear day. You wouldn't want to go to Gary today, though."

"And you had religious training when you were younger?"

"I was a good student."

"You seem to have kept your faith."

"Well, I believe in repentance. I have to aspire to something."

Horowitz didn't quite tell the whole truth about his reason for being in prison. He'd been convicted on multiple counts of conspiracy to commit murder. It was nothing personal, just that he'd long served as a fence for criminal gangs in Chicago and elsewhere that did, occasionally, kill people. He'd had a wife who divorced him and two adult children ("Both college graduates, one from the University of Chicago!") who'd disowned him, and several grandchildren whom he'd never meet.

"No one visits you here?"

Horowitz looked down and shook his head.

Tobias suggested that the man come see him in his office if he had trouble sleeping, was feeling suicidal, or was experiencing a steep weight loss for no apparent physiological reason. He'd quickly resolved that the man was struggling with depression and not doing a bad job of it, but that his recovery might not last, not in here, in prison.

"That's funny," the old prisoner said, looking down at first and laughing. "Here I was trying to recruit you and I see you're trying to recruit me. It may seem a contradiction to you but, you see, I don't believe everything in the Bible. I know they're just stories." Then he stood and tugged on his prayer shawl with both hands at his shoulders. "But religion at least has a history. People like you? The alchemists couldn't turn lead into gold and neither can you."

TOBIAS NEVER INTENDED to remain in Joliet long and, indeed, scouted out opportunities in Chicago on days off, which became more frequent in his second year as he discovered that his work was not closely monitored in any case, and as he realized that a short hop to the bigger city could always be justified as research, or the need for a consultation. He was looking for opportunities, that's all. He could join a large practice, be a kind of junior partner as if he were in a law practice, maybe be *mentored* by an elder statesman, a prospect which offended him because of the likelihood that the man would know less than he or, worse, be a woman effectively dressing him down, or he could join a research hospital and throw his hat into the ring of new scientists, be one of the people who would publish, but that would mean a lot of hard work if he were to do it well. Or, he could fly solo, which was the course he settled on. He turned down a contract extension to stay a third year at the prison, concluding that Joliet was a "sad backwater," and signed a lease for upscale office space on Michigan Avenue in Chicago, within earshot of the Art Institute. He rented an apartment, too, on Fullerton Avenue, a nice stone and brick brownstone with bay windows, and he could walk to Lincoln Park, to its zoo and greenhouse, and even stroll by the small marina there and size up the different boats. He was making the right choices in life, as he knew he would.

CHAPTER 5

SOMETIMES TOBIAS RODE the bus downtown. He'd snap the *Tribune* in half or in quarters and read it while stuck between a window and some heavy-breathing person in the aisle seat, or he'd grip an overhead strap if he were standing as the bus shunted and shuddered along, the morning paper tucked under his arm. Oftentimes, he would sneak a peek at the gum-chewing, young secretaries or retail salesmen he shared space with as they glumly rode to work, too, and make judgments about them – this one was fat and had lost interest in sex; that one was nervous about closing a deal or meeting a quota; another had recently been handed a terrible medical prognosis. It was all in their body language, the drape of their clothing, or just what was lurking behind their wide eyes. Nothing was normal; everything was a sign. His only indulgences outside of work were fine cigars and occasionally dining out. He favored intimate restaurants in the South Loop or on boutique-lined side streets that intersected with North Michigan Avenue, the latter because he often enjoyed walking up the avenue and across the Chicago River, ambling under the glow of all the window displays from upscale shops along the way if it were dusk, even stopping to inspect the wares at times, whether camera equipment or Burberry raincoats. Other times, he'd stop to pick up a meal-to-go at a supermarket, and he infrequently fried a hamburger and baked a potato himself at home, simple meals like that. He found time to enlarge his music collection, occasionally visiting a dedicated record store on Wabash Avenue and sampling their collection in a soundproof listening booth prior to purchase. He tended to favor reissues of Fritz Reiner and the Chicago Symphony Orchestra.

His practice held steady over the years. He had enough clients to pay the rent, to garner invitations to local conferences, and he even once was quoted in the Sun-Times for his views on a serial murderer who had been shot dead by Downstate police after he was cornered in an abandoned farmhouse. "Maybe he was mistreated as a child," Tobias had intoned. "By his mother, most likely."

It was a comfortable enough life, and Tobias was growing fatter, his cars a bit pricier, and he'd saved enough to buy a condo in the Mies van der Rohe buildings on Lake Shore Drive. He was able to purchase for his parents, when they died in turn, nice headstones, too, but he did not keep artifacts of his parents' lives – the shofar, the Haggadah, the Hanukkiah – these were put up for auction and fetched modest sums.

Yet, while watching the local PBS station at home one evening, his interest was piqued by a new series on "The Children of the Holocaust." Viewers were exposed to the classic scenes of emaciated prisoners and piles of human corpses, even a still of Gen. Dwight Eisenhower visiting Ohrdruf at the end of the war, all interspersed with interviews of middle-age Americans in New York City and Miami and Los Angeles, men and women who had been born to Holocaust survivors. The documentary included pictures of their parents from before the war, typically professional people of some means enjoying tea at an outdoor café in Vienna or Zagreb or Bucharest, and sometimes the children were filmed with their parents in the present time as they asked and answered questions or shared stories. Psychiatrists talked about adult children who had not adjusted well, describing their trauma and depression, their failure to fully participate in the American dream. Tobias was skeptical – not about the Nazis – but the need to always make excuses, or so it seemed to him.

Tobias had treated a handful of Holocaust survivors, but the only one he respected was one Jacob Diamant. Jacob had fought the Nazis and their collaborators during the war, which is what made him stand out. The only son of a Jewish farmer who lived near Zambrow in East Central Poland, his parents had urged him to flee in early September 1939, literally within hours of news that Germany had invaded the country from the west. His father had connections among the Christians, including the more militant, right-wing nationalists who'd long wanted to strip Polish Jews of their citizenship but would buy his milk and eggs in times of personal famine. At least these nationalists hated the Germans, too. The senior Diamant employed two Gentile men on his small farm, and he told all three of the young men – the two Christians and his son – to find an army somewhere and fight back. Jacob's mother shaved his head and cut his beard, including his side curls, and one of the Gentile farmhands gave him a change of peasant clothes to wear. "Be strong in yourself" Jacob's father told him in Yiddish, and he gave each man 100 Zlotys. It was the last time Jacob saw his parents and two sisters.

"It's not far-fetched," Jacob told Dr. Silver during their first session. "You see, most Jews knew the catastrophe was on its way. We knew it for decades, we knew it before Adolph Hitler was born. Most of my friends and I, we all belonged to *Hashomer Hatzair*. Do you know what that is? No, you probably don't speak Hebrew. Not even a little? Well, it was the Young Guard, that's all. We drilled and practiced with wooden rifles. Some of us had better training, though. Real knives we'd stab into sand bags and small pistols we could take turns firing in the woods. So, we ran, Jerzy and Piotr and I, and we joined the *Armia Krajowa*. Mostly we hid out in the woods and disrupted lines of communication and things like that, but sometimes we did ambushes. That was tricky because the Germans liked to retaliate against civilians. I learned to eat pork and grass, too."

Diamant had not sought therapy for bad dreams or unextinguished angst due to the genocide. He said he was an admirer of Primo Levi, the Italian engineer and writer who continued to work in Auschwitz and tried to live a normal life after the camp was liberated. It was only after Diamant's wife died of breast cancer, then his only daughter more recently committed suicide, that he was knocked low.

Tobias was not indifferent to human suffering or unimpressed with examples of bravery and resilience. "It must be painful to have fought so hard to live and then see the lives of your new family taken away like that," he told his patient. "Do you know what happened to your family in Poland?"

"Oh, yes. They're recorded at *Yad Vashem* in Israel. Do you know about *Yad Vashem*?"

Tobias shook his head.

"No? It's all right. You're an American Jew. Your people probably came over prior to 1924. Have you read about the immigration laws in America?"

Again, Tobias shook his head.

"Well, it doesn't matter," Jacob continued. "I didn't want my daughter to know too much about the past, either. Why burden people with the past. They just want to have their own lives. I suppose your parents were like that, too."

Jacob Diamant was a short, agile man, and his original Polish accent had been considerably abraded over the years. He spoke a tempered, even cordial English with perfect grammar and diction, and that first day he'd dressed nattily in sturdy leather shoes, pressed trousers with a sharp crease, and a muted tweed sport jacket. He seemed more philosophical than lost, more reconciled than reactionary. Tobias asked him what he did for a living, work being so much a part of identity in America.

"I build bridges," the man said. "Not with my hands, though they get dirty and raw sometimes when I'm out in the field. I'm a civil engineer for the State of Illinois. As a child I played with an American-made Erector set and made toy bridges in all sorts of shapes, breaking down the old ones and using the same parts over and over again for new designs, some of which I thought would win me patents. But that was when I was a child. You dream big and are impressed easily when you're young. When I was a bit older, I built earthen bridges like some people build sand castles, and then I built a real, functional wood bridge over a small creek on my father's farm. No nails in the trusses or anything like that, either. I used a hand drill for all the holes and stout pegs I carved from the seasoned roots of a beech tree we'd pulled out of the earth. I hoped to go to university in Warsaw to study engineering. The dream survived the war and now it's a nice metaphor for my life, don't you think?"

Tobias signaled his approval of the man's story. "You sound like a natively optimistic person," he said. "Research shows that people who exhibit optimism live longer. So, why do you need me?"

Jacob rubbed his chin. "Why do I need you? I think a better question is what can you offer me. It's like shopping for a car. You should tell me about all the options."

"Touché," Tobias replied. "I am in your debt."

"No, not at the fee you charge. I am certainly in your debt."

"Touché again."

"Well, to answer your question seriously, it's just this," Jacob Diamant said. "I thought I would like to talk to someone. It's a very modern thing to do. But I didn't want to burden my friends. Everyone has their problems. My friends tried to console me after the deaths of my wife and daughter. They said how well I was dealing with things, or they said God had a special purpose for me. That's why he had given me so many challenges. I have a friend who cried more than I did! But it got me thinking. Am I too passive? Am I just a cold person under this cosmopolitan exterior? So, I came to you, I come to you, to seek validation. I need an outside appraisal, not of my house or a piece of jewelry I'm thinking of buying but of me. Am I a cold person, someone like, say, Primo Levi, or should I be more like Eli Wiesel?"

Over the following few months Tobias and Jacob discussed many topics, conversing much like two old friends on a park bench. They analyzed strategy during World War II – was Eisenhower right to land at Normandy, or should the Allies have continued a march up Italy, where they'd already gained a foothold? What if Germany had developed a trans-Atlantic bomber to attack America first – they were working on such a thing. Jacob asked if Tobias knew about the Evian Conference in 1938. "Roosevelt tried," he said. "I was very impressed when I read the news in the papers. It was publicized in my country, I mean Poland. The government even sent a delegation. But it was not an offer to receive refugees. The government said they wanted to deport Jews just like Germany was doing. That was hard to take. And you know what the representative from Australia said. 'As we have no real racial problem, we are not desirous of importing one.' I remember hearing those words on Shmuley's wireless. Shmuley was a friend who perished and I'll always conjure him as a 17-year-old. But you know all about the Evian Conference, at least. Do you?"

They talked about more immediate matters as well – where had Jacob had met his wife ("She was a Holocaust survivor, too; she worked in a flower shop,") and what she was like ("A very quiet person, actually. Wistful or sad, sometimes I couldn't tell,") and why his daughter had taken her life ("She could never find happiness. She knew too much about tragedy in the world to allow herself to be happy. It was always the rainy season of hurt for her.")

There was no conclusion to the therapy sessions, no resolution of a crisis as that had never been a treatment goal as such. Jacob merely wanted to talk, to come down slowly from the more recent tragedies in his life, kneading the blows along the way. Then he stopped coming.

CHAPTER 6

TOBIAS SILVER HAD FOUND it difficult to meet women, in spite of being successful. In part, this was because of his job and focus – he wanted name recognition, not a trophy bride. He was building a career, not a home or family. And while doctors in larger practices or on staff at major hospitals could always mingle with nurses and administrators, he was committed to his solo practice. Who could he speak to – a secretary he might bump into in the elevator, the girl behind a candy kiosk in the lobby? He didn't attend any religious services nor did he belong to fraternal organizations such as Kiwanis, not to mention the Shriners. He knew of medical teams that went on missions to Haiti or even Africa, but they typically included dentists and eye surgeons and the like, not psychiatrists, plus they tended to hold hands and pray at night inside their tents. It wasn't for him. He saw women patients, but most were as unappealing as they were vulnerable – the woman who'd gained too much weight and lost too much body tone after three pregnancies, the woman who was too homely to ever have been courted, and, of course, the women who'd been betrayed by their husbands. Not to mention, they were *patients*. But there were comely women who were available, who'd drop subtle hints. He'd mentally undress them, imagine what it might be like to bed them, even rehearse lines from "Same Time, Next Year," in his head. If professional ethics weren't enough to dampen his interest, to dissolve desire into harmless fantasy, though, there always was the possibility of being outed. It was just as in civil society – some people obey the law because they're good citizens, others behave only because they fear the consequences. Nevertheless, opportunity still was most likely to walk through the door with his next appointment.

The patient, Dora, was attractive enough, he'd thought, and certainly upper crust. She was the kind of middle-age woman he would have liked to sidle up to at a hotel bar in a distant city, ask politely if the seat next to her was taken, and then closely observe her as her nostrils flared and eyes widened before introducing himself by name. "I'm here for a medical conference," he might say, something that would be sure to impress. Then he'd act as if he were interested in whatever she might have to say and after a while they would move to a small table in the corner and then, as if the curtain were rising on Act 2, they'd retire to one of their rooms or the other. Dora, about 40 at the time, had a raven's black depth to her hair, perhaps dyed, Tobias thought, that was cut in a chin-length crop and curled at the tips like a speakeasy flapper from the Prohibition era. She dressed well for her sessions – two-piece wool suits, linen blouses and colorful silk scarves. Expensive jewelry, too, but nothing large or gauche, no trinity earrings or heavy, diamond-studded broaches, just real pearl necklaces and tasteful gold pins.

"A woman in my position can't be seen out and about with other men," she told him one day. "I don't travel much. I did go to a spa in Arizona once and I met an interesting man there but it can't become a pattern."

"Is that what troubles you? You're longing for, shall we say, adventure with another man?"

"Oh, Doctor, let's not employ euphemisms. I'm longing for a man between my legs."

The woman appeared to have good breeding and manners and Tobias tried to get at the root problem, namely how could it be that she really was having problems finding a lover on the side if that's all she wanted. He asked when was her first time – it was while attending Woodlands Academy of the Sacred Heart in Lake Forest, after one of the few dances with boys from another Catholic school that the girls were allowed to attend.

"Were your parents open about sex?"

The woman laughed out loud theatrically. "They bought me books about all the great women saints. The nuns taught us to wait until marriage, then a miracle would occur."

"You couldn't go on normal dates?"

"I just told you. I fucked the first boy I ever danced with."

Tobias enquired further into that experience; it hadn't gone well. Young Dora and the boy had snuck off to a nearby wood, the mosquitoes were active, and the boy was out of his mind, not violent or abusive, but he was only interested in penetration, then he ejaculated quickly. He admitted it was his first time, too, for which he apologized, then he pulled up his pants and ran away.

"Coming of age is hard on everyone. It's not just you."

"I married the next man I slept with."

Dora's husband was a successful stockbroker in a gilded building on LaSalle Street, a managing partner as far as Tobias could tell. He must be diligent, smart as well, Tobias knew, but still he felt a smug superiority over the man. He – Tobias – was a healer and an intellectual. Dora's husband was someone who could spit out money like a silkworm spins silk, perhaps, but ultimately was only good at making money. It was a very hostile, reductive picture of a man he hadn't met.

"Are you feeling guilty about something, or just making up for lost time?" he asked Dora.

"I don't understand the question."

"Women who are promiscuous, or desirous of becoming so, often are punishing themselves for something. Or they're punishing someone else, most likely their parents or their husband. Did your father sneak around?"

Dora shrugged. "I never thought about that."

"Does your husband sneak around, as far as you know?"

"Well, the firm has a suite at the Pick Congress Hotel permanently reserved."

"The Pick Congress? It's all right, but nothing special. Why not the Drake? Well, the Drake is probably too far away."

"Doctor, the point is that he can get the key and sneak off anytime he wants. The other men can, too."

"And the women in the firm?"

"There are some women brokers. I bet they use the suite, too."

"Ah, so maybe you are seeking to get even with *them*?"

The woman stood up, kicked off her heels and slipped from the red bolero jacket she'd worn that day, then she began unbuttoning her ivory-colored blouse. "Look, doctor, I can't be seen with another man out and about but I know you want to fuck me and what does it matter why I want to fuck you. I'm not going to report you to anyone if that's what you're afraid of."

Women wanting to sleep with their therapists turned out to be not that rare. Some doctors linked it to the transference, the love that came of dependency and hoped-for salvation, and certainly Tobias knew the theory. Yet there were pragmatic reasons women would do this, namely opportunity and confidentiality. He'd brought it up with a fellow therapist once – *'Did women patients ever try to seduce you?'* – and the colleague saw through the question immediately.

"Of course, we have to say no," the other therapist, Milton Gross, replied after acknowledging that there were times, there were opportunities, there was even attraction. "I once had to send a patient to another doctor. I couldn't tell her why. There was just something about her I couldn't get past. She probably thought I didn't like her or respect her. But if they bring it up, if they give you subtle hints that they find you attractive, if they say things like why can't their husbands be more like you and so on, you must tell them those can be normal feelings to have for one's therapist but it's not real attraction. The important thing is that they shouldn't feel shame or guilt of any kind. And, yes, maybe the setting has something to do with it. There are plenty of jokes about that couch, you know. Sure, I was approached once or twice in my career. But you can't do it. You just can't."

Dora and Tobias had regular sex for several months. She insisted he bill her, which he did, as this provided the perfect cover story. The insurance statements would prove to her husband, who might become suspicious with what she did with her afternoons, that it was only therapy, not an affair. Then, one day, Dora failed to appear for an appointment, and for the next. Tobias hesitated before calling his client – that's what she was, but so was he, he understood – but when he did call Dora said that she'd found another therapist. He was taken aback.

"Another therapist?"

"Well, you could call him that. Or her. What's it to you, anyway?" Then she hung up.

THE EXPERIENCE WITH DORA brought back bad memories of a girl Tobias had seen fleetingly years earlier on the campus of the University of Chicago, while doing his undergraduate work. He'd been walking through one of the castle-like, limestone buildings there when he spotted a girl dressed in a tight-fitting cashmere sweater and wool pencil skirt, whose hair was straight and crisply cut, someone with real North Shore breeding. She seemed to be reading a note in her hand and smiling to herself as other students flowed around her on either side like a school of fish. He couldn't help but stop and stare when her sixth sense caused her to snap her head in his direction, then she turned and briskly walked away. It was weeks later when he saw her again, at the start of the following term.

"Anyone claim this seat?" he asked her on the first day of class for the History of Western Civilization, one of the staples of undergraduate education at Chicago at the time. He'd approached her from behind but recognized her immediately, despite the high-collared pullover she'd worn on this day, and the fact that her hair was an inch or two longer than before. He hadn't noticed her shoes the first time he'd seen her but he recognized them as high-quality leather flats. It was the same girl.

The girl turned her head up to look at Tobias. "I don't think teachers assign seats anymore," she said, but nothing else. Not an invitation, but not quite a rebuff, either. Tobias wondered if the girl remembered him and seated himself, then he stored his books under the seat.

"I love the part where the Athenian fleet is destroyed at Aegospotami," Tobias said, leaning over as if to whisper in the girl's ear. She did not turn at first to listen more carefully to the words, but she could not suppress a smile.

"So, you've read Thucydides," she finally said, turning her head down and only slightly in the direction of Tobias. It was a very sly gesture, very sexy, he thought. "So, why are you taking this class, then?"

"It required," he answered. "Should I feel guilty?"

Finally, she smiled openly. "Me, too," she said. "Then I'm finished with required courses. My name is Jennifer, What's yours?" With that she extended her long, slim, very pale hand, and Tobias took hold of it, but lightly. He was so glad she hadn't recognized him from before, which is how he thought of his first encounter with the girl. It had been an encounter, even though it was hardly that, and he didn't really know if she recognized him or not.

The two went out for coffee after class – the teaching assistant who led their section spent most of her time deeply apologizing for having to follow this vector in history because the beginning of Western civilization was the end of civilization everywhere it was exported, she argued, and they settled on a small café on East 57th Street. Tobias was so thrilled that this beautiful young woman was walking by his side as they strode down the street, as others *moved to the side* to let them pass, that he felt himself grow giddy, even hard. He didn't know which was more embarrassing.

The café was nearly full for an early afternoon at the start of the Spring trimester and the girl – *Jennifer is her name*, Tobias had to keep reminding himself - joked that everyone must be cutting classes already.

"Oh, they'll be at Harper Library until it closes," Tobias said. "I don't know if it's that they're so committed to success, or that they just couldn't stand failure."

Jennifer wanted to talk and Tobias wanted to listen. She was from Winnetka, a well-to-do north Chicago suburb, and her dad was COO at the Allstate Insurance Co. Her parents had been divorced for several years, and her dad had remarried – "Uh, yeah, it's exactly what you think," she said – and though she'd thought of going to school "out East," as she put it, she explained that she wanted the kind of grittier, more diverse experience she'd find at a school such as the University of Chicago. "It was either here or Columbia," she said. "I was accepted everywhere, not that I applied everywhere. But, you know what I mean."

Tobias was struck by the girl's reference to diversity – there weren't many blacks in the College so maybe she was referring to the neighborhood. Or, to people like him. She had her own elitism, but it seemed more tied to her individuality than any kind of class or ethnic structure, and though she was really saying that she was slumming by attending a school like Chicago, the fact that she was doing it meant she could at least put her money where her mouth was, or at least her father's. Tobias relied heavily on scholarships to attend the school but he decided to keep that from her; he thought he might have a chance with the girl.

Their first date was at Ida Noyes Hall that Friday night, and it was her idea. When Tobias explained that he didn't know how to dance, Jennifer said it didn't matter because she didn't really want to dance, only to attend the event. They were to meet there, at the steps to the venue. This was Tobias's sophomore year – Jennifer was a year ahead of him – and he still lived in Pierce Tower, one of the dorms at the corner of 55th Street and University Avenue.

"You got a date?" his roommate had asked him. The roomie was pre-med, as was Tobias, and he'd stacked his books in the order that he would study them that evening, chapters and pages all marked with yellow stickers.

"Don't wait up for me," Tobias told him.

"I'll still be reading when you come crawling home with your tail between your legs," he said. "I know that girl. She's using you."

"Oh, yeah? For what?" It was bravado Tobias was showing, but he had wondered the same thing.

"Not all girls are superficial," he told his roommate. "You'll see."

Though it was raining steadily the evening of the dance Tobias did not want to walk under an umbrella the several blocks to Ida Noyes at 59th and Woodlawn. Instead, he donned a cheap London Fog raincoat, the kind with raglan shoulders and a plain zipper front, and a waxed cotton fedora, something fishermen wore. He almost wore slip-on rubber galoshes over his leather shoes, then looked at them in horror before opening a window to his 7th floor room and hurling them as far as he could. One landed over the fence that bound a nearby soccer field; the other fell short.

"That's right. You won't need your rubbers tonight, old pal," his roommate cackled.

WHAT DID THE GIRL want from him, indeed, Tobias fretted as he walked in the rain to his destination? The sun had set and the streetlights seemed dim now; his shoe leather squished as he stepped on little wet leaves leftover from the winter. A few students gaily came and went on the same sidewalk, and as he passed near the library he saw the real "grinds," the students who only studied, who would grind it out like prisoners at hard labor, pile inside the library for more late night work. Tobias had no illusions that he would get laid, not yet, not that evening, but he thought this relationship might really go somewhere. He was cautiously optimistic. He had shaven closely that evening and put on talc afterward – he hated himself when he showed a dark, Richard Nixon-like shadow on his face, yet his clean face now seemed puffy, unmanly even. He couldn't let it bother him, though. The girl had seen something in him and that was all there was to it.

The dance hall was poorly decorated, a half-hearted attempt to mimic a '50s high school hop with a bit of a Roaring 20s theme blended into the concoction. Streamers and crepe ribbon hung from rafters and hooks, but tackily, with no art or design evident, and a strong flood light was reflected from a single revolving mirror ball. No matter, as few people were dancing. Mostly, this was an occasion to chat up a girl, or for a group of girls to coyly huddle as a boy tried to break into their circle, and off in this or that corner the more earnest students still debated Ho Chi Minh and Mao, even Leon Trotsky. But Jennifer Ellison created a buzz when she entered the arena, accompanied by Tobias Silver, whom she had met at the front door. For one thing, she was at least three inches taller than he. She'd worn a fur wrap, which she threw over her shoulder once inside the building. Tobias himself walked one step behind her as she approached this and that friend, asking how everyone was, listening to their replies as if she cared, as if she were an accomplished politician who could remember everyone's name, and then she moved and greeted more people. It took Tobias a few minutes to understand what was happening. This was her cotillion and she was coming out, a debutante of her own design, and he was a merely an accoutrement. But why? What was the end game? He went along with the masquerade in the hope that some reward would be coming his way eventually.

"Can you get me some punch," Jennifer asked him at one point. He hesitated, but only because he hadn't seen a punch bowl. "It's over there," Jennifer told him, pointing to a long table with a white tablecloth off to one side. "A paper cup is all right. Get yourself one, too."

He looked her up and down when she spoke to him like that. Her frame perfect under the thin fabric of the close-fitting chemise; her thin calves were as smooth and shapely as Queen Anne furniture legs, and her short heels looked steady, firm and strong, too. He caught himself staring at her chest, as well. She noticed it all and just smiled at him condescendingly. He chased down the punch as ordered.

Tobias met a friend at the punch table, who asked who the babe was that he had accompanied to the dance. "Where'd you meet someone like that?" the friend asked. "Does she go to school here? Really? She's your date? No way. Do you even know her name?"

Tobias dipped the ladle in the punch bowl and made a motion as if he was going to punch the friend in the face, then he claimed that he'd been sleeping with the girl for weeks, that she licked his dick, and he was the only man who'd ever given her full satisfaction. "That's all that matters with these girls. Who can give them the biggest orgasms?"

"Oh, yeah," his friend replied. "As long as her eyes are closed." Tobias bumped the other boy on the shoulder with the butt of his hand, then he filled two cups with punch and returned to Jennifer. She had already moved on to speak with other people at the party.

SO, WOULD SHE DO him or not, Tobias wondered? As the evening wound down that was all he could think about, despite his diffidence earlier that evening. Yet, the mixed messages flashed before him like an old movie marquee. He didn't even know where the girl lived. An apartment? One of the few sororities at Chicago? He'd be willing to go to a motel, but it would seem so tacky to suggest such a thing to a girl like Jennifer, and he didn't even know if she really was willing to have sex with him. He asked if he could walk her home.

"Do you know where I live?" she replied demurely.

"Maybe I've been stalking you all along," he said. It took her a moment to realize this was a joke, and she agreed that he could walk her home.

Jennifer Ellison lived in a historic elevator building on Dorchester Avenue, not far off campus. She'd have to let herself in with a key through its double doors, and she told him boys were not allowed past the tiled and chandeliered lobby after 11 pm. He then understood that this is where they'd say goodbye for the evening but he wasn't out of small talk yet. He asked Jennifer is she lived alone or had a roommate; he asked how long she'd lived in this residence.

Was it a furnished apartment? Did she have a car?

He wanted to ask if Daddy paid the rent but thought better of the question – it would seem jealous and petty.

"You want to come up, don't you?" she said.

All he could do was shrug his shoulders sheepishly.

"Look," she told him. "I just broke up with my boyfriend but I didn't want to go to the dance alone. I have a lot of friends I wanted to see. A lot, but I couldn't go alone and I didn't want anyone to think I was dating someone new. Women can go out with men and there doesn't have to be anything sexual about it. Where have you been for the last few years?"

She didn't speak condescendingly to Tobias; there didn't seem to be a hint that she was trying to put him down or put him in his place. It was just that it was so obvious to her that this wasn't really a date, that no one looking in from the outside would even imagine such a thing, not even at a school like Chicago where, sometimes, geniuses could score with beautiful women.

"You don't remember me, do you?" he spurted out. Standing in the broken light under the sole chandelier hanging from the hallway ceiling Jennifer looked at Tobias quizzically. "The first time we met, that we saw each other even though we didn't speak," he continued. "Inside Mandel Hall, or one of corridors leading away from it? You caught me staring at you and you turned up your nose at me and then hurried away. I thought that was maybe why you wanted to get to know me better in class, that maybe you knew you'd been unfair."

Jennifer squinted and looked off to the side, then shook her head. "No, I don't think so," she finally said. "I don't think I ever saw you before that first day in Western Civ. I hope I haven't misled you in any way." With that, Jennifer Ellison bent her head and gave Tobias a dry peck with her lips on his cheek, then she turned toward the gated elevators. The following Monday Tobias transferred to a new section of the required course, the History of Western Civilization.

CHAPTER 7

Tobias had once given a lecture on Alfred Adler, the Austrian-born psychiatrist and originator of the "inferiority complex" theory, at a conference in Atlanta sponsored by the Centers for Disease Control and Prevention. It was a high water mark in his career; the talk was related to his work with African-American prison inmates, both in Joliet and as a consultant to Cook County Hospital relating to some of the more violent criminal suspects brought there for observation. In those instances he would read the arresting officer's report, make his own observations, perhaps ask the subject a few questions (and often be spat at, which is why he eventually began donning personal protective equipment and a face shield when confronting some of them), and invariably would prescribe a drug, often Stelazine, because that would stop them cold, whether they were truly psychotic or merely experiencing existential rage. He made a little money from this part-time work, what he later learned younger people might call a side hustle.

Tobias was not the keynote speaker at the CDC conference but more than 20 people attended his break-out session, which he was assured was a respectable number. He spoke about the inferiority complex as it related to allegedly aggressive behavior of African-American men – all the young lions were compensating for their low status in society, he argued, a refinement of the old manhood theme from his Joliet days but more in line with Adler. Violence was inappropriate behavior, he argued, but nonetheless reflected the famous inferiority complex. Better such men seek excellence in sports or music, which many did, he noted. That would be the more appropriate response to their inferiority complex.

Such a thesis, and the endorsement of a long-forgotten Jewish psychiatrist, did not sit well with the audience. One tall Black man stood up and asked

Tobias if similar forces might not also be at play for, say, the owners of professional sports teams, as well as people who needed concert halls and classroom buildings named after them, or who simply swelled the ranks in professions such as law and medicine. Tobias understood immediately – people like *him* were compensating like crazy, too. Tobias looked at the man while bobbing his head up and down almost imperceptibly, like a buoy in the water, because he knew the man's question really was an accusation. "Yes, the evidence does support that," he said. "No one people are better than any other, or motivated by higher ideals. I can assure you I do believe that." The other man sat again, surrounded by a rustle in the audience like a flapping of wings, and Tobias hated that he had been forced to back down.

MORE YEARS PASSED, the vanity of youth far enough behind him to be an amusement, the indisposition of old age not yet waiting around the next corner. Tobias had not made the great breakthrough he'd longed for professionally; the goal posts were receding, and he was losing the great game. He had once been ambitious, and he'd thought he was on a good trajectory, but one day as he stood to enter the elevator at his Michigan Avenue office building, still smartly dressed in a long wool coat and freshly shined shoes, he had an epiphany.

This was it. This was all there was ever going to be. No, his life would not be considered bad, not by ordinary measures, not by ordinary people, but it would never meet expectations. His expectations. He had a career, a home and a car, even appropriate romances with women his own age, but in the end it was only a life. He had settled, just like most other people.

Tobias understood his handicaps: he had no base, that is, no large, institutional backing from which to conduct experiments, no wide-ranging connections from which to recruit collaborators and, most frustrating to him, no brand nationally to attract attention for his findings even if he were to publish something somewhere. Freud, Jung, and Adler became more ossified with each passing year, even the change of seasons. It was all about data, not case studies; controlled experiments that could be replicated, not inner workings of the mind revealed; trees, not the forest. Psychology had become a prisoner of its own research, linking variables and insinuating cause and effect but proving nothing. The days of holding lay audiences rapt while you drew back the curtain on carnal desire and dark secrets, while not entirely gone, were now the province of women's magazines and daytime talk shows, even a source of humor on the popular "Frasier" television series. He was not a sound bite. He was an army of one. He had been bold to become a psychiatrist when he was younger, he told himself. But the world was changing, as it always does, and people like him were being left behind. Time is insidious that way; it's like erosion and you just don't notice until it's done. Yet his practice was self-sustaining, if hardly spectacular. Patients still came via the Yellow Pages – choosing a doctor that way was analogous to throwing a dart against a map on the wall and deciding where to vacation next year or what stock to buy, he mused – and though referrals from doctors he'd met over the years had tapered off, an occasional one or two would arrive.

CHAPTER 8

Tobias saw few interesting patients in the ensuing years. Morrie Stein proved to be one of his more absorbing contacts, however. A veteran journalist, Stein had started out as a paperboy delivering the morning news to Northside homes and apartments from the back of his bicycle in the 1960s, when a kid could still do that in America, and he later wrote a column for his high school paper, "The Morrie You Know," which was all about the high bacteria count in the school's indoor swimming pool and government surplus foods being sneaked into cafeteria lunches, but also well-researched obituaries for past graduates who had died in Vietnam. Sensitive, generous and diligent he was, but his grades were not stellar and not only did Northwestern University pass on him, he couldn't even get into the main state school at Urbana-Champaign. His family was not wealthy – Dad sold menswear at a Sears on Lawrence Avenue, and Mom worked in a neighborhood candy store on Kedzie Avenue, near a Ravenswood elevated stop – so he settled on Northern Illinois University in DeKalb, the former teacher's college, majoring in journalism. It all worked out, though – after the Watergate scandal broke he was well-prepared and every newspaper in the country was hiring. He started his career promisingly at the *Chicago Sun-Times*, a Number Two daily but in a major market, plus he could save on rent by living at home.

The paper put him on the police beat at first, weekends and nights, and he outfitted his first car (a compact Ford Mustang II he'd purchased at a deep discount) with a police scanner. The police beat always was the "sink or swim" deep end of the pool for beginning journalists in America. Murder, rape and arson, followed by more murders, plus the occasional feel-good story, such as one about a police captain who was a Big Brother to the orphaned son of a local gang banger were his staples. And then more overnight murders, more bodies found floating in the Chicago River or behind a dumpster in a Westside alley.

Morrie's first big story was the tale of two teen girls who'd been found dead near a rural road in LaSalle County. He'd heard the initial alarm on the police scanner, and he promptly grabbed his jacket and note pad and drove to the scene. He found the way easily enough, just follow the procession of squad cars traveling at high speed west on US30 all the way to Shabbona, then south toward Mendota. It was a dry day in early fall when the bodies were discovered – tall brown grass had partly hidden the corpses but walking close by, his press pass held out like a superstition symbol in case anyone would challenge him, he could see their naked bums that looked like they'd repeatedly been spanked with a paddle, then their bruised legs and knobby spines. The bodies lay parallel to each other as if they'd been forced to lie still together, out of sight of passing cars on the nearby two-lane. Morrie looked for signs that they'd been dragged to this spot but didn't see any, no telltale matted grass or clothing that had caught along the way. There wasn't much serious crime in the rural areas of his beat, yet Morrie knew he'd have to visit the families and call in a photographer to get the money shot, which would be a mother wailing and burying her head in the bosom of a neighbor. It was one of the things he liked least about the police beat – voyeurism masquerading as empathy, filling a news hole pretending to be notes from the front.

The girls, aged 12 and 13, often walked along the less-traveled roads near their homes, Morrie learned. They were best friends and they probably shared their concerns about school and hopes for the future, this nasty teacher, that cute boy, would they be in the same classes when they reached high school? How lovely it is to have a best friend at that age, he thought. After surveying the scene, after speaking to police and noting the gawkers and rubberneckers who'd begun arriving, just standing behind the hastily erected yellow tape barrier with folded arms, asking each other what had happened, Morrie walked off toward a boulder in the distance and leaned against it. There were no sirens wailing any longer, no crackling audio on the radios, either, and the wind soothed him like white noise in his ears. He tried to fathom the girls' last, terrifying moments when they must have realized they were going to die. "Why, why?" they may have cried. Why, indeed. He wondered how a day can be bright and warm and optimistic and then a moment later momentously black. Later, from the pictures their parents shared with him, he thought they were normal looking girls – each a little chubby, kind of plain, one had acne – just average girls who would grow up, marry, have two or three kids each, and maybe join their respective church sisterhoods. Maybe bake apple pies for the county fair, maybe take a cruise to Alaska when their children were grown ("Breathtaking! A vacation of a lifetime," they'd proclaim) and more. Then they'd get a nice obituary in the local paper. Yet they were dead right now.

His stories about the girls – how they'd met in one of those vinyl clad, tacked-together apartment complexes off the Interstate; how one had survived leukemia; pictures of them holding little frogs cupped in their hands that they'd plucked from the retention pond in back of their building; what they were up to that fateful last day of their lives; even a motorcycle club's honor guard on the way to the cemetery for their internment – won First Place in a statewide journalism competition. He hadn't entered his stories, that was his editor's doing, but he accepted the award, even went to the ceremony at a Downtown hotel to pick it up. But once home he stuffed the wooden plaque, it was shaped like a map of Illinois, in a little used drawer in a spare room and walked away.

MORRIE STEIN DIDN'T OFTEN score with women, either. It was his good manners, he told himself, or his stout upbringing, that women must have found boring. He'd dated in high school but only young women who would decry all the sex and drugs the other teens were having, and he would have to agree with them. A brief kiss on the stoop of the girl's house was all he expected in those days.

"Be a *mensch*," his mother and father always told him, and he was.

Morrie stood 5-feet-10, not a bad height per se, and he'd retained a full head of wavy brown hair well into middle age, which he counted as an asset. He was no muscle-bound beach bum but he had kept his weight down nicely. What flummoxed him, though, was when people said he reminded them of Woody Allen. This all started in the late 1970s when Woody Allen still made movies that were funny and, indeed, there was a resemblance. Morrie had the same long face, a nerdy, stumblebum way of speaking, and quite a large, droopy nose. The comparison to the film star troubled Morrie so much that he avoided certain types of clothing – no plaid wool sport coats, for example, and no bucket hats, ever. Worst of all were the heavy, rectangular eyeglass frames he shared with the comedian. He tried to wear slimmer wire frames but his prescription was such that the lenses then were conspicuously thick on the sides.

Morrie's first intimate relationship had been in college; the young lady was from Woodstock ("No, not that one, silly," she'd told him when they met for the first time). Woodstock, Illinois, which was to become a pricey outlying Chicago suburb, a kind of Connecticut home in the Heartland, still was rural at the time. Liza Lynch ("Liza with a Z and a hard 'i' just like the actress," she'd said) was studying to be a registered dietician and she'd gently chastised Morrie for his food choices while both were in line at a dormitory cafeteria.

"Trying to bulk up?" she asked. Morrie had chosen two cuts of meat loaf, two pieces of Texas toast, an order of oily, skillet-fried potatoes and a slice of apple pie with a scoop of vanilla ice cream on top.

"What do you recommend?" he asked after turning to look at the girl behind him in line.

"Stop staring at me and maybe I'll tell you," she replied.

Liza was fair-skinned, even pale, and her long, strawberry blonde hair easily betrayed Celtic roots. She was devoid of make-up and her unplucked eyebrows might have seemed bushy had her color not been so faint. Morrie was smitten by her freshness. He learned that she was a farm girl who'd "walked beans," that is, pulled out weeds by hand in the soybean fields, and she'd detasseled corn every summer. She even helped deliver a kid goat for her high school FFA club.

"Have you ever seen pigs do it?" she asked on one of their early dates. "I mean bulls and cows, you can see how it works, but pigs give me the shivers."

"Why are you telling me this?" he asked at the time.

"Morris Stein, you are a virgin, aren't you!" she said. "I do not believe it."

They saw each other a lot that semester and Morrie even visited her in Woodstock after classes let out for the summer. The Lynch family invited him to stay in their 1890s I-home, so named because many rural and farm homes from Indiana to Iowa looked the same – slender clapboard siding almost always painted a washday white but sometimes in brick, and small wraparound porch with minimally turned posts – and Morrie was consigned to the spare bedroom for the stay. "Of course, Mama," Liza said when the temporary boarding arrangements were announced. Only during walks across nearby fields, hidden behind thick brush and gangly hackberry trees, could they get it on.

Back home in Chicago later that summer Morrie's father debriefed him on his trip to the country. "Are you a man now?" he asked with a wink, and his mother, who was seated nearby doing needlepoint, blushed and looked away, pretending not to hear.

"Leave me alone," Morrie said, and then he ran upstairs.

TURNING TO A PSYCHIATRIST was as much push as pull for Morrie. A friend at work encouraged him not to be a Sad Sack, said he should be proud of his career even if it never would go further than the Tri-state area. "Look, people count on you to be fair and honest," the colleague argued. "You lead a moral life. That's important, even if no one recognizes that anymore." Yes, it was true, Morrie told himself. Nobility comes in assorted flavors. Nonetheless, he felt he was missing out.

His mother, shortly before her death, also had encouraged him to try therapy. "There's nothing to be ashamed of," she said. "Look at Mike Wallace. He's come out with his depression and look how successful he is. And who was that man who ran for vice-president with George McGovern?" There was a mixed message in both references – Morrie would never be a celebrated journalist like Mike Wallace, and the allusion to former Missouri Sen. Thomas Eagleton, who had to withdraw from the 1972 campaign because of his prior psychiatric treatment, was downright alarming.

Morrie eventually moved on to the suburban beat, and he tried various strategies over the years to make his life more agreeable, including some based on suggestions from pop psychology magazines and morning talk show hosts, such as volunteering (Habitat for Humanity and stocking a local food bank), find a new hobby (golfing, but he didn't want to commit to lessons or an expensive golf club set) and travel (the British Isles and Ireland, then the Scandinavian countries because they all spoke English there).

"How's the Queen?" his suburban desk editor asked after he returned from a vacation in London.

"Fine, fine," Morrie said as he hung his jacket on a clothes tree and logged on to his computer. "She waved to me from the balcony at Buckingham Palace."

"Well, you look refreshed. And next year you get three weeks' vacation. Remember that."

THE BIG LAYOFFS at the *Sun-Times* began in 2010. The Internet had been stealing eyeballs for several years, which impacted both subscription sales and display advertising, and Craigslist had decimated the classifieds, hence the newspaper's owners tried to cut their way to profitability. The features department was dismantled first. After all, lots of travel companies and health care providers would provide free copy to the newspapers – *Top 10 Vacation Spots Revealed* and *New Hope for Diabetics*, plus Hollywood had all sorts of canned celebrity interviews available. The business section was raided next – no serious business executive consulted hometown newspapers for anything anymore, and how many local business executives were out there, anyway? The guys in Armani suits, or even Brooks Brothers, just came for the Mercedes and Jaguar ads, which also were in retrenchment. And the suburban desk could easily fill some of its space with handouts and press releases from any and every local government agency and public utility in their market area that wanted to tout a new upgrade or amenity, leaving only the occasional bond issue or rate hike or upcoming election to keep the people minimally informed. Put another way, you could put out a paper with half the staff. Morrie Stein, more than three decades of yeoman service behind him, found himself among a rising tide of unemployed Americans.

Morrie, 58 at the time of his first visit to Dr. Tobias Silver, expected the office to be staged like a Victorian parlor but this one was much darker than expected. The curtains were drawn when he arrived, and he needed to squint as he tried to make out the doctor's features in detail. Why would the man want to sit in his own gloaming, he wondered? Tobias sat in a large armchair with good posture; he sat upright with his legs crossed and arms neatly folded on his lap. Morrie could catch a glint of light reflected off the doctor's eyes but could not make out their color; save for the white of the eyes he might have been looking at a sculpture, not a human. Tobias was so immobile that Morrie concluded he was studying him. Well, of course, that's just what this sort of doctor does, he remembered.

"So, what brings you here, young man?" Dr. Silver finally asked. Morrie winced at the reference to age but perhaps the doctor just wanted to establish rapport. That would be the innocent construction, and he accepted it.

"Work," Morrie replied. "I'm 58 and out of a job. And women, too, I guess. I can never get it right with them." Morrie sat up on the edge of his chair, his hands now resting on his knees.

"And women, too? That'll cost you extra."

The little joke played well, so was a good start. The doctor asked about Morrie's youth, his relationship to his mother ("Oh, my mother, sure, everyone knows about that, but she was a very decent woman, not demanding or needy at all,") as well as how he'd gotten into journalism, then more details about his personal life. *Had he ever assaulted anyone? Was he a closeted gay? Was there one recurring dream he had that stood out from the others?* Morrie was eager to get down to work, that thing all psychiatrists like to say they do with their patients, and he figured this was just what he was doing.

"Would you like to know if this is the first time I've seen a psychiatrist?" he asked.

"If you would like to tell me," Dr. Silver replied.

"I don't do drugs, you know. I mean, prescription drugs. I don't believe in anti-depressants. So many people have different reactions to them."

The doctor nodded once but didn't say anything.

"Plus, they give you constipation, don't they? Or so I've read."

When the doctor finally spoke up again he asked what Morrie hoped to achieve in therapy, what his goals were.

"Well, you're not an employment agency, but I would like to get back into the business," he said. "I just wonder why it is that I'm out on the street and some of the people I worked with for years, they're no better than me, yet they still have their jobs. I don't think I've done anything wrong, yet I've been made redundant."

Morrie had been provided Tobias Silver's name, along with those of two other therapists, during his exit interview at the *Sun-Times*. One was a Ph.D. psychologist; another held the rank of Master of Social Work; and Tobias was the sole M.D. among the lot. Each of them had agreed to accept a reduced fee for three months of therapy as part of the newspaper's Employee Assistance Program. He thought that picking one over the other was a crap shoot – how do you evaluate therapists who operate one-on-one behind closed doors and you can never get a valid consumer review of them because of the stigma attached to all things mental health? The other two were out in the suburbs, probably in some medical office building or perhaps just a converted home on a side street on the edge of town with a discrete wooden shingle hanging from a post in the front lawn. In the end, he chose Tobias for his office in the Monroe Building. It was on a famous boulevard that fronted Buckingham Fountain and all the hybrid elms in Grant Park, and he knew he'd feel better stepping back into a cosmopolitan milieu when leaving his appointments than if he were suddenly stuck in some sprawling suburban surface parking lot wondering where he'd left his car. Plus, he could ride the 'L' to his appointments. Yet, he had momentarily questioned why a real doctor – a University of Chicago and Pritzker School of Medicine graduate at that, which he knew because he'd read up on the man on a medical website – would be part of a discount employee assistance program.

The 50 minutes of that first session passed quickly. Morrie spoke about a few of his stories, but only in brief, and both men lamented the decline of daily newspaper journalism in America. "My parents used to take the *Daily News* every afternoon," Tobias said. "They wanted to get the latest news when they came home and they didn't think much of television news."

"Oh, yes," Morrie said. "Walter Cronkite once said that all the copy from the evening news on network TV wouldn't fill half a page in *The New York*

Times. But, there's a lot more competition for people's attention these days, and people don't want to pay for the news anymore, at least, not many people."

They settled on business matters – Tobias said he'd bill the *Sun-Times* for three months if Morrie completed the right forms, which he did – and he assured Morrie that there was nothing unique about his dilemma, that a lot of people faced unemployment in a time of rapid technological change. Morrie could only laugh at that guidance. "You know the difference between a recession and a depression?" he asked.

"Yes," Tobias answered. "A recession is when your neighbor is out of work. A depression is when it's you."

When the session was over Dr. Silver rose from his perch first. "I'm so glad to have met you," he told Morrie. "Let me walk you out." The doctor smoothed the front panels of his suit jacket and, with a sweeping gesture, directed Morrie toward the door. "Next week, same time?" Dr. Silver suggested once the door to the outer reception area was open. Only then, with the little sconce light falling on the doctor's face, did Morrie get a good look at the man. He thought Silver was rather jowly, his skin patchy and puffy, the color not pink but more like a grey and tan, and he saw that Tobias had thick eyebrows and coarse hair, and his nose was somewhat hawk-like but not overly large. Morrie knew he was staring at the doctor too long yet he was struck by how unyielding the man was as he did so. He suddenly sensed an indifference, even a latent disparagement, in the doctor's untroubled affect. Maybe he'd been expecting too much from this man, he worried. The doctor must see many dozens of patients a year and it would be hard to establish a true rapport with each one, which was the innocent construction again. He was delivering a service; would Morrie expect anything more from, say, a chiropractor? He noted that the man didn't even offer to shake his hand, though. The two men stood looking at each other a few moments longer, then Morrie turned and walked on, listening carefully as the door latch behind him clicked shut.

It was late afternoon when Morrie left the Monroe Building and the rush hour already had begun. He looked fondly at the luminescence from the taillights of all the cars and taxis as they slowed and accelerated almost cyclically on the wide boulevard in front of him and even the honks from disparate horns pleased him, not unlike listening to Canadian geese in flight. All going somewhere, he thought. Everyone had a life, it seemed. He could have moseyed over to Wabash Avenue and climbed the steps to the elevated platform; the Brown Line stopped there and would take him directly home, but what was the hurry, he asked himself. He walked south on Michigan

Avenue, a bit against the herd, and stopped in front of a large plate glass window by the Artist's Café in the historic Fine Arts Building, a late 19th century structure built in the Romanesque style of the day, big limestone blocks and high, arched windows. He stood silent watch as diners ate their meals on thick china plates and lifted large tumblers filled with mineral water, perhaps not as gaily as in a Renoir or Toulouse-Lautrec painting, but with a certain level of abandon nonetheless. Morrie personally favored Edward Hopper's vison of America, not just the famous *Nighthawks* painting, but in so many others, a New England lighthouse on a seemingly barren coast, a strong sidelight coming in from the west, or an intimate hotel lobby, a older but staunch businessman in a heavy wool suit is carrying his topcoat across his arm while two women sit in upholstered chairs reading, everybody going about their business without disturbing anyone else. Very, very staunch, he'd always thought. As for *Nighthawks*, he's been to a Steak 'n' Shake diner in Chicago many times, but it was like a Hollywood set, a Las Vegas impression, with its polished chrome trim and red and black checkered décor everywhere. Only happy families ate there, or so the corporate owners would have you believe, while out on the state highways the Waffle House places with a million and one ways to serve your eggs were perhaps a bit too pathetic, filled as they were with terse, unshaven truckers who'd been on the road for a week and broad-shouldered state troopers who came in for free coffee and any leads on the latest outlaws. Hopper would have painted a Waffle House instead of a Steak 'n' Shake if he were still alive, Morrie knew.

But, as he stood regarding the palmy diners at the Artist's Café, a young lady with long blonde hair and a statuesque Roman nose turned to look up at him—maybe she'd think he was a stalker, he fretted—and she smiled kindly before turning her attention back to conversation with the other dinner guests. Morrie moved on.

Dr. Tobias Silver, too, had nowhere special to go that afternoon. He regularly parked his car in a garage on Harrison Street and as he walked he weaved easily between the gathering throng on the sidewalks, taking good strides, his arms swinging at his sides, as he went to claim his car. He gave the appearance of a confident, untroubled man. Once home he'd heat a frozen meal in the oven, watch the national news, then spend most of the evening in his ample library, his Athenaeum, as he liked to think of it. He would pull down a classic text on ancient Chinese dynasties or a coffee table book on Medieval art or just Nietzsche's "Genealogy of Morals," which he'd been rereading, people inventing religion and reward in the afterlife because they'd been defeated in this one. When he reached the garage he nodded to the attendant, who greeted him with a, "Yessir, Dr. Silver," and after the man retrieved his car and pulled up alongside him near the exit he promptly jumped out, and held the door open for Tobias, who tipped him a single dollar bill, as he always did. "Thank you, Dr. Silver," the attendant said. "Have a good evenin', Dr. Silver."

"You, too," Tobias said as he slid into his seat, checked the rear view and driver side mirrors, and then pulled into traffic, part of a school of fish now going this way and now that way, moving in concert as if all one collective conscious mind.

IT HAD BEEN YEARS since Morrie Stein attended Friday night services. He didn't have children to model or any observant Jewish friends who might invite him to tag along. He knew that some people become more religious as they age or simply seek a return to a community they once felt close to. He understood that he might be subject to the same sort of devolution. Nothing like a crisis in life to make one more prayerful, of course, just like the adage that there are no atheists in a foxhole. He knew all the risk factors compelling belief, most of them involving loss or hurt. Morrie's parents had attended services at the imposing, armory-like Albany Park Hebrew Congregation on north Lawndale Avenue on many an occasion – it was across the street from a city park where both Christian and Jewish children would play in the afternoons after the nearby elementary schools let out for the day, and just north of a Jewish community center. He'd infrequently been to the latter building or the small park when he was younger as he attended elementary schools in Ravenswood, then high school in Irving Park. In a city of neighborhoods such as Chicago it was like being across the border in another country. His parents liked the Albany Park Hebrew Congregation, though, because it was large, and seated many hundreds, which meant they could maintain a certain level of anonymity, maybe hide their pedestrian lives, and because it was almost Unitarian in outlook, following a watered-down liturgy that made no assumptions about any congregant's knowledge base. It was at this temple that Morrie had celebrated a group bar mitzvah years earlier with other young men of the right age. Returning to his empty home after meeting with Dr. Silver, waving to a little girl who was riding her tricycle on the sidewalk in front of the house next door, he decided that this was just what he would do – attend Friday night services at his parents' former favorite temple. He would follow in the footsteps of his youth, a time in his life as real and valid as the future and just as important to him. He would walk the two miles or so to this shrine.

Morrie hadn't gone on long walks of late but as he did so on this day's close he allowed himself to enjoy the rattle and screech of the "L" trains, the huff and sputter of cars pulling into driveways and the avian-like cries of children playing anywhere. He was so happy he'd decided to walk. His life was in crisis but life goes on; he wasn't bitter at all. Morrie knew there wouldn't be many people present at a reform temple for Friday night services but that was just as well. He didn't really want to pray so much as absorb spirit and contemplate meaning.

He remembered that the old temple was at the corner of Wilson and Lawndale, yet when he arrived he discovered only an empty lot with not so much as remnants of the rubble from the building's apparent destruction. When you're young, very young, everything that is always was. That's how it seems when you're young. The congregation had been there forever. So, what happened? He knew the neighborhood hardly had a Jewish presence anymore and that synagogues and temples sometimes were sold to church groups, sometimes just donated, but the relic apparently had not been repurposed in any way. What was the hurry to knock it down? Shifting sands and recurring dust storms cover up the past; conquering nations do the same. Is that what the world still thought of Jews? He snapped his head and looked south, across the street. Where was the Max Strauss Center, which was the name of the Jewish community center he remembered? Built in the slimmed-down, rectilinear style of the 1940s it was no architectural gem but that just meant it was an efficient structure and certainly not old at 60 or 70 years on. It was a community center with a gym and playrooms and offices. Surely there still was a use for a building like that. But it was gone.

Children still played in the city park across the way, on the heavy metal and wood merry-go-round, on the shiny slick metal slides that scorched tiny bums in the mid-day sun in summer, and on the swings made from wood boards carried by rusty chains. But there were not as many children as he recalled seeing in his youth. Everything always seems bigger and more important when you're younger, so maybe the park was never quite as busy as he recalled, he thought. Morrie understood the problem with recalling the past. Memory makes things bigger, more prominent than they were. Or does it? The past can't always be considered a lie because there really was a past. On this day, however, there were only a few children on the swings and slides, maybe two or three mothers doting over their babies in prams as they sat on the park benches. The sun had dropped behind the apartment buildings to the west, yet a gentle light fell broadly over the scene. There should have been more vitality here, he was sure.

Morrie could think of nothing to do but return home. On Drake Avenue, though, just three blocks east, would be *Beit Itzchok*, an Orthodox synagogue that he'd never attended but which had the highest prestige in the area because of its history of learned rabbis. He would stop in there, he decided. True, he was an *"am ha'aretz,"* one of the common people deemed to be negligent of their religious obligations even if not otherwise sinful in the eyes of the Lord, but this was the modern age in a truly secular society, and he doubted the old, observant Jews he expected to find there would pressure him in prayer in any way. *Beit Itzchok* had been known as a discrete architectural gem, a small Greek-inspired temple with yellow bricks and limestone trim. Morrie looked forward to visiting there; the evening would not be a failure or foolish, sentimental diversion after all.

The synagogue was not there. It was gone. One could make out where it had stood from remnants of the foundation walls, i.e., a manmade gorge that had only partly been filled with rubble and debris. He approached the plastic barrier fencing that surrounded the site, more symbolic than secure, just a visual cue to "keep out." The little synagogue apparently had only recently been demolished. Was it the last to fall? That would be somewhat of a distinction.

As Morrie stood in the middle of the sidewalk a woman pulling a collapsible shopping cart halted in front of him and waited patiently for him to move out of the way. He looked quizzically at her before realizing what the situation was; she continued smiling, and he apologized and stepped aside, apologizing again as she passed him, and he watched as she continued down the street dragging the little cart behind her. She was an older woman who wore a silk headscarf that she'd tied beneath her chin. She must have been an old-timer in the neighborhood, and he thought to run after her, to ask what had happened. To ask where all the Jews had gone. All gone.

IT WAS AT MORRIE'S suggestion that therapy sessions were to continue on Friday afternoons. He'd have all week to search for jobs, maybe do a little freelance copywriting or editing, and then have something to report as he looked forward to the weekend and a respite from the previous week's pressures. He'd worn a suit and tie to his first meeting with Dr. Silver, though not his old Florsheim Imperials, genuine articles that had been made in Chicago, and he decided to continue doing so. Dress every day as if it mattered, even if times are hard, he'd once somewhere read.

It's never good to be caught looking at your watch after asking a patient a question. It suggests bad intent. But that's what Morrie saw Tobias do during a later therapy session. Dr. Tobias Silver's question had referred to what Morrie liked best about being a journalist. People typically are happy to talk about their work, their successes and their contributions, particularly if they think they'd done a good job. So, why wasn't Dr. Silver listening attentively, he wondered? Somewhat instinctively Morrie pulled back the sleeve on his left arm and looked at his own wristwatch. He decided to ignore the slight.

"I remember interviewing a former college professor from Notre Dame," he said. "Joe Montana had been one of his students. But the man's daughter was born with Down Syndrome, and he quit his post to help care for her full-time. When I met him he'd already taken a job with the insurance company he'd once sued for an increase in benefits; now he helped them deal with new disability claims because he'd made himself an expert on the law. I asked him how he felt about no longer teaching at a national university. I mean, think of the status he'd given up. But that wasn't it, he said. It was just that for the first time in his life he had a job where the primary goal was to make money for his employer, not molding young minds or doing research or creating new knowledge or anything else of intrinsic value. That's how I felt about journalism. It had intrinsic value. It's wasn't a job I did only because I needed the money or because I wanted to help the company make money. That's all changed, I guess."

Tobias nodded enthusiastically. "Very commendable," he said. "You were very fortunate to have a job you loved. You did love it, right?"

Morrie was surprised by the question. "Of course, I loved it. I *was* fortunate to have a job like that. And I was very good at my job because I thought it was an important job. Forget about passion. It's an overused term. The job had real value, that's all."

"No doubt. No doubt," Tobias said after he sipped from a glass of water and set it back down on the side table next to his chair. "You've indicated that you won some awards, too. Tell me about them."

Morrie told him about a kickback scheme related to new sewer lines he'd written, and another about a builder's encroachment on rare habitat. He said nothing about the two murdered girls, however.

"Not every story can be sexy, can it?" Tobias commented, which Morrie thought was an inappropriate remark and essentially negative at that. Tobias followed up his comment by asking if he'd ever won any national awards.

"Like the Pulitzer Prize?" Morrie said.

"Hmm, yes, like the Pulitzer. Oh, scratch that. You haven't won the Pulitzer or you would have told me already."

Tobias asked about his job prospects and Morrie said there might be some if he were willing to relocate, which he said he was, and especially if he was willing to go to a smaller market.

"You're on a common career path," Tobias said. "You rise, you crest, and then you go down."

"I didn't say anything about going down in my career," Morrie retorted, somewhat defensively. "It would just be a smaller market, that's all. Fewer readers but just as valuable. I'd probably be an editor or even writing coach because of my experience. That's all I meant. Anyway, even if I were to remain a reporter I'd still have to produce the same quality journalism for a thousand readers as for a hundred thousand."

Tobias nodded his assent. "That's a good line," he said. "Try to remember it if you get an interview."

Tobias apologized that he couldn't help him with actual job openings and suggested they instead get back to the real work of psychotherapy. "If you have problems, you'll still have them even if you get hired somewhere," he said. "The problems people have are never the ones they think they have. I trust you know that or you wouldn't be here. That is correct, isn't it?"

"What's correct? That I'm in denial about what my real problems are or that I know that I have real problems beyond simply being out of work?"

"Hmm, yes."

It was cat and mouse time.

JOB PROSPECTS DIDN'T IMPROVE much over the next several weeks. Morrie was able to lunch with a few old friends, all of whom were sympathetic but without anything concrete to offer, not counting the one who pulled out his wallet and asked if he could use some "scratch," as he put it. Morrie did hear that he was one of four finalists for a job with the *Register Star* newspaper in Rockford. A human resources staffer did a preliminary phone interview, then called back the next day to set up a two-hour window where Morrie could visit with several editors in person. It was good news, and the caution about having to pass a drug screen hardly concerned him, though being subject to a six-month probationary period if hired seemed demeaning to him. He'd probably want to move to Rockford, but he could afford the long commute at first if it gave him the time he needed to find the right house there. The appointment to meet with management was set for three weeks hence. "And just so you know," he was told, "we'll be talking to candidates from Milwaukee and Kansas City, as well as another former reporter at the *Sun-Times*. We're not at liberty to tell you who that is." It gave Morrie pause: they all wanted to work in

Rockford? The contraction throughout the industry was quite real. Morrie brought it up with Tobias.

"How does applying for a job like that make you feel?" Tobias asked.

"I shouldn't have to go on probation. I can tell you that."

"Maybe you don't want to be judged?"

"How so?"

"You're afraid that you're not really good enough. Half the people in the world couldn't get the job they currently have if they had to apply for it again. There was an article about that in *The Wall Street Journal*."

"Do you know about Gannett newspaper properties?" Morrie said. "That's their policy, too. As part of the annual performance review they often ask employees to reapply for the job they already have. They use it as a tool to demote people."

"Some people quit rather than accept a demotion, don't they?"

"That's what I hear."

"And you know why, don't you? You're a smart guy, Morrie."

Morrie looked to the side to consider the question, then snuck a glance at Tobias again, who was staring intensely at him. "Sure," he said. "They're humiliated. That's what really breaks people."

Tobias moved on; he asked whether his patient was having any luck in meeting women and Morrie suggested that telling someone he was out of work and living on savings could hardly be a successful pick-up line. Tobias congratulated him on retaining his sense of humor, then asked if the real problem wasn't just that he never thought he was good enough for women. Morrie's interest was piqued.

"What do you mean?" he asked.

"You told me that you loved your mother the first time we met. Remember?"

"I think I said she was a very good and decent woman. I loved her, of course, but not in the way you guys always like to talk about."

"Ah, I see you've read up on Freud. Perhaps an encyclopedia entry? Tell me, did you try to please your mother when you were younger?"

Morrie shrugged. "Please her? Sure. Every boy wants to please his mother and father."

Tobias interrupted him. "I didn't ask about your father."

"What?"

"You thought you could never outperform your father, therefore you could never win over your mother. Was that the problem?"

Morrie scrunched his mouth before speaking again. "Is this what you call cutting to the chase? Look, I respected all women because I respected my mother. It had nothing to do with sex. If anything, I underestimated how much other women might be interested in sex just because of her. And I was not intimidated by my father. He sold slipcovers, for God sake."

"Morrie."

"What?"

"Why are you getting so angry?"

Morrie Stein finally found a job. It was not one he would have coveted in ordinary times nor was it the one in Rockford – they'd called from the *Register Star* to cancel his appointment two days out saying they'd decided to promote from within. But a small optical manufacturing company in Lisle had decided to publish a newsletter for its client list and wanted an experienced "wordsmith," as they put it in the *Chicago Tribune* ad, to write and edit the copy. Layout experience was required, which Morrie did not have, but there were new computer software programs that could help with that. Morrie weighed the job offer carefully – the pay was mediocre and the work conditions were not great as his office would be next to the busy photocopy room and didn't even have a window. Benefits were meager, too, just one week of paid vacation for the first five years and Major Medical only for health insurance, but he wouldn't have to pay the premium. Parking out in the suburbs was free, of course. A father and son owned the firm and even though Morrie didn't like the way the older man looked at him during the interview, as if he were questioning why a fifty-something former newspaper reporter would apply for a job like this, the son had been quite enthusiastic, which helped seal the deal because it was the son who mostly ran the day-to-day operations. Morrie came early his first day on the job – "Reporting for duty," he joked while saluting his new bosses, then he felt embarrassed – and he was surprised to learn that the owners wanted him first to whip up little biographies about them for their new website, something that would list all their accomplishments and awards over the years, seminars attended and such, as well as invent a few quotes that would highlight their commitment to their customers, passion about their business and heartfelt support for all the brave men and women serving in the armed forces. When Morrie asked if they had any newspaper clippings or testimonials from others that would document assertions he might make in the little biographies, the son asked if that was really necessary while the father accused the press of fabricating quotes all the time, so why did Morrie need to see "proof" of anything. Then the son handed him a disposable camera and told him to take some pictures on the workshop floor. He looked at the little pocket camera and then again at the two men.

"If this is for publication don't you think you'll need a professional photographer?" he asked. "Someone with lighting equipment, not to mention, well, a real camera?"

"It's all right. It's all right," the father said. "They'll just be test shots. We'll hire someone to do the real photos later. What, you can't even snap a few pictures?"

Morrie dropped down into a nearby seat; he felt faint for a moment. The son approached and asked if he was all right but the father asked if he was on any medication. "You didn't take this job under false pretenses, did you?" he demanded to know.

Morrie was stunned. "What?" he asked, speaking both warily and with an incredulous, tortured expression on his face. "What?" he asked again.

The father turned to his son. "I told you he was probably on medication," he said. "That's probably why they fired him at the newspaper. I don't even remember ever seeing his byline."

Morrie thought about offering to quit before he was fired, but he hadn't even filled out all the proper income tax and Social Security paperwork yet. He sighed, laughed self-deprecatingly at himself, and headed for the door. He wasn't going to give them the satisfaction of saying goodbye.

TOBIAS WANTED TO ANALYZE what had happened at the optical firm even though Morrie recounted the experience more as anecdote than plaint. "You didn't really want the job, did you?" Tobias asked while looking fiercely at him.

Morrie looked away. "No, I guess not," he said. "I guess I was lucky to find out how shitty it was so fast."

"You were too good for a job like that, you thought."

"I don't know why I took it. Maybe it was the title. I'd be editor of my own little magazine. Was that so silly of me?"

"Not if you couldn't get anything better," Tobias said while arching his eyebrows.

AFTER THREE MONTHS OF THERAPY Morrie began to wonder where it was leading. He couldn't accuse Dr. Silver of being the kind of person who handed out aphorisms and platitudes like Hallmark greeting cards, of merely applying thin salves to deep wounds. He tried to see a purpose and method to the doctor's tactics, though. Perhaps it was tough love, the doctor pushing him hard at times so that he would accept basic truths about himself. Morrie knew the Serenity Prayer and liked it a lot - *God grant me the serenity to accept the things I cannot change; courage to change the things I can; and wisdom to know the difference.* The prayer didn't sound like a banality to him. It was a good rule to live by, he believed. But, increasingly, he felt that the Tobias wanted him to accept that he had found the station in life where he belonged, much like water always seeks its own level. That he would not accept.

The bargain basement priced therapy sessions with Dr. Silver had come to an end and Morrie Stein had not yet found permanent employment. When he told Tobias that he'd have to discontinue the sessions Tobias asked if the reason was financial. "What do you think?" Morrie replied.

Tobias was unmoved. "If you had cancer would you discontinue treatment because of money?" he asked.

"But I'm not dying, at least not tomorrow, or next week," Morrie said. "I'm just out of a job. Maybe a little depressed, too, but I'm not suicidal."

"Don't you own your home?"

"Yes. Why do you ask?"

"You have an asset, that's all. There are home equity loans. You're not really bankrupt."

"That's right. And I don't want to be bankrupted."

Tobias considered his patient further; he deeply resented patients who didn't want to pay for their mental health care. He had as much or more training than the most famous surgeons; didn't people know that? And a surgeon's job was easier – cut open a person, take something out or reconnect this tissue to that like an electrician rewiring your house, and then stitch him back up. But psychiatry was the master class in the medical arts and only certain people could do it properly. He was one of them, no less than a Picasso or a Beethoven in their respective fields. Put another way, a true artist supersedes even the best training; he has gifts that cannot be taught. People would gladly mortgage their homes and empty their retirement accounts to pay for cancer treatment, and vainglorious millionaires and the nouveau riche would pay any price to own a Picasso. But psychiatrists constantly had to sell themselves. Tobias wanted to make sure that his patient knew he was still in command.

"That's good," Tobias finally said to Morrie, speaking with a vaguely menacing and conniving expression on his face. "Very, very good. I'm proud of you. You're standing up to me. Because I think you're benefitting from therapy and it would be a shame to see the progress you've made go down the drain I'm prepared to continue offering my services for free, at least until you get back on your feet. How does that sound? Hmm?"

MORRIE HAD BEGUN TO SEE Dr. Silver in the early spring; now the sessions had rolled over into the late fall. He'd managed one good temp job in all that time, a two-week contract at the Encyclopaedia Britannica to help write an entry on local law enforcement. A criminologist from the University of Maryland-College Park was having trouble getting his piece down to a manageable length, even for the Britannica, and an old friend from *The Sun-Times* who'd long ago joined the encyclopedia's staff had reached out to him. Morrie was glad for the work, but more so for the vote of confidence. If you don't have your reputation you don't have anything, he always believed. The temp job was just one splintered plank to hold on to after the shipwreck, though.

"I can't promise this gig will lead to anything," his friend had told him.

"No promises. Understood," Morrie had replied.

"You know, we're actually laying off people in most departments," the friend continued. "It's the fucking Internet. First it was Bill Gates giving away Encarta encyclopedias with Windows, then along came Wikipedia."

"I still have my full set from the 1960s," Morrie said.

"Oh? Britannica or Funk & Wagnall's?"

Morrie was chagrined. "Okay, you win. We got one volume for $1.99 every week from the A&P store on Lawrence Avenue. I bagged groceries there for a time."

"Didn't we all. Didn't we all," his friend said.

Morrie felt good about commuting daily to work Downtown just like in his old police beat days, even if only for two weeks. Work is not drudgery when you're out of a job; it's something you thirst for. He always liked riding the 'L,' the bump and rattle of the train car on its uneven tracks, the crackling sound of bad loudspeakers announcing the next stop, and if a fellow passenger sat too close to him or stepped on his toes while rushing to the exit he would just smile because he had a job, he had a life, if only for two weeks. Movies set in Chicago always spotlighted the 'L,' no less than movies shot in Paris would feature the Eifel Tower. The cameramen often showed the trains from under the platform girders on Lake Street or Wabash Avenue in the Loop, streaks of light and slashing shadows if filmed during the day, a striking incandescent glow and Edward Hopper window lighting if at night, and sometimes passengers inside the train cars, inside the womb where real people lived.

It was just a two-week contract and Britannica was laying off full-timers, not hiring – he kept reminding himself of that, counting each day as if it were a holiday about to end too soon. But that's what they always say, isn't it, he secretly thought. The *Sun-Times* and the *Tribune* and every major newspaper in the country, before readership started to decline around 2000, would feed qualified job seekers the same line. It was to manage expectations, to judge reactions, to make the hounds chase the fox more resolutely. The fact is companies always hire someone they really want. A job at the encyclopedia would check quite a few boxes for Morrie. It had a name, one he could toss out with aplomb if he were to meet an old acquaintance who wanted to know where he was working these days. It had depth, too, depending on exactly what position was available. Nationally recognized scholars wrote all the articles, true. But he would be working with them. The pay was a problem, of course. Britannica was notorious for poor pay among the lower rungs of employees and why not, the publisher must have thought. They had no shortage of applicants from good fields who wanted to work there. This was even true of the proofreaders, some of whom had earned Ph.D.'s in this or that English or other liberal arts concentration. Well, that would be a gut-wrenching comedown for him, to look for missing apostrophes and dangling participles, making little marks with soft lead pencils on the margins of page proofs but never being allowed to change anything on his own initiative.

The contract work was extended for another week, which gave Morrie some hope that he had found a home, and they put him on another task in-house, this time dealing with the Burnham Plan and Chicago's plethora of good city parks. He didn't know much about the subject but the encyclopedia had its own large library of resources; his friend said they wanted him for the job because he was a Chicago native and would know what sounded right and what missed the mark. But it was only for an additional week. Morrie was given a nice send-off after that third week along with a promise that they'd call him again if more temp jobs opened up. But the Encyclopaedia Britannica still was laying off full-time employees; he should keep looking elsewhere if that's what he needed, his friend emphasized.

Morrie did not find full-time work and was not called back by the encyclopedia. And there'd been a new round of layoffs at the *Sun-Times* and now one at the *Tribune* – he had to read about these developments in the alternative press because none of the television stations bothered to cover the troubles in print journalism any longer – and he finally had to admit that he really would have to change careers. He could sell real estate – one large firm was advertising that they could help new hires get a real estate license in two weeks! The men's department at Macy's was hiring suit salesmen, a job that another veteran journalist he knew had already taken. What could there be to a job like that? Take arm measurements? Get down on one knee to measure inseam length? Some styles wear better on different people so good taste might be a qualification, but most customers just wanted the latest fashions, either that or some classic style.

"And a nice shirt to go with that, sir?"

He thought of teaching journalism. When he investigated that possibility he discovered that most of the adjunct positions already had been taken by both practicing and former journalists and that the pay was less than what a house painter made per hour. How is it that most journalism classes are taught by adjuncts, anyway, he wondered? What do the tenured faculty do?

Road closed ahead. That's what every sign he saw seemed to announce. Morrie told himself that he'd take a factory job before he did anything as servile as telling an overweight, middle-aged man that a pair of brown flannel pants looked splendid on him.

WINTER AGAIN IN CHICAGO, the television stations agog with weather alerts and stories about the rising price of road salt or the best snow tires to buy, and all the window displays on State Street were sprinkled with Ivory soap flakes and the potted trees on Michigan Avenue all were strung with Christmas lights. It's said that the incidence of depression increases during the holidays, that it's the contrast between one's own troubled life and the apparent happiness and satisfaction in everyone else's that's to blame. It was for that reason that Morrie forced himself out of the house, if for nothing more exciting than a stroll down the narrow aisles of small ethnic stores on Lawrence and Lincoln avenues, or long walks through the barren yet hardy landscape in nearby Horner Park, a winter scene like something from a Siberian forest.

Morrie had gone through all his liquid savings and was now eating into his retirement account. He never worried much about Chicago's high property taxes before but now he found himself wondering why he had to pay for some child's second-rate public school education or subsidize the teachers' union at all, just like all the disgruntled old white men who loved to write nasty letters to the editor at both daily newspapers. He stopped shaving every morning; he'd already stopped getting up early. He'd only eat half his meals, too, then leave the dishes out before getting around to cleaning up a day later, then two days later. He'd sit in front of the television for hours and not remember what he'd watched in any detail. He had no interest in meeting women, either, other than possibly romancing a rich widow and living off her sizeable estate – it was a fantasy he allowed himself to enjoy but didn't really believe in. His sessions with Dr. Silver had become moribund, too. Morrie would drag himself to the office, not out of hope or desperation, but mostly to submit. He had begun to accept that if he was failing it must be his fault.

"How are we doing today?" Tobias asked him the last time. He'd started speaking in the editorial "we" several weeks earlier and Morrie didn't like it but didn't openly object. He didn't want a fight. He didn't like the snarky look on the doctor's face, either, a message that said, "You didn't do anything this past week, did you?" Morrie didn't object to that, either, because he had come to believe the sneer and snark were justified, that he deserved it. What had he done lately, after all? It was self-flagellation.

"My father died in December, you know," Morrie said. "I didn't even say a prayer on his *yahrzeit.*" He expected a response from Tobias because he'd never talked about his father's death before – it had been a hit-and-run accident and the culprit was later caught, then convicted of manslaughter but released after four years, no civil suit on the agenda as the man was judgment-proof – but Tobias rarely changed his aspect anymore, just letting Morrie drone on like lamentations heard from a distant chamber.

"I said I missed the *yahrzeit,*" Morrie repeated, looking up at the unyielding doctor. "Isn't that terrible of me? Or do you even know what that is?"

Tobias cleared his throat and crossed his legs the other way. "Yes, I know what that is, Morrie. So, you feel guilty about this? Or do you think saying a little prayer after he's decomposing in a pine box six feet under the ground might do him some good, like leaving baskets of food and gold bracelets for recently departed Pharaohs to help them in their journey to the other world?"

"Tobias, I'm hurting. That's all I'm saying." Morrie's eyes were moist.

Dr. Silver had a box of tissues on the big walnut desk in his office. As he never sat there during sessions it's possible that his patients didn't pay much mind to it. But Silver did something he'd never done for a patient before, at least not for a male patient. After squeezing his mouth as if he'd just tasted something disagreeable, he grunted, rose from his seat and walked slowly to the desk, so slowly, in fact, that it was unmistakably an act of distasteful obligation, and he snapped a tissue from the box, then turned to Morrie and held it with only the tips of his fingers. It was as if to say, "Here, take it," an order and a concession, like giving a dog something to help it lick its wounds. Morrie raised his head and looked up at the therapist – Morrie's posture had been poor in the moment, leaning far forward in his seat – and he licked his lips as if he were indeed a hungry, beaten dog. He stared hard at the single piece of tissue, and he knew that if he took it he would continue to be imprisoned by the man but if he declined he would be truly alone.

NASCENT TEARS PROVED to be a turning point in Morrie's life. He'd hit bottom and survived. Maybe it was just a dead cat bounce, yet he felt that his life still mattered because he was still living it. He realized that he'd been humiliated by his doctor, an insight that soured him like the taste of old vinegar.

At their next session Morrie was so bold as to ask Tobias why he'd gone into psychiatry. He was blunt – was it the Jewish doctor thing? Tobias replied sarcastically by asking if his patient was thinking of applying to medical school himself. Morrie understood the question well. He'd interviewed homeless people before – under a bridge, at a shelter, guys who were begging for change at a highway off-ramp – and they would ask the oddest and most unlikely questions but often related to the kind of work he did, namely journalism, something they'd never thought of before yet somehow, no more than on a whim, they thought they could do from that point on. Thoughts of what these homeless individuals could become were not merely random but were instantaneous, devoid of a clock of any kind. Their lives existed outside of time. Tobias's remark suggested that he understood the phenomenon well himself – who was this hapless person who thought to ask a real doctor how he'd become a doctor as if he might try to become one himself, as if that's all there was to it, flip a coin, snap your fingers, *dream it* and it will be done. Tobias was not only ridiculing and reviling marginalized, disconnected, *farblunget* people such as the homeless, he was making fun of him, Morrie Stein.

Clearly, Tobias was annoyed that his patient had dared to challenge his motives, his reasoning behind his choices in life. The commoner does not question the King. It wasn't that Morrie Stein intended to become more aggressive in confronting his therapist but he was becoming inured to the pain of his own circumstances, and he found strength in that, implacability in the face of failure and submission. It was both revelatory and liberating, much like the old Janis Joplin lyric, "Freedom means having nothing left to lose." Yet Morrie had long thought the song's theme contained a gratuitous sentiment, fortitude without really needing to be staunch, bravery without doing anything, because it's only bravery when you have something to lose and are willing to risk it all. Bob Dylan spoke to him more directly – "How does it feel? To be on your own, with no direction home, a complete unknown, like a rolling stone."

"And just what are you smiling at?" Tobias asked.

"I was thinking about why neither of us served in the Army," Morrie answered.

Tobias scrunched his face as he was increasingly wont to do over the disparate, often obscure references his patient was making of late. "I've treated veterans before, Mr. Stein," he said.

Morrie whistled softly and shook his head. "Oh, boy, we both know what that is, sir," he said. "That is one big, fat, defense mechanism, a big, fat, juicy obfuscation. I didn't ask if you treated veterans. I asked if you were a veteran."

"Humph," Tobias snorted. "And why didn't you serve?"

"The draft was over when I got out of college. I wasn't sorry to see it go. I'll admit to that. But why didn't you go, Tobias? You're older than me."

"I was in medical school. The country needed doctors. That's an occupational deferment. And they didn't want psychiatrists when I got out."

"You asked, of course."

"Oh, fuck you, Morrie."

THE SESSIONS CONTINUED THROUGHOUT the winter and into the early spring. Morrie had suggested that they meet in a nearby cafeteria or bar, any place that might have a booth in back where they could talk freely as none of this was real therapy anyway, he explained. Tobias was astonished and said he would not agree to such a thing ever, yet he continued to see Morrie in his office without payment. It was after one session in early March – '*Has it been a year already?*' *he mused* – that Morrie witnessed a homeless person digging into one of the city's heavy welded steel trash receptacles on Michigan Avenue. The man was distributing garbage all around him as he looked for things of value inside the misbegotten cornucopia of tossed papers, foam coffee cups and half-eaten sandwiches, and he didn't pay attention to passersby as they eyed him with scorn or just walked around him. The man was not so poorly dressed – not at all – as he wore good shoes, a light tan raincoat, knee-length, and even a chapeau as if this were the 1950s, but Morrie knew that only homeless people and beggars stick their arms deep into trash bins looking for little treasures. He felt some personal relief as he spied the man, reassured by the fact that he had not sunk that low, confident that he never would, but nonetheless he felt sad for the man and not a little contempt for all the good people of the city who just ignored the one-act drama in real time. He decided to approach the man.

"Sir, what are you looking for?" he asked. "Maybe I can help you."

The traffic continued to whir and whine as it passed the busy intersection, a policeman blew his whistle and windmilled his arm to direct all the cars and taxis that needed to turn, and the chatter of pedestrians and the rustle of their shopping bags or just the little clicks of women's high heels on the sidewalk reminded Morrie of one of those rainmaker shakers he'd had as a child. He waited for the man to reply, not sure that he would because he could see how engrossed he was in his dig.

"What?" the man said rather loudly and scornfully when he finally turned to face Morrie. "Who are you? My secretary threw out my notes for a brief I need to prepare over the weekend for a court appearance Monday. You want to help me search for them in this load of crap?" The man looked off into the distance and shook his head, and then he turned his attention back to the trash receptacle.

It was a Friday afternoon, as usual, and Morrie sat in a crowded Brown Line rail car for his ride home. He had scored a window seat, which would make the trip more pleasant. He could mark the progress on a roofing project where the rails crossed an alley – most three-flats and six-flats in Chicago had flat roofs with rubber or tar coatings, so it would always be a simple if messy job – or he could watch children playing stickball and skipping rope in the street near the end of his 30-minute trip. Yet, at the Belmont stop, halfway through his journey, he saw a group of Hasidim scurry across the platform to transfer from the Brown Line to the Red Line. Their appearance corroborated all the old stereotypes and sentimental street fair artist renderings of such Jews – the long wool frocks, some with satin edging, the broad brim beaver hats, and the long side curls hanging below their ears, especially those. He could easily tell the leaders from the followers, by both the relative ages and the way some hurried and waddled at the same time, little ducklings following the adults. They were heading home and then to *shul* before sundown. Maybe he should attend a Jewish seminary himself, he suddenly thought. Not necessarily an Orthodox one – he couldn't see himself outfitted like a 17th century Pole and what did that have to do with Zion, anyway – but there were Conservative and Reform trends he could adhere to. Why not? He thought of the old Joni Mitchell song, she's seen life from both sides now. That should be a precondition for the rabbinate, the priesthood, even the presidency, he thought, otherwise it's too easy to believe your own myths and false premises.

Like he was really going to do such a thing, he mused followed by a giggle. Like he was one of those homeless people who, with a flip of a switch, could conjure themselves in another occupation, another life, another world. For a moment he thought Tobias might be right about him and he shuddered.

FOR THE FOLLOWING FRIDAY'S appointment Tobias had pulled open one panel of the curtains against the far window to let in the indirect light from the late afternoon sky. He had dressed differently, too, in a lime green sport jacket over dark navy gabardine slacks. It was a very spring-like outfit, very Bermuda-like, and the garb didn't so much hide his growing girth as create a new vogue for him. Morrie noticed the changes immediately, and he signaled his alertness by theatrically covering his eyes when he looked toward the now exposed window, then squinting when he turned his attention back to Tobias while scanning him from tip to toe.

"What's with the new look?" he asked somewhat flippantly; he was fiddling with some items in his own pocket as if to illustrate that he didn't really care about the change.

Tobias just smirked and pointed to the usual seat for his patient to park himself.

"What is the occasion, Tobias?" Morrie persisted.

"Do I need one to dress differently?"

"Nothing is done without a reason. Isn't that what you people always say?"

"I'm glad you've been listening."

"Maybe it's your depression that's lifting, Tobias."

"You're forgetting who the patient is, Morrie."

The relationship had been combative for months, two warthogs in a closed pen charging each other before retreating, stalking and ignoring, always rising anger followed by sudden indifference. It wasn't just Morrie who had been struggling the last few months; Tobias had showed no respect for his patient, yet had failed to break him. Bend him, yes, which was tantalizingly close to victory. *'We break them down so the we can put them back together again.'* That still was Tobias's operative principle for his most serious cases, but some required more effort than others. Was the patient that stubborn or just stupid? In deep denial, or just a deep depression? Either way, failure to break the patient was failure, not of the cure, nor even of the patient, but of *himself*, Tobias Silver. Like a compulsive gambler who must always play one more hand, roll the dice and place another bet, he wasn't ready to quit on the therapy yet. Money had nothing to do with it, it was his jaws that wanted to taste victory. Tobias had broken and tossed out patients before, and had been disdainful of many others, those patients who weren't really ill, and he was just their human placebo. But Morrie Stein's resistance troubled him to the point of wondering whether the patient had a secret agenda, not unlike him. Well, game on. Who would break first?

Tobias cleared his throat and asked if his patient would like a drink of water. Morrie turned his head slowly in the direction of bottled water on a tray on Tobias's desk, then up again at Tobias. "Sure," he said, then added, "With ice." There was no ice bucket in evidence. Tobias grabbed one of the plastic bottles and handed it to Morrie, who continued to search the room with his eyes.

"So, what shall we discuss today, Morrie?" Tobias asked.

"I saw a group of Jews on the train last week," Morrie related. "I was on my way home after our session and I wondered what it would be like to be a rabbi."

"How did you know they were Jewish?" Tobias asked. He had taken his own bottle of water with him to his seat and had been sipping it while listening to his patient. "What gave them away?"

Ah, the attack and parry again, Morrie knew. This is what he had come to love about his sessions. He no longer believed Tobias Silver could be of any help to him; the sessions were not even some brief respite from a dreaded looming doom or even like standing under an awning in a thunderstorm but you know you'll have to move on while it's still pouring down anyway. Respite? Retreat? Not at all. He had come to enjoy the sessions like good burlesque. They were the highlight of his week.

"They were all circumcised," Morrie answered drolly.

"They were Hasidim, right?"

"Well, that was a pretty good tell," Morrie said.

"I've seen them out and about, too," Tobias said. "Did they try to convert you?"

"That would be the Chabad. But these Jews were in a hurry to pray. It was getting to be late in the afternoon."

"You think God hears their prayers? Come, now, you don't believe that."

"I believe that having something to believe in helps people. It doesn't matter if it's true or not."

"An example, please?"

"Well, you, for example," Morrie said. "That's why most patients seek counseling. It's like Mommy planting a kiss on an owie." Tobias seethed behind a tight-lipped grin.

"OK. You came here today to tell me about the Jews you saw on the train last week. So, let's find out what that means. Have you been thinking about the Jews lately?"

Morrie opened his mouth as if he were about to continue speaking but he stopped short. It was something in the way Tobias had said "the Jews" that alerted him. Morrie never liked the way people talked about "the Jews," whether from an anti-Semitic or even a philo-Semitic perspective. There were groups of Jews and Jews in history and Jews who prayed all the time and those who even stole but who were "*the* Jews?" He had once argued with colleagues at the *Sun-Times* that the most dangerous word in the English language was the definite article "the." All hate speech against the other, whether "the Negroes" or "the queers" or "the Jews" or "the Reds" included the definite article. Each group may share a characteristic, which might be something self-identified or assigned to them from outside, but it wouldn't be them, sort of like distinguishing people with a disability from disabled people. Morrie decided to explore these points with Tobias.

"Toynbee wrote that the Jews have no reason to exist in history anymore, not to mention what Hitler thought. Just what do you mean by speaking of 'the Jews?'" he asked.

Tobias's eyes widened. "You're an intellectual, Morrie Stein! Good for you. And here I thought you were just a reporter for a second-rate newspaper, someone Ben Hecht might have tossed into one of his novels for comic relief."

"I think it's you who has a problem with Jews," Morrie continued, undeterred. "Don't you know that stigmas only hurt if you believe in them yourself?"

"Are you Jewish?" Tobias asked.

"What? You know I'm Jewish. We talked about my parents."

"Morrie, I'm pulling your leg. Of course, I know you're Jewish."

"Yes, of course. Well, let me ask you this. Did you think I was one of *them* the moment you saw my name?"

Tobias put the fingers of one hand to his chin and slowly rubbed it. "'One of them?' What do you mean? One of whom?"

"The Jews, of course, that transcendent entity across generations that you can't kill even when you put a stake in their hearts."

Tobias tapped his chest with the fingertips of his right hand. "I have to answer your questions? I don't answer to you."

"That's not the point. Do you think I'm one of them? It's so clear you don't like me, yet you accepted me as your patient."

"I might be a surgeon who doesn't like black people but that doesn't mean I'd misdiagnose one on purpose."

"A revealing analogy, Dr. Silver. Let me put it this way. Do you believe there really is any such singular entity as the Jews, some mathematical set that would continue to exist even if it were an empty set? That's what I'm asking about. Do you believe they are some kind of irrepressible pack of dogs running wild in history and needing to be hounded in return? You know, 'the Eternal Jew?' But there is no such thing as 'the Eternal Jew.' It's only the stereotype that's eternal."

Tobias drank from his bottle of water again. "Do you mind if I light up a cigar?" he asked. "This is getting interesting, Morrie. You're exceeding expectations." Tobias walked round his desk and pulled open a drawer, then withdrew a cigar from a cylindrical glass tube, snipped the end with a cutting tool, and lit it with a chromed Zippo lighter that he flipped open, then snapped shut. "Oh, I'm sorry," he said as he stood behind the desk. "Would you like one? They're only drugstore quality but at least they don't come in packages of five wrapped in cellophane." Morrie shook his head.

"So, where were we?" Tobias said when he returned to his chair. He pulled his ashtray closer on the side table, drew in a puff, and blew the smoke out slowly from a whistle thin gap between his lips while looking directly at his patient.

"I'm not going to flinch," Morrie said.

Tobias tapped the cigar on the rim of the ashtray even though hardly any ash had built up. "You are so good, Morrie," he said. "When did this happen? Are we getting laid again?"

Tobias sighed and rolled his cigar between his thumb and two fingers, and smoothly inserted it into his mouth while appearing to look up at something in the ceiling. Then he leaned far forward in his chair – it was the attack and parry again. "You missed your calling, Morrie," he said. "You should have worked for the Soviet KGB. You dissect language and pick up on all the clues very well. And now you have concluded that I am some kind of unreconstructed Jew hater. No, I don't believe in 'the Eternal Jew.' But there are these little Jews like you who make me sick, always whining, always falling, always running to someone to save them. You embarrass me, sir. I don't know how you can stand being you."

Morrie inspected the room. He felt as if he'd been thrown into a Eugene O'Neill play but there are only two actors and no audience, no fourth wall. The sofa was threadbare, its brown velour worn shiny in places like the seats of old wool trousers, and the curtains were old as well, with folds that sagged, the heavy jacquard fabric and faded floral print pattern looking more funereal than cheerful. He looked at the ceiling light fixture – three bulbs behind an etched and frosted glass shade but one was out. Tobias Silver was just an old man living in a Banker's Box of obsolete theory and bad intention that people only stumbled upon by circumstance. He studied Tobias, who did not move. It was becoming so clear to Morrie that Tobias Silver only had a dinky, little private practice to crown his glory. It was nothing. Still, he might tell himself that even if he was a failure as a businessman and professional at least he wasn't as failed as some of his patients; it was so clear to Morrie that Jews like Tobias Silver who hated other Jews had convinced themselves that no matter how despised they might be in the eyes of the world at least they weren't as despicable as these other Jews. That was the secret of Jewish self-hate, wasn't it?

"Tell me, Dr. Silver, when you were an ambitious young man, was it because you wanted to show the Gentiles you were as good as them, or you wanted to show the other Jews that you were better than them, maybe that you were not really one of them at all? I can understand wanting to be better than the competition whoever they are, to be a winner, to prove yourself. That's the way of the Western world, of capitalism, of the International Olympic Committee. But I don't understand wanting to be better than the Jews. The German scientists and musicians thought they were the best in Europe, yet there were so many Jews who were just as good as them, whether in Germany itself or Russia or even America. The Germans wanted to prove they were better than the Jews, who were the only people they felt really threatened by. Not for taking over the banks or newspapers or even governments. It was not a tangible, material threat they feared, but a psychological one. Maybe they weren't better than the Jews after all? I think you can understand that, Dr. Silver. So, tell me, why do you need to prove you're better than the Jews? Why do you need to prove you're better than me?"

Tobias put down his cigar and shifted about in his seat; he sniffed loudly before speaking again. "You know I can't continue to see you if you're going to be like this, Morrie," he said. "Don't you want to continue seeing me? You must see some value to our sessions or else you wouldn't continue to come. I'm not even charging you. It's because I want to help you."

Morrie wasn't falling for it any longer. Tobias didn't want to help him, yet he had wondered why a doctor would continue to see him without receiving payment. Morrie finally figured out why. It was because he – Dr. Silver – must have seen some value in the sessions for himself. And, what could that premium be, if not the naked truth about his own, blunted life? Did Dr. Silver worry that he was too much like Morrie? It was Narcissus not liking what he saw in his reflection but he was Narcissus so he had to look.

"I'll be leaving now, Dr. Silver," Morrie said. "Don't get up."

He didn't.

At the door Morrie stopped and turned to address Tobias one last time. "Did you ever read John Cheever's *Falconer?*" he asked. "Writers know something about life, too." Tobias took the cigar out of his mouth and nodded. He had read the novel.

"It's the scene when Ezekiel is still in prison for killing his brother. He wants to get out of prison, and he doesn't know how he's going to do it but he knows he is going to do it. While he's still in his wife visits him. It's the usual passive aggression from her because she married him before she discovered he was a homosexual, yet another unmentionable, inscrutable, despised personage in our culture, and he's told her what goes on in a men's prison, so she knows. But on this visit he tells her that at least he's never taken it up the ass. He has some standards, even in prison, even there, defrocked and divorced from normal society as he is. He's never taken it up the ass. He's got that, at least. Later in the book, after he's finally escaped, he's riding on a bus and it's raining outside, and he doesn't know where he's headed but he's not going back to prison so he walks to the front of the bus, and he gets off. He just gets off. He gets off the bus and that's the end of the book."

Morrie didn't wait for a reply. He didn't care whether Dr. Silver understood or not. He just turned and got off the bus.

ABOUT THE AUTHOR

ABRAHAM AAMIDOR has reported for the *Champaign-Urbana News-Gazette*, the *St. Louis Globe-Democrat* (now defunct), and *The Indianapolis Star*. He won more than 40 local, state and national writing awards in his journalism career, including twice a Finalist in the national Missouri Lifestyle Journalism Awards and twice a First Place in the Indiana Associated Press Managing Editors Feature Series contest. His previous books include *Chuck Taylor, All Star: The True Story of the Man behind the Most Famous Athletic Shoe in History* (Indiana University Press, 2005, 2017); *Shooting Star: The Rise and Fall of the British Motorcycle Industry* (ECW Press of Toronto, 2009), and several other non-fiction books. His novel, *Letting Go*, was published by The Permanent Press in 2018.

Aamidor was born in Memphis and grew up in Chicago from age 7. He is the son of Holocaust survivors and the only member of his birth family to be born in America. He's a former VISTA (Volunteers in Service to America, now associated with AmeriCorps) Volunteer and met his wife, Shirley, an immigrant from England, while in the program. Shirley and Abe have two sons, Joe, a consultant in the clean energy/smart building space, and David, a Lt. Col. in the United States Army.

CPSIA information can be obtained
at www.ICGtesting.com
Printed in the USA
JSHW021936091122
32912JS00003B/18